EXTERNAL CONSTRAINTS ON ECONOMIC POLICY IN BRAZIL, 1889–1930

External Constraints on Economic Policy in Brazil, 1889–1930

Winston Fritsch

Associate Professor of Economics
Catholic University of Rio de Janeiro

University of Pittsburgh Press

Published in Great Britain by The Macmillan Press Ltd

Published in the U.S.A. 1988 by the University of Pittsburgh Press,
Pittsburgh, Pa., 15260

Printed in Hong Kong

Library of Congress Cataloging-in-Publication Data
Fritsch, Winston.
External constraints on economic policy in Brazil,
1889–1930.
(Pitt Latin American series)
Bibliography: p.
Includes index.
1. Brazil—Economic policy.   2. Brazil—Commercial
policy—History—20th century.   3. Coffee trade—
Government policy—Brazil—History—20th century.
I. Title.   II. Series.
HC187.F757   1988   338.981   87–19209
ISBN 0–8229–1147–7

For Lilian

Contents

List of Tables

TEXT TABLES

APPENDIX TABLES

Preface

The object of this book is to describe the conduct of economic policy in Brazil during the country's heyday as an export economy, the 'First', or 'Old', Republic as the formally liberal regime of the Constitution of 1891 – which extends from Abolition and the downfall of the Empire to the Revolution of 1930 – became known in Brazilian political historiography.

An important motivation of this work from an early stage has been to study and, as far as may be, critically to revise some conflicting explanations of the political rationale in the use of the basic core of policy instruments available to the federal government during the First Republic - that is, monetary, fiscal, exchange rate, coffee price support and foreign indebtedness policies. Until a few years ago most would agree that this was not a controversial issue. The bulk of post-1930 literature explained the conduct of economic policy during the First Republic as being straightforwardly conditioned by the corporative interests of the coffee trade, based on a sketchy analysis of the system of political domination and control built up by the civilian plutocracy in the late nineties and the resulting hegemonic position which the larger coffee planters of São Paulo and their commercial and banking connections came to occupy within it. The alleged unrestrained exercise of the political muscle of the coffee interests in shaping economic policy was illustrated, according to this traditional view, by the notions that the Executive was always prepared to lend support to coffee valorization schemes and that the secular depreciation of the milréis resulted from politically motivated decisions aimed at benefitting the leading sector of the export-producing bourgeoisie.

During the past decade, however, the traditional interpretation has been challenged from two different sides. On the one hand, it has been forcefully put forward in influential works by economic historians, that the conduct of economic policy was predominantly influenced by the application of orthodox principles of monetary, fiscal and exchange rate policy.[1] The argument is constructed in such a way as to reveal the adherence of a great number of influential contemporary public men to orthodox principles of financial policy, at least in their public statements. From this is derived the strong claim that these doctrinaire principles actually shaped policy decisions in a

xi

permanent way. However, this recent literature was not explicitly put forward as a criticism of previously accepted views on the unchallenged political dominance of São Paulo coffee interests – which, in effect, it accepts. Nevertheless, the fact that the essential ingredients of orthodox ideology were, *inter alia*, a deep aversion to expansionary monetary policies and a preference for overvalued exchange rates – and, as such, run against the perceived immediate interests of the coffee sector – gives these recent contributions a strong, although implicit, revisionist flavour.

On the other hand, recent works on the political history of the period have tried to qualify the naïve understanding of the character and strength of *Paulista* hegemony implicit in traditional interpretations and the simplified vision of the nature of political conflict during the First Republic, often based on a superficial analysis of the contradictions between the interests of coffee and those of other politically represented groups.[2] The statements about the rationale of the economic policies followed before 1930 presented by this second line of revisionism differ little, however, from those found in traditional literature[3].

The present state of the literature is thus a curious one. The works of the revisionist *economic* historians implicitly reject the view that macroeconomic policies were always geared to the interests of the hegemonic group while lacking, because they are essentially an idealistic interpretation of historical processes, a convincing explanation for the political rationale of the orthodox policies actually followed on occasion in a state in which exporters and, particularly, the coffee interests had an overwhelming influence. At the same time, the writings of revisionist *political* historians call attention to the over-simplified analysis in traditional historiography concerning the character and strength of the position held by the political oligarchy of São Paulo in national politics, but still stick to the latter's train of thought in their references to the political rationale of economic policy making.

Although the design of this work at its inception was considerably motivated by the desire to investigate the validity of these conflicting broad generalizations in the history of Brazilian economic policy, this is not the only and not even the chief determinant of the scope of the present study. As research progressed, it became clear that in spite of the remarkable growth in the academic literature on the economic history of the First Republic and the improvement in the availability of statistical data relating to the period witnessed in recent years, there were still two important lacunae to be filled before a proper assessment of the rationale of federal economic policies could be made.

First it was essential to develop a fuller understanding of the nature of the recurrent macroeconomic disequilibria affecting Brazil during this period and, especially, of the adjustment processes accompanying these shocks in an extremely open export economy. As will be shown in this work, the fundamental structural characteristic of the Brazilian economy during the period here studied was its extreme vulnerability to two types of exogenous shocks affecting its balance of payments position. The first of these originated from periodic supply shocks in the coffee sector resulting from large variations in the yield of coffee trees depending on weather conditions which, given the weight of the product in the value of exports and its price inelastic international demand, could cause a sharp fall in export earnings in the absence of *ad hoc* measures destined to support world prices. The second shock was that of the swings experienced by the world economy during the first three decades of this century, such as the large growth and subsequent collapse of world trade and international investment flows to primary producing countries in the decade preceding World War I and in the second half of the twenties, or the postwar boom and collapse of primary commodity prices.

Nevertheless, even though there seems to exist wide agreement that this great vulnerability of the Brazilian export economy to exogenous external shocks made it extremely dependent on the smooth functioning of the world economy, and/or on foreign financial assistance, to avoid major macroeconomic disequilibria, the existing historiography pays, at most, cursory attention to world economic events and practically ignores the relations between Brazilian authorities and foreign lenders in the analysis of economic policy decisions. Consequently special attention will be devoted here to correcting these shortcomings by giving emphasis to the study of the ways in which international developments affected the context in which economic policy decisions had to be made and how Brazil's relations with her creditors conditioned these decisions themselves. Indeed one of the contributions attempted in this book is to try and show that any work that fails to take these aspects explicitly into consideration is bound to misinterpret the rationale of economic policy making during the period.

Secondly it became clear that an adequate appraisal of the aims and results of policy actions, as well as the understanding of the

macroeconomic adjustment mechanisms through which they operated, demanded a much firmer grasp of the changing institutional
framework within which policy was implemented than that available
in the existing literature. Indeed, the way in which the frequent
external shocks affected Brazil's macroeconomic stability depended
crucially on certain institutional features of the economy which both
conditioned the policy reactions to external disequilibria and influenced the ways in which the shocks were internally transmitted.
Some of these features of a more structural or permanent character
are widely acknowledged in the literature[4]. However, at most a
cavalier treatment is usually given to the description and analysis of
the effects of the changing institutional set-up of the country's monetary system – during the First Republic Brazil was twice on and off a
fully backed gold standard, varied many times her note-issuing authority as well as the legal constraints placed upon the creation of
high-powered money – or of the several different schemes used to
finance coffee price support, which had quite distinct macroeconomic
implications.

Since monetary and coffee policy were perhaps the most important
stabilization instruments used at the time, this has been a source of
irritating imprecisions in several works and, in effect, the foundation
of many unwise generalizations in the analysis of policy making. In
the following pages, therefore, some space will be devoted to the
description of institutional and operational aspects of monetary and
coffee stabilization policies which is fundamental for a sound grasp of
the more relevant and interesting issues to be discussed. The discussion of monetary and exchange rate management provides, in
addition, the opportunity for useful insights into both the working
and the rationale for the adoption of the gold standard and floating
exchange rates in peripheral countries during the period here studied, the academic interest of which goes beyond that of Brazilian
economic historiography.

Rio de Janeiro   WINSTON FRITSCH

Acknowledgements

During the years in which I have been working on the subject of this book I have incurred many debts.

First of all I should like to thank those who commented on and encouraged the development of this research from an early stage, as a dissertation submitted for the PhD degree in the University of Cambridge. In this regard, I owe a special debt of gratitude to Professor Donald E. Moggridge, who not only supported this research project from its inception and consistently gave competent counsel, but more than once provided the encouragement I needed not to abandon it under the pressure of growing professional duties. Professors Susan Howson and Ian Drummond closely followed the development of my early work and also provided wise and generous advice; to Professor Howson I also owe invaluable support in obtaining Lord Rothschild's consent to consult the files relating to the 1924 British financial mission to Brazil. To Professor Marcelo de Paiva Abreu I owe the stimulus of his unfailing and friendly interest in the development of this study, as well as many valuable suggestions. Last but not least, I must express my deep thankfulness to my wife Lilian, whose intellectual companionship and loving self-denial enabled me to finish this work.

I should also thank Dr Derek Chisholm, Mr Jorge Fodor, Dr Luis Aranha Corrêa do Lago, Dr Paulo Neuhaus and, especially, the late Professor Carlos Díaz-Alejandro, who read drafts of parts of my work at different stages and made helpful comments, as well as my students for their warm and interested reaction to the ideas put forward in this book. My colleagues at the Department of Economics of the Catholic University of Rio de Janeiro provided the intellectually stimulating environment in which its final version was written, and should also be thankfully acknowledged.

Many people in Brazil, Britain and the United States helped in the search for and use of sources. In this connection, both Lord Rothschild, who generously allowed me to use papers from the archives of N.M. Rothschild and Sons, as well as the late Mr J.W.F. Rowe, who took the trouble of returning to 'the mists of antiquity', as he put it, to discuss some points relating to his seminal 1932 work on Brazilian coffee policy, should be especially thanked. I am also grateful to Dr John Atkin, to Mr Carl Backlund of the Federal Reserve Bank of

New York, to Mr Clarence Lyons, Jr. and Mr Gerald Hairnes of the National Archives of the United States, to Mr Washington Luis Pereira de Souza Neto, to Mr Cláudio Pacheco of the Banco do Brasil, to Mr C.D.H. Robson of Rothschilds, to Mr T.M. Rybczynski of Lazards and to the staffs of the Public Record Office in London, of the Cambridge University Library and of the Biblioteca do Ministério da Fazenda in Rio de Janeiro.

Mrs Maria Ilda Marques Augusto sacrificed part of her vacations to prepare the final typescript in a very short time and is also to be thanked.

W.F.

Brazilian Currency Notation

The reader should be aware that, throughout the period covered by this study, the Brazilian monetary unit was the *milréis* and that for large amounts the *conto de réis* or *conto*, for short, equal to one thousand milréis, was used. It should also be noted that following contemporary usage, exchange rates are here expressed in pence per milréis.

1 The Shaping of the First Republic: an Introduction

1.1 BIRTH AND CONSOLIDATION OF THE NEW REGIME

The outstanding fact in Brazilian nineteenth century economic history was the great development of coffee production from the 1830s. On the one hand the rapid spread of coffee plantations in the hinterland of the state of Rio de Janeiro consolidated the southward drift of the dynamic nucleus of economic activity begun with the gold rush of the eighteenth century and gave birth to a class of wealthy slave-owning planters who became the political mainstay of the imperial regime established after Brazil's political independence from Portugal in 1822. On the other hand it defined the pattern in which the country was to be integrated in the new international division of labour emerging during the *Pax Britannica*. Its main characteristics were the growth of the new staple's exports to the United States – which towards the end of the century would become Brazil's largest market – and other dynamic coffee-consuming countries such as the German States; a great dependence on industrial imports, especially from the United Kingdom, until the decline of British competition and import substitution in cotton textiles and other British industrial staples substantially reduced her share in Brazilian imports in the last decades of the century; and a growing foreign long-term debt in the form of both government loans issued in London for fiscal reasons since political independence through Rothschilds – who became the sole agent for the Brazilian government by the middle of the century – and, later, of public utility company loans, mostly railway loans, which increased substantially from the late 1860s.

The greatest policy problem during the early coffee boom was how to overcome the potential obstacle to the continued development of the coffee industry posed by the increasing difficulty of procuring slaves to work the labour-intensive plantations as a result of strong British diplomatic and military pressure to end the slave trade in the South Atlantic. This was resolved, nevertheless, by the illegal importation of African slaves as well as by transfers from the stagnating cotton and sugar plantations in the north-east. However after 1850,

1

when the Brazilian government was eventually compelled to enforce an effective prohibition of the contraband trade in slaves, the problem of labour scarcity became acute as coffee plantations continued to spread southwards towards São Paulo and railway development began to open new areas in the interior of that state.

Although some São Paulo coffee planters started private schemes to finance the coming of European immigrants, free labour mobility in a growing economy with an almost unlimited supply of land soon made it unrewarding from a private point of view. The new planters began to press for government subsidies to immigration at the same time that liberal agitation for the abolition of slavery grew. The imperial government, however, not only failed to answer the demands of the São Paulo planters but it was also politically unable to take bold steps towards abolition.

From 1870 onwards political tension between the old slave-owning rural oligarchies and the rising rural and urban groups interested in abolition and the diffusion of wage labour began to undermine the political stability of the Empire.[1] The Republican Party was founded and radical criticism of the great constitutional powers granted to the Emperor – who could, for instance, dissolve parliament and nominate provincial governors – and of the fiscal power concentrated in the central government began to be voiced. Finally attrition between the government and some high-ranking members of the Army, among whom pro-republican sentiment had become widespread, proved fatal to the regime. In spite of the very favourable economic conditions prevailing from the mid-eighties, not even the personal prestige of the aged Emperor, the belated abolition of slavery in 1888 or the promises of political and economic reform made by a succession of short-lived cabinets could prevent the military coup which proclaimed the Republic in November 1889.

The building of the new republican institutions took place during the nineties and had two decisive moments. The first was the drafting of the strongly unfederalistic Constitution of 1891 – a reaction against the excessively autocratic and centralizing character of the old regime. The new constitution granted more extensive fiscal powers to the states (for instance, the export tax was withdrawn from the federal government), allowed them to raise foreign loans and to organise armed militiae without any interference from the federal government and made state representation in the federal Chamber of Deputies proportional to population. This, given Brazil's regionally uneven demographic spread and income distribution, had the effect of concentrating political power in the hands of a few states.

The second was the crucial process of reconstruction of a workable federal political system under civilian rule and parliamentary institutions in a vast country in which old-established regional political oligarchies and emerging modernizing groups with entirely different political, economic and even cultural outlooks coexisted. This achievement was the work of the new groups who assumed control of the leading states' governments following five years of military discretionary rule and recurrent civil war. First they took control over the federal executive at the time of the return to civilian rule and constitutional government. The political elites of São Paulo – representatives of the emerging but already powerful free labour coffee sector who were unencumbered by political compromises with the old regime – led this process, skilfully playing their dual role which guaranteed the backing of the relevant trade and financial interests and the development of a natural political *rapport* between their leaders and the strongly anti-monarchist military controlling the transitional governments. Finally, at the turn of the century, they consolidated the new regime by designing an informal system of political checks and balances between the federal government and the leading regional political cliques, which allowed a relatively smooth functioning of formal parliamentary rule under strong presidential powers.

This system consisted basically of granting federal favours – including, if necessary, military support – to the controlling rural political oligarchies in the lesser states so as to enable them to consolidate regional power and, in return, provide the federal government of the day with a comfortable and docile congressional majority. The smooth functioning of this system was based on the more stable nature of regional political leadership and control by the hegemonic groups in the leading states, rooted in larger and well established business interests – such as the coffee planters and their trading and banking connections in São Paulo – and, on the other hand, on the enormous leverage given by federal resources to the poorer states' controlling oligarchies to amass the support of regional landowners and on the absolute coertion which could be exerted upon voters by the latter in these backward areas in the absence of secret balloting.

The 'Oligarchic Pact', as this system of power centralization and political control is sometimes referred to in the literature had, however, three important sources of instability. The first stemmed from possible divergences between the political elites of the leading states of São Paulo and Minas Gerais on fundamental aspects of federal policies; as will be shown in the following pages, such divergences were not infrequent during the twenties (over the conduct of monetary and coffee policy). The second was the occasional difficulty of appeasing the 'intermediate' states of not inconsiderable political weight, such as Rio Grande do Sul, Bahia, Rio de Janeiro or Pernambuco, which not only had a more complex internal power structure but also nurtured legitimate ambitions to have a stronger say in the conduct of national affairs and demanded greater representation in the federal executive. This problem gave rise to political difficulties for the leading groups in the negotiations preceding some presidential elections. Finally there was the criticism voiced by dissenting politicians, intellectuals and independent sectors of the press against the undemocratic aspects of the regime which found a sounding board in the rising urban middle classes lacking effective political representation and in a significant fraction of young army officers. This discontent was indeed the source of recurrent political strains, especially after the war, and, together with a serious political fight between the leading states over the 1930 presidential succession and the devastating impact of the Great Depression, can be counted among the contributory causes of the Revolution of 1930 and the collapse of the First Republic.

1.2   ECONOMIC POLICIES IN THE CONSOLIDATION PERIOD

The early years of the Republic were times of great economic instability. Following the overthrow of the imperial government the long upswing the Brazilian economy experienced during the eighties gave way to a brisk inflationary boom followed by a depression lasting until the early days of this century.[2]

The early boom, which was sustained roughly up to 1895, originated in the extraordinary monetary expansion and the exchange rate collapse during the first two years of the new regime. The former was the result of the implementation of a plan for monetary reform, returning note-issuing rights to a number of domestic private banks, carried out by a succession of short lived cabinets, which more than doubled the monetary base in these two years.[3] The sudden interruption in 1890 of the large foreign capital inflow of the late eighties, probably coupled with an outflow of private balances after the revolutionary change of government and an 8 per cent fall in export earnings in 1890, led to an 18 per cent depreciation during that year.[4] In 1891, when the demand-generating effects of the credit expansion began to spill over into higher import levels, import growth more than offset a mild recovery of exports causing the balance of trade to shrink further and the exchange rate to collapse. By July 1892 it stood at 37 per cent of its November 1889 high.

This large depreciation had two important consequences: it boosted profitability in the tradeable goods sector; and caused a sharp growth in public spending measured in domestic currency, since the federal government's expenditures abroad, in the form of foreign debt service and payments for supplies for the army, navy and publicly-owned companies, rose in proportion to the fall in the rate of exchange.

To the inducement afforded by the low exchange rate, domestic producers responded by intensifying import substitution of some non-durable consumer goods and expanding the productive capacity of export sectors, notably coffee production. Although the economic historiography of the period places great emphasis on the industrial growth which apparently occurred during this period, the transformation produced in the coffee producing sector during these years was of far greater importance in shaping the future course of economic policy. Since the slight fall in the relatively high international coffee prices prevailing in 1890 was more than compensated by the dramatic fall in the exchange rate of 1890–2, and world coffee prices recovered in 1893, export prices in domestic currency had more than doubled by 1894.[5] Coffee growing being largely a domestic business, this led to a great extension of new planting in the newly opened areas of the state of São Paulo, helped by easy money, large inflows of Italian immigrants and the recent railway development in the state.[6] However, faced with a price inelastic international demand, dependent chiefly for its growth upon income growth in the consuming countries, in the depressed condition of the international economy in the mid-nineties this large increase in coffee planting meant disaster not only to the planters but to Brazil as well, as soon as the additional supplies started flowing to the market.[7] This point will be dealt with in greater detail below.

As referred to above the exchange rate collapse also posed a serious transfer problem to the federal government. At a time when the government's capacity to borrow abroad was severely restricted it was not enough to solve the purely fiscal aspect of this problem, viz., tapping domestic resources for the non- inflationary financing of the growing expenditure. Even though a deflationary fiscal policy could have positive balance of payments effects, the authorities still had to face the crucial problem of how to relieve the pressure their remittances abroad would put on the Rio foreign exchange market, following the depletion of their London reserves, before a substantial adjustment in the balance of trade could take place. A review of the aftermath of the early exchange rate crisis will illustrate this point.

Following the 1891 exchange rate crisis the government's attempts to redress external equilibrium were doomed to failure. By 1892 growing concern regarding the balance of payments position led to attempts to prevent its further deterioration by reducing the outstanding note issue.[8] In December the banks of issue had their issuing rights withdrawn and a deflationary programme was drawn up, which, however, was abandoned in 1894 when the growth of public expenditure – made worse by the escalation of civil war in the south of the country – had to be met with a fresh issue of Treasury notes. Import demand kept on rising and the slight recovery of exports in that period had no sustained impact on the trade balance. The Treasury tried to relieve, for as long as it could, the pressure its demand for foreign exchange would exert on the Rio exchange market. It did this by swapping gold-indexed internal bonds for private foreign exchange balances and by getting short-term accommodation in Europe, but, towards 1894, it became increasingly difficult to do so and the exchange rate slumped to new all-time lows. In 1895, with a similar crisis approaching, the Treasury found relief in the possibility of using the proceeds of a £7.2 million loan – one of the few federal external long-term loans raised in the decade, purportedly for the extension of a public railway – to defend the rate. With this breathing-space and the return of political normality, the authorities went back at once to the deflationary strategy outlined in 1892 and in addition, towards the end of the year, Congress approved a large tariff increase in an attempt to redress the budgetary imbalance.

But it was too late. As an inevitable outcome of the extention of coffee planting, ever larger outputs came to the markets in 1896 and 1897 and world prices slumped badly[9] with a devastating effect on Brazil's capacity to pay, despite the sharp contraction of imports brought about by the 1895 credit squeeze, the higher tariff, and the contraction of money incomes. The very small trade surplus of 1896 and the apparent exhaustion of the Treasury's foreign reserves towards 1897 – signalled by the renewal of heavy official purchases in domestic foreign exchange markets – caused once more a large fall in the exchange rate[10].

As 1897 passed, with the perception that the structural nature of the coffee crisis made an early export recovery unlikely, it became plain that the extent of deflation required to attain equilibrium in the balance of payments current account was politically unfeasible. In early 1898 the President in a letter to his already chosen successor stated that after studying several alternative policies he and the Finance Minister '. . . were convinced that the safest and most effective way will be to raise a large foreign loan which would serve as a basis for the reconstruction of our finances' and urged him to go to London to negotiate it with the government's bankers.[11] In April, as the President-elect sailed to Europe, a representative of a leading British bank operating in Brazil was sent to Rio to discuss the details of a plan for financial assistance drawn up in London. In June it was agreed that Brazil would get a £10 million credit to be drawn upon over three years to meet interest payments due on a large part of Brazilian external liabilities and the suspension of their amortisation payments until July 1911.

The Funding Loan of 1898 is a watershed in pre-war economic policies. The weakness of the Brazilian negotiating position, the authorities' extreme concern with the budgetary consequences of low exchange rate levels and their lack of understanding of the economic costs of deflation led to their agreeing to take new and far reaching fiscal and monetary deflationary measures following the loan. Indeed the long reached consensus that the central problem was the collapse of the exchange rate and that its solution rested on monetary deflation, and the opinion that past failures to pursue this course stemmed from difficulties directly or indirectly related to the burden of foreign obligations and the low level of official reserves, exacerbated the government's anxiety not to miss the unique opportunity afforded by the loan. The determination with which the Campos Salles administration stuck to its programme, in spite of its domestic consequences, bears witness to this.

On the fiscal front an internal consumption tax was progressively extended to cover a large number of products and the collection of 10 per cent of the tariff duties 'in gold' was implemented. This meant that a 10 per cent fraction of the – mostly specific – tariff duties would be paid at the par value of the milréis by means of special 'gold cheques' issued to importers by the banks operating in foreign exchange against payment of its equivalent made in domestic currency at the ruling sterling premium.[12]

Monetary deflation started in 1899, according to a scheme that was as odd as it was simple: the Treasury would deposit with some chosen foreign banks, to be subsequently destroyed, the equivalent in domestic currency, at 18d, of its drawings on the London loan.[13] In July 1899 some items of revenue were earmarked to provide the requisite funds for this, at the same time that the powers of the Banco da República, the government's banker since the 1892 reform, to issue Treasury notes were withdrawn.[14] Finally Rothschilds' recurrent worries about the level of Brazilian funds in London were placated by the pledging of half the revenue from the new gold tariff as well as other sundry foreign currency revenues to the progressive building up of Treasury reserves in London.[15]

The deflationary interlude at the turn of the century[16] was the direct cause of two events of paramount importance. Firstly it was responsible for the banking crisis of 1900 which led eventually to the creation of the Banco do Brasil, an institution destined to have increasing influence on Brazilian economic management. Secondly the recovery of the rate of exchange from 1898 in the absence of a compensatory rise in international coffee prices, brought for the first time to the forefront of national politics the debate on official intervention in the industry.

The banking crisis of 1900 was one of the severest in Brazilian economic history and resulted in the government take-over of the Banco da República, the largest domestic commercial bank in the country. The panic which followed the suspension of payments by the Banco da República in September 1900 was due to the effects of the sudden monetary contraction on the bank's already weak liquidity position.[17] Coming together with the credit squeeze, the July 1899 curtailment of the bank's power to use Treasury note issues to relieve its cash position and provide accommodation to domestic banks endangered the liquidity of the banking system, and the agreement the bank signed with the government in February 1900 to settle its debts to the Treasury, with a large sum being due at once, gave it a further blow. But it was not until the winter that the events which were to precipitate the crisis occurred.

Towards July the London and River Plate Bank – the bank which led the funding loan negotiations in Rio – came out with an attempt to lead a speculative rise in the exchange rate[18] and was followed by the Banco da República.[19] At that time most foreign banks held funds awaiting transfer to Europe in the expectation of a recovery in exchange but the rise was so violent that the threat of a large scale flight of their deposits prompted them to challenge the British bank.[20] They succeeded in doing so and the exchange rate, after being quoted in July at more than 40 per cent of its June average, fell again to its former levels during August and the Banco da República had to cover its speculative position at a heavy loss. This proved to be the *coup de grâce* to the bank's solvency. In early September it approached the government for a large currency loan, but with no success, because of the latter's commitment with its foreign creditors. Negotiations went on, but rumours that the positions were irreconcilable leaked, leading to a run on the bank and the suspension of payments on 12 September. The bank's importance in the domestic banking structure and the government's position as its main creditor led to immediate official intervention. Government-appointed directors took over the administration on behalf of the shareholders to proceed with the liquidation of the bank's outstanding debts and its eventual reorganisation.

The fundamental aspect in the five-year period of government control of the Banco da República was the maturing of the idea that it was desirable, and with luck feasible, to have some degree of official influence over the exchange rate. The main reason for its desirability was that this would enable the authorities to smooth the seasonal pressures on the exchanges arising from the underlying fluctuations of the balance of trade.[21] Besides, after a decade of currency upheavals, government officials and public opinion in general were very critical of the alleged destabilising influence that speculation by the larger foreign banks could have on the market and knew that the Banco da República, being a private concern, was under no obligation to countervail those influences even if this was thought to be in the national interest and the bank had the funds to do so.

As the year following the crisis went by there were clear signs that the worst was over. The increase – although at much reduced prices – in the quantity of coffee exported, the acceleration of the rubber boom and the depressed level of imports caused a sharp and sustained increase in the trade surplus at the turn of the century which, together with the relief provided by the funding loan, greatly improved the balance of payments position.

The drawings on the funding loan stopped in 1901, thus ending the period of large reductions in high-powered money associated with them.[22] The exchange rate moved erratically upwards, but by the end of 1901 the Banco da República was already able to manage 'to impress a relative stability on exchange and to correct the excesses of speculation[23]' and successfully stabilised the rate at around 12d – some 67 per cent above its 1898 average – where it was to be kept for the next three years.

The steady recovery experienced from 1902 was not shared by the country's main export sector. Since the advent of larger crops in 1896, there had been a marked loss of profitability in coffee production. The sudden increase in output had caused world visible stocks to rise from an average of 2.8 million bags during the period 1890–6 to 6.0 million bags in 1897–1900 and led to a halving of world prices. Agitation for official help to relieve the planters' plight had been mounting for some time, but the federal administration consistently took a rather detached view based on the belief that the coffee situation would automatically be put right in the long run with gains to the average productivity in the industry by the elimination of the less efficient producers.[24] Even when expectations that output would stabilise at new levels were proven false by the bumper crop of 1901, which put world stocks at 11.3 million bags or almost three-quarters of annual world demand, the government remained unimpressed, and let the rise in exchange rate put an additional strain on the planters.[25] But now all concerned knew that the future of the industry hung in the balance and, although planting in São Paulo was stopped in 1902 by the imposition of a prohibitive tax, it was clear that should another large crop occur before a sizeable reduction in world stocks had taken place, some measures would have to be taken to avoid a price collapse of unforeseeable consequences.

The continuity of austere economic management beyond the end of Campos Salles's presidential term in 1902 was guaranteed by the establishment consensus in appointing Rodrigues Alves – a conspicuous advocate of deflationary policies and a member of the inner circle of politicians responsible for framing them – as the only presidential candidate and of Senator Leopoldo de Bulhões, a man of impeccable orthodox credentials,[26] to the Finance portfolio. The easing of credit conditions in European capital markets at the beginning at the huge pre-war world international investment boom coincided with the improvement in Brazil's credit standing as her London reserves grew, enabling the government to launch a large programme of port expansion and public works in Rio, financed through foreign loans. However, in spite of the expansionary effects these investments were bound to have, they did not reflect a deliberate departure from the beliefs in the beneficial effects associated with tight monetary and fiscal policies by the school of thought responsible for the policies which followed the 1898 loan, as the figures on the note issue and the budget surpluses show.[27]

In May 1904, in his annual message at the opening of Congress, President Alves stressed the importance of the permanent reorganization of the Banco da República.[28] With the bank's soundness restored and its importance as an effective instrument of exchange rate policy widely acknowledged, the authorities' opinion was that its transformation into an institution permanently controlled by the government and capable of performing some basic central banking functions would be the last stepping-stone towards the completion of the financial reconstruction programme.

After protracted discussions, at the end of the following legislative session in December 1905, the basic statutes of the new institution – the Banco do Brasil – were approved.[29] According to these, the government was to hold a controlling interest in the new bank – its governor and the director of exchange operations being directly nominated by the Executive – which besides conducting its normal commercial business could provide ways and means advances to the Treasury up to a proportion of anticipated revenue, rediscount short term bills, have its capacity to manage the exchange rate strengthened by being granted the monopoly of issue of gold cheques and, last but not least, have the right of issuing notes at par against gold when full convertibility was eventually declared.

Ironically, however, after this reform, at the very time the achievements of the deflationary policies were reaching their peak by paving the way towards the long-term aim of full convertibility of the milréis at the old legal parity – a policy goal strongly held within government circles[30] – its political wisdom was to be increasingly challenged by the events to come.

2 The Pre-war Gold Standard

2.1 THE COFFEE VALORISATION-EXCHANGE STABILISATION DEBATE AND ITS CONSEQUENCES

Although since 1901 ever smaller coffee crops and the exchange rate stability achieved until 1904 had taken a little of the heat out of the debate on coffee problems, in 1905 unexpectedly large foreign capital inflow and export earnings resulted in upward pressures on the exchange rate which were beyond the powers of Banco da República, to offset.[1] At the beginning of the year the bank let the rate float and after two unsuccessful attempts to peg it at higher levels, was finally able to regain control of the market in September and managed to stabilise it at around 30 per cent above its pre-rise level.

This sharp exchange rate appreciation, by setting milréis prices back to their 1902 levels, reminded the planters that the only course open to them was action directed at raising the level of international prices. In August 1905 delegates of the leading producing states succeeded in securing the President's pledge to press the passage of a bill authorising a federal guarantee for foreign loans contracted by them to finance valorisation schemes.[2]

One month later the flowering of the 1906 crop presaged an output of unprecedented magnitude.[3] Nevertheless, despite these early signs of greater financial risks in supporting the price of the commodity, federal backing for loans relating to valorisation was approved in general terms in the Budget Law. In February 1906 the governors of the states of São Paulo, Rio de Janeiro and Minas Gerais – the largest producers – signed an agreement laying down the details of the valorisation plan to be presented to Congress. It asked the Union's guarantee for a £15 million loan to be raised by São Paulo to buy the surplus coffee at prices ranging from 55 to 65 French francs per bag[4] or its equivalent in domestic currency; a tax of 3 francs to be levied on each bag exported would provide revenue earmarked for the service of the loan. But by fixing a minimum price in terms of foreign exchange the signatories of the agreement were not unaware that the planters would not be protected from further exchange rate rises and they also inserted in the plan a bold proposal for exchange stabilisation based on the issue of notes fully backed by gold, convertible at an exchange rate level to be subsequently agreed upon.[5]

As its details became known the plan came under heavy fire. It was held that it would make nonsense of the moral suasion exerted by the federal government upon the states against the growth of their foreign indebtedness[6] and in April the soundness of coffee price support as a commercial proposition was condemned by Rothschilds as 'an artificial expedient [which] must result in catastrophe'.[7] The exchange stabilisation clause also proved to be a major obstacle to its approval by Congress, for although a temporary pegging was not opposed by several sectors of opinion, orthodox politicians responsible for the "financial reconstruction" policies followed since the 1898 funding-loan were utterly opposed to changing the old 27d par.[8] It soon became apparent that the central issues were not only the level at which to stabilise the rate, but also the Finance Minister's determination to get terms that would not block the way to further exchange rate appreciation in the future.[9]

Thus when the President addressed the reassembled Parliament in early May it became evident that his former enthusiasm toward the plan had gone. He disapproved of the producers' lobbying for stabilisation at a 12d rate and criticised the idea of a permanent stabilisation below par, thus in effect condemning the idea on which the controversial clause of the Bill had been based. To general amazement he went further, to argue that the coffee-producing states were financially strong enough to uphold their position in foreign capital markets and doubted the wisdom of artificial intervention on commodity prices.[10]

Although some days later Affonso Penna, the incoming President, practically settled the exchange rate issue by declaring himself in favour of drafting an independent stabilisation bill to peg the rate at 15d,[11] many believed that until November, when the incumbent government's term of office ended, there would be no action towards monetary reform. As time was running short, São Paulo leaders summoned the other states' representatives to redraft the agreement, dropping the stabilisation clause. Its new version, presented in July, established minimum prices in milréis and allowed for the collection of the 3 francs export tax by the states should the federal government not guarantee the necessary financial arrangements. Therefore, when the coffee valorisation bill was finally passed at the end of the month the early valorisation plan had been utterly defeated: not only had exchange stabilisation not been assured at the level proposed by the producing states, but the federal authorities had successfully avoided committing themselves to backing the financing of the scheme. At that time the equivalent of 20 million bags – twice as much as those of the two preceding years – had already been harvested.

The state of São Paulo, responsible for around 80 per cent of the coming crop, would not accept as inevitable the gloomy outlook of a major crisis in its chief industry. State representatives were sent to Europe to negotiate a loan, but were refused on all sides. During July, with the coffee already flowing to the ports, they desperately tried to buy time through the issue of a £1 million loan from the joint Brazilian branch of the Disconto-Gesselschaft and Norddeutsche banks to be repaid in one year.[12] In August, as a last resort, they attempted to enlist the help of the large coffee importers in support of the scheme and approached Hermann Sielcken, partner of one of the largest American coffee-importing firms. The large roasters had an obvious interest in preventing a large fall in prices since the increase in world stocks in the previous few years had been mainly financed by them. Sielcken was non-committal at first as he feared a repetition of the 1906 crop in the following year but, in September, when reliable estimates predicted a small crop for 1907, he agreed to secure the support of other large American and European firms to carry on the coffee purchases.

The basic lines of the deal were that the importers would advance 80 per cent of the funds needed for the purchases to be made by the state at a price not above the ruling New York price on the security of all the coffee bought, which was to be warehoused in New York and some European ports. Even though São Paulo at that time clearly had not yet enough funds to meet its 20 per cent share of the purchases plus the storage cost of all the coffee bought under the scheme as well as the interest on the advances provided by the importers, the purchases started at once. Finally, however, in December the state's financial position was strengthened and the success of this first stage of the price support operation assured by means of a £3 million long-term loan raised with the help of Sielcken and others in London and New York, secured by an export surtax as proposed in the original scheme. This brought the other producing states back into the scheme, for it was argued that concentrating the burden of the new tax on São Paulo planters would place producers from other states at an unfair advantage.

In June 1907 the valorisation managers were able to announce that, having bought a surplus of over 8 million bags and effectively prevented a large fall in prices, they would end their intervention in the market. But this daring action by the coffee interests was not yet an unqualified success: São Paulo would have to carry over its stocks for some time before it could start selling without having a damaging effect on prices, and would still have to find ways to finance the enormous storage and interest costs associated with the plan.[13]

By this time a profound change in Brazilian monetary policy had taken place with the passage of the new exchange stabilisation law in December 1906. The central element of the legislation was the creation of a Treasury Conversion Office which would issue convertible notes against equivalent amounts of gold deposited with it at the rate of 15d. Opposition from the defenders of the return to the 27d legal parity who saw in the proposal a subtle manoeuvre to avoid further revaluations, led to the introduction of a legal limit of 320 000 contos (£20 million) to the Office's note issue, which if reached would bind Congress to taking a decision on a new stabilisation level.

Quite apart from constituting a surrender to the wishes of the coffee interests, the reform represented a much broader and inevitable political reaction against the damaging effects the continued pursuance of the established monetary and exchange rate policies would necessarily have on large sectors of the Brazilian economy.[14] Since the upward floating of the milréis in 1905, the authorities had been warned of the limited ammunition available to the official bank to control the impact that the acceleration of the foreign investment boom and the strong trade surpluses would have on the exchange rate. Their short term creditor position represented by the Treasury's reserves in London had been built as an effective device for fighting the temporary downward pressures on the exchanges which had been the chronic problem of the nineties; however, now that the direction of the external pressure had been reversed, new means would have to be found to fight the disrupting exchange rate appreciations.[15] It was not unnatural that the Brazilians should try, as several Latin American countries had done in the previous few years, to solve this problem by adhering to a gold-exchange standard.[16]

Besides the formal aspects of the Brazilian pre-war gold standard outlined above, it should be noted that the purely passive role of the Office – buying gold and converting its notes at the established rate – devolved on the Banco do Brasil a crucial role in monetary management. Although the Conversion Office was the only note-issuing authority, it was now primarily the bank's ability, through its foreign exchange operations, to maintain the exchange rate between the gold import and export points defined by the legal stabilisation rate and the transaction costs of moving gold across the Atlantic that would prevent the volume of the monetary base from changing. If, following external disequilibria, the offsetting action of Banco do Brasil's foreign exchange operations failed to prevent exchange rate movements large enough to induce gold flows in or out the Conversion Office vaults, the credit fluctuations associated with the automatic changes in the Office's note issue would affect domestic monetary stability, unless fiscal and domestic debt management policies were tuned to countervail its effects.

Even though domestic policies aimed at offsetting the effects of gold flows on the monetary base were not an uncommon practice under the pre-1914 international gold standard,[17] they were not followed to any large extent in Brazil. In fact, still reflecting the anti-inflationary bias of contemporary opinion on economic policy, there was some discussion about the advantages and ways of sterilising the monetary expansion induced by gold inflows. There were proposals that budget surpluses or internal borrowing should be used by the Treasury to withdraw part of the inconvertible notes in circulation 'to neutralize the pernicious effect of the addition to the circulating medium' which would be caused by the issue of the new notes.[18] However, with the growing budget deficits from 1908 on and given the relatively small size of domestic capital markets – which could not absorb large issues of the common 5 per cent Treasury consols, the *apólices*, without a large discount – very little was to be done on these lines. The fact was then that, as long as gold movements resulted from the Banco do Brasil's failure to countervail the pressures on the market exchange rate, they would have their full effect on domestic credit conditions.

This link between balance of payments fluctuations and domestic credit conditions created by the 1906 monetary reform is fundamental to the understanding of the macroeconomic dynamics of the pre-war cycle. The working of the Conversion Office meant that the balance of payments adjustment mechanism usually associated with the 'normal' working of a gold standard – i.e., fully stabilising changes in current account induced by changes in the money supply caused by gold movements – would be operative. But the conventional belief in the smoothness of adjustment in this context results from an artificial reduction of the analysis to self-correcting income and comparative cost variations affecting the balance of trade and overlooks the importance, overwhelming in the Brazilian case during the decade preceding the war, of large surpluses on the balance of payments on capital account and their volatility.[19] Normally following export booms such surpluses tend in general to aggravate an already buoyant current account position. In these conditions the operation of the gold standard adjustment mechanism is felt through a marked compensatory trend in the trade balance caused by strong import growth.[20] In the absence of exogenous developments making for export growth this export economy's golden age can only last as long as the capital inflows continue unabated. If they falter after the downward trend in the trade balance has gathered momentum the results can be very damaging because of the speed with which the subsequent readjustments take place.[21] Because of the lagged response of import demand to changed credit conditions, a large overall balance of payments contraction is bound to occur in the short run leading to heavy reserve losses. If these losses can be sustained for long, the squeeze on money incomes they bring about will eventually correct the external disequilibrium at the cost of reductions in output growth, but if they are large relative to the domestic monetary base a crisis of serious proportions may arise.

To sum up, the Brazilian gold standard of 1906 closely linked domestic monetary stability to the behaviour of the balance of payments, in a way which could strongly reinforce the usual expansionary or contractionary effects of, respectively, external surpluses or deficits. Up to the outbreak of war in 1914 exogenous developments affecting the international coffee and rubber markets and the flow of long-term European capital would, therefore, be decisive in determining changes in the level of domestic activity.

2.2   TIDING OVER THE 1907–8 WORLD RECESSION

The Conversion Office was opened in December 1906 with a £1.7 million Treasury gold deposit and throughout the first half of 1907 new note issues were made mainly on account of further deposits made by the government and the commercial banks.[22] As the outstanding Treasury note issue was not contracted, remaining practically unchanged until the second half of 1907 at slightly above 660 000 contos, the issue of over 92 000 contos by the Office up to June represented a marked departure from the eight years of deflationary policies.[23]

In 1906 the balance of payments had been strong as the sale of the large coffee crop at artificially controlled prices and growing rubber exports had caused a substantial improvement in export earnings and foreign investments continued to grow.[24] Industrial investment was picking up again partly as a consequence of the extensive tariff increases voted in the budget for 1906, which had greatly enlarged protection for a number of agricultural and industrial import substituting activities.[25] Higher imports resulting from the recovery and the tariff changes, enabled the government to balance the budget in spite of a 13 per cent increase in expenditure. Thus by mid-1907, with the disruptive upward pressures on the exchange rate brought under control and the easing of credit conditions, all the indications were that, barring some disaster with the valorisation scheme, Brazil was set for a period of economic prosperity.

The coffee position was, however, still very delicate. In June, when the end of the purchases was announced, a flurry of rumours in the American and European press about the collapse of the scheme led São Paulo to apply formally to the federal authorities for a £3 million loan. As this application certainly implied the existence of a previous informal understanding with the federal government a £3 million short-term advance was provided by Rothschilds with the proviso that a long-term loan for that sum would be put on the market when a favourable situation offered. This was eventually done in October.[26]

This loan was not a definitive solution to the recurrent problem of financing the Brazilian share of valorisation costs. Nevertheless it was significant in the sense that it represented the first instance of open federal support for valorisation. When submitting the state's request to Congress the President explicitly recognised the *national* importance of the coffee problem[27] and in fact a close link then existed between the success of the exchange stabilisation policy, which had been the central plank in his electoral platform, and the behaviour of coffee prices. It was feared that if prices collapsed before the small crop expected for 1907 was exported it would be difficult to prevent a large gold outflow, particularly since rubber prices had been falling in the first half of the year. Federal support was thus given not with the sole intent to protect the planters' incomes but primarily, to defend the country's exchange earnings.

However the real test for both the exchange rate policy and the support of coffee prices started when the recession affecting the American economy from the second quarter of the year developed by October into a severe crisis which rapidly spread to London.[28] Its initial impact on Brazil was felt through a perverse contraction in export earnings at the period of their normal seasonal peak and in a temporary cessation of capital inflows. Rubber prices were particularly affected because of the contraction of British and American demand, which represented nearly 90 per cent of total exports, and fell by a third between September 1907 and February 1908.[29] Coffee prices were not affected but export earnings suffered the effects of the end of the valorisation purchases and the much smaller crop of 1907. Credit tightening in London prevented long-term Brazilian borrowing from September 1907 to March 1908 except for the £3 million coffee loan, and money lent at short notice to the Brazilian branches of foreign banks after the stabilisation of the milréis was returned to their head offices.[30]

Despite the reversal of previous trends the Banco do Brasil successfully fought to maintain the exchange rate within very narrow limits. However it should be observed that the behaviour of the Banco do Brasil was not prompted by any deliberate intention to isolate the domestic money market from the deflationary forces resulting from gold losses, but rather by the government's desperate attempt to maintain confidence in the stabilisation experiment. In fact by far the most important role in the adjustment of the balance of payments was played by immediate Treasury action to speed up the reduction in the volume of its outstanding inconvertible issue from October 1907 to June 1908, which accounts for 85 per cent of the 3.7 per cent decrease in the monetary base.[31]

The international crisis was deep but short-lived. Credit conditions in London eased towards the end of the first quarter of 1908 bringing a revival in foreign lending.[32] Coffee prices and output did not change much from the previous year's figures but rubber prices rapidly regained their early 1907 levels and the sale of the new crops reversed the downward trend of exports towards the end of 1908. Notwithstanding these signs of an upturn in the central countries, small gold losses were allowed to continue and were instrumental in preventing an upsurge of effective demand until export recovery was well under way.

The only significant mark left by the crisis was a radical change in the framework of coffee valorisation which shows that the weakness of the scheme lay not only in the capacity or otherwise of the producing states to finance their part in it, but also stemmed from the way the 80 per cent Euro-American share in the purchases was financed. Once valorisation began, the importers financed their part by issuing warrants against the coffee consigned to them by the producing states for acceptance by American and European banks. In this way a continuous flow of short-term funds was provided, and the valuation foreign bankers placed on the coffee they accepted as security was the main determinant of the price which the scheme could sustain. During the period when the bulk of the purchases was made this mechanism worked smoothly. However, in early 1908, it appears that because of the monetary stringency in Europe the coffee warrants had started piling up for rediscount in the Banque de France.[33] In May the bank announced that it would only accept coffee bills at 15 per cent below the valuation at which the commercial bank advances had been made, inducing some of the bankers supporting the scheme not to renew their short-term credits on maturity.

The only way this unforeseen situation could immediately be faced was by selling part of the coffee stock. Sales started later in May, but it was clear that, in the bearish atmosphere then prevailing and with the coming of the next crop only two months away this alternative could not be pursued for long without a disastrous effect on prices. In July the sales ended and it seems that the basis of a plan for consolidation of the problematic short term liabilities, secretly negotiated with a consortium of large banks, had already been outlined. In August the São Paulo Chamber agreed to submit for federal approval a proposal for the raising of a £15 million loan for that purpose, and passed legislation to limit the maximum amount of coffee to be exported in the following years[34] as well as to raise the export surtax from 3 to 5 francs to provide additional security for the new loan. Federal support was made public in October. Congress approved the request for a guarantee later in the year and the loan was floated in December.

The funding of the valorisation debt had two important consequences for Brazil. The first was that, through a condition imposed by the lenders, Brazilians lost control over the management of coffee sales and an international committee based in London was formed to plan the liquidation of stocks.[35] This could be dangerous to the extent that the committee's decisions – over which Brazil had very limited influence – would control world coffee prices and indirectly determine Brazil's export earnings. Secondly, the imposition of limits on Brazilian coffee exports to volumes that were lower than the output capacity of the São Paulo plantations could cause a rapid increase in prices and would induce exporters to sell the year's crop as soon as they could, before prohibition became effective. This concentration of large exports in a shorter period of time would aggravate the country's seasonal export instability and complicate the task of exchange rate management.

2.3 THE BOOM OF 1909–12

From the recovery from the world crisis in 1909 to the end of 1912 Brazil enjoyed a period of very rapid export and output growth. Because of the sharpness of the upturn in world economic conditions in 1909 and the changes affecting the marketing of Brazilian coffee crops pointed out above, the early stages of the boom were marked by a sweeping improvement in the balance of payments which induced sizeable gold inflows causing a large monetary expansion.[36]

However, the extent to which the external disequilibrium was allowed to influence domestic stability was not unrelated to political changes affecting the country's economic management.

In June 1909 the sudden death of President Penna, one and half years before the end of his term of office, brought in a caretaker government, headed by the Vice-President, and the Finance portfolio was returned to Leopoldo de Bulhões. Still faithful to his old ideas about the economic advantages of overvalued exchange rates and critical of the stabilisation level adopted in 1906, Bulhões would not miss an opportunity to prove its 'artificiality'.

Such an opportunity was afforded when in the last quarter of the year the normal seasonal growth of exports was greatly reinforced by the rocketing of rubber prices and the scramble to export the São Paulo coffee output, which turned out to be 20 per cent higher than the quota allowed by the new valorisation regulations. As imports had only begun to recover from the contractionary monetary policy imposed since late 1907, the trade balance swung into an abnormally high surplus during the last quarter of 1909 as shown in Table 2.1.

The sharp increase in net foreign exchange earnings was immediately translated into upward pressure on the rate of exchange. By the end of September the Banco do Brasil could not stem the tide and market rates rose towards the gold import point.[37] Correctly anticipating these changes the foreign banks which financed Brazilian foreign trade responded by importing gold on a large scale to meet their enlarged operations. As a consequence net monthly issues of Conversion Office notes rose to new records in November and December, the relation of the outstanding issue to its statutory limit jumping from 28 to 70 per cent.

Table 2.1   Brazil: 1908–10 quarterly trade balance (*in £ millions*)

Quarter	Exports	Imports	Trade surplus
1908 I	11.4	10.1	1.3
II	7.4	8.4	–1.0
III	9.4	8.3	1.1
IV	15.9	8.5	7.4
1909 I	16.4	8.5	7.9
II	7.1	8.2	–1.1
III	16.1	9.7	6.4
IV	24.2	10.5	13.7
1910 I	14.6	10.6	3.0
II	10.3	11.1	–0.8
III	19.6	12.4	7.2
IV	18.4	13.7	4.7

Source: Brazil: Ministério da Fazenda (Directoria de Estatística Commercial), *Commércio Exterior do Brasil*. Officinas da Estatística Commercial, Rio de Janeiro, several issues.

Early in 1910 the trade balance position returned to normal levels. Gold imports dried up and there was even a mild net outflow from the Office's reserves during the first quarter as whole. However, the Finance Minister had been impressed by the strength of the external position and saw in it a sign of the need to revalue the exchange rate. In April, growing capital inflows reactivated the upward pressures on the exchange rate and Bulhões, forecasting that the Office's issue would soon reach the legal limit, sent the interim President a proposal recommending its abolition and the pegging of the milréis at 16d, transferring from Congress to the Executive the power to authorise 'the successive rises in the exchange rate established by the Office'.[38]

It was unlikely that Congress would accept losing its power over such a sensitive issue as exchange rate policy, but as the Executive had *de facto* power over the exchange rate through its influence on the Banco do Brasil's exchange management, the rumour that the government had made up its mind over a new stabilisation level was sufficient for foreign exchange dealers. Even though the Bulhões proposal had been drafted when the amount of gold-backed currency was still just 73 per cent of its legal maximum,[39] gold inflows grew rapidly towards the end of April and the 320 000 contos ceiling was reached in 14 May when the Conversion Office was closed, since no decision had yet been taken concerning its new regulations.

To break the opposition to its exchange rate policy the government staged a repetition of the tactics used in 1906. The Banco do Brasil drove its rate up to the proposed stabilisation level and, in July, with the approach of the export season, led a further rise to over 18d in September. However, this rapid change appreciation alienated important political support from the government and threw it into open confrontation with domestic producers. The São Paulo government, considering that the year's coffee output would be small, announced at once its decision not to apply the export prohibition, thus giving exporters the opportunity to fight the high exchange rates by refraining from selling their stocks and, in mid-September, the majority of the Senate Committee discussing the new exchange stabilisation bill was critical of the government's manipulations and favoured a 16d rate.[40] The private banks immediately started driving their rates up towards this figure but on 22 September the cabinet, completely out of touch with majority political opinion, decided not to alter the Banco do Brasil's rate.[41] In spite of the serious official reserve losses which this decision entailed, it was stubbornly maintained until the newly elected government took office on 15 November. By then the support of the overvalued official rate had cost the authorities almost all the Bank's foreign exchange credits and about three-quarters of the Treasury's London reserves.[42]

With the inauguration of the new administration the political deadlock was promptly solved.[43] Legislation was passed in December authorising the stabilisation of the milréis at 16d, extending the issuing limit to 900 000 contos and the Office reopened in the following month. The short-term economic consequences of the currency upheavals during the provisional government and the subsequent revaluation were not very important. However, the permanent effect of the revaluation on the level of imports would be a source of strain in the long run. The decision to revalue had been taken amidst intense optimism in regard to the evolution of the country's foreign exchange earnings. This optimism was proven unjustified by subsequent developments and the maintenance of the overvalued rate when the favourable external position began to change would be the source of damaging deflationary pressures.

The first serious reasons for alarm, with the worsening of the balance of payments prospects, appeared in 1912 and were connected with unfavourable trends developing well before that. The federal budget had swung again into deficit in 1908–9 when the fall of imports affected tariff revenue. After that, in spite of a substantial recovery in imports, the deficit continued to grow due to the sudden rise in expenditure from 1910 when amortisation payments on the part of the federal foreign debt funded in 1898 were begun again. There was also the renewed growth of expenditure on public works after 1909.[44] However, until 1911 the widening deficit could be covered by the large foreign loans financing the government's public investment programme and the favourable foreign exchange position enabled the Treasury to transfer the debt service without putting too much pressure on the exchange rate.

Nevertheless the increase in public expenditure alarmed Brazilian creditors. In spite of government pledges to balance the budget[45] the deficit continued to rise, the difficulty of financing it grew and in 1912 the government could not place a single long-term loan abroad. See table 2.2.

Table 2.2   Brazil: 1910–13, federal revenue, expenditure and credit operations* (in thousand contos)

Year	Revenue	Expenditure	Deficit	Gross Long-term Borrowing		Net issues of short-term foreign bills
				Foreign	Domestic	
1910	525	624	99	96	33	–
1911	564	682	118	142	28	–
1912	615	789	174	–	65	47
1913	654	763	109	184	41	–9

* *Amortisation of long-term debt is included in the expenditure figures.*
Sources: Brazil: IBGE, *Anuário Estatístico do Brasil*, 1939–40, Serviço Gráfico do IBGE, Rio de Janeiro, p. 1410.
Brazil. Ministério da Fazenda, *Balanço Geral da União*, Imprensa Nacional, Rio de Janeiro, 1910–13, *passim*. Table A.15.

As the high level of imports and the seasonal decline in exports were already responsible for a large reduction in Brazil's foreign exchange earnings in the first half of 1912, the fall in net capital inflows appears, on the basis of the scanty evidence available, to have been an important cause of the gold outflows and the credit stringency felt that year. Although the beginning of the war in the Balkans in October caused London interest rates to rise and prevented the floating of Brazilian loans for the rest of the year, the deflation of 1912 did not last long. The coming of the export season improved the balance of payments position, and renewed gold inflows relieved the liquidity squeeze later in the year. Nevertheless it was clear that, in the event of a continuing fall in foreign capital inflows, the prevailing balance of trade trend would have to be reversed promptly if exchange rate stability was to be preserved without large reserve losses and the ensuing consequences for domestic monetary stability.

There was little that could be done by way of restricting import demand. The absence of sophisticated instruments of monetary policy at that time meant that the only way to curb imports short of devaluation – which was not contemplated – or tariff increases – which required too large a measure of political consensus to be rapidly carried through Congress – and without a loss of the Office's gold reserves, would be by contracting the paper money component of the monetary base. There were in principle three means of financing the note withdrawals: budget surpluses, and domestic and foreign long-term borrowing. The first alternative was clearly unrealistic, since with the already large budget deficit and the decrease in tariff revenue that the fall in imports would cause, the size of the expenditure cuts required would be politically unacceptable.[46] The second was limited by the small size of Brazilian long-term capital markets and the effects of a continued growth in Treasury bond issues on their prices. The third alternative – a repetition of the post-1898 policies – depended once again on the government's ability to borrow abroad.

The possibility of an improvement in exports in the short term looked even more remote in late 1912. In fact, besides the growing federal budget deficit and the doubts as to the future trends of foreign capital inflows, an even more worrying change as far as the viability of the pre-war growth model was concerned was the deterioration in the prospects for export growth.

Rubber prices had fallen sharply after an extraordinary rise in 1910 and there was widespread concern over the long-term prospects of the wild rubber industry in face of competition from the new British and Dutch plantations in South East Asia. Even though in 1911 Brazil was still by far the largest world producer, it was known that the large areas planted in the Straits and the Dutch East Indies were already entering full production and that there was a marked productivity differential in their favour. These fears were proven founded, and Table 2.3 illustrates the impact of the increase in supply of plantation rubber on world prices and the swiftness with which it destroyed Brazilian pre-eminence in world markets.

Table 2.3   World rubber output and prices: 1909–18

| Year | Output (metric tons) | | | Prices (pence per lb)* |
| | Plantation | Wild | | |
		Brazil	Rest	
1909	3 600	42 000	24 000	82
1910	8 200	40 800	21 500	102.5
1911	14 419	37 730	23 000	60
1912	28 578	42 410	28 000	58
1913	47 618	39 370	21 452	44
1914	71 380	37 000	12 000	34.5
1915	107 867	37 229	13 615	31
1916	152 650	36 500	12 448	37.5
1917	213 070	39 370	13 258	37.75
1918	255 950	30 700	9 929	35.5

* Average London spot price of fine Brazilian (Pará) rubber.
Sources: Output: Macedo Soares, J.C. de; A Borracha: Estudo econômico e estatístico, L. Chauny et L. Quinsac, Paris, 1927, p. 28.
Prices: Idem, p. 62, and The India-Rubber Journal, several issues.

The unfavourable trends in rubber exports had, however, been compensated by the substantial rise in coffee prices which started in late 1910 as the result of the ultimate success of the valorisation programme. Until the middle of that year, the Valorisation Committee had refrained from selling from their stocks so as to force a reduction in other stocks held at the consuming centres.[47] The importers had been able to resist, owing to the fact that in 1909 world supply was higher than demand, but the small Brazilian crop of 1910 put an end to their opposition. Since for the next two crops the yearly coffee output remained below world consumption levels because of the restrictions on new planting instituted in 1902,[48] the London Committee was able to gain complete control over world prices and force a continuous rise until the end of 1912.[49]

Thus, since the collapse of rubber prices began in 1910, the growth of exports maintained until 1912 derived almost solely from the increase in coffee prices. However, as the distribution of coffee exports between countries was highly concentrated – the United States, France and Germany alone absorbing over two-thirds of them – further price increases could sooner or later provoke retaliatory action by the leading consumers.

In May 1912, completely out of the blue as far as the Department of State or the Brazilian Foreign Office were concerned, the U.S.

Attorney-General started anti-trust proceedings against the American agents of the Valorisation Committee in New York, which would eventually lead to the embargo of 950 000 bags of coffee stored in the city.[50] In spite of intense Brazilian diplomatic protests no political compromise could be found and on 16 January the London Coffee Valorisation Committee announced the sale of the whole of its New York stock.

The liquidation of the New York stocks is a watershed in the history of pre-war valorisation. It marked its practical termination and, as will be seen in the following section, also the end of the large coffee price rise started in 1910, which was one of the last factors still sustaining the long pre-war boom.

2.4   COLLAPSE AND CRISIS: 1913–14

Following the sale of the New York valorisation stock the long rise in coffee prices came to an end.[51] The growing trend in the world supply of rubber, combined with the effects on demand brought about by the tight monetary conditions in Europe and the associated business downturn in the United States, caused another sharp fall in world rubber prices from the start of 1913, and Brazilian rubber exports shrank by a further one-third during the year. However, because of the record export levels achieved in 1912, the still expansionary trends prevailing at the beginning of the year delayed the transmission of the sharp reversal in export demand to domestic business conditions, and imports remained at very high levels.

No matter how clearly these events foreshadowed a severe balance of trade disequilibrium they do not seem to have been fully anticipated by the government. In the first months of 1913 the authorities' main concern was still the budget position since the credit stringency in the world's leading capital markets had made it increasingly difficult to finance the very large recent growth of expenditure within the framework of the gold standard.

Again, as the official overseas reserve position deteriorated, a foreign loan was seen as the only feasible short-term solution to the government's financial and exchange rate management problems. Furthermore there were now difficulties even in financing public expenditure in domestic currency since Francisco Salles, the Finance Minister, feared that successive large issues of *apólices*, with which public contractors and suppliers were currently being paid, would affect their prices, and could damage foreign confidence and jeopardise his attempts to raise a large foreign loan abroad.[52]

Although credit conditions in London improved during the first quarter of 1913 and a short-lived wave of Brazilian borrowing – mostly public and railway issues – went on until June, the very high levels of imports, which were maintained until the second half of 1913, compounded a huge trade deficit in the second quarter of the year and Conversion Office gold losses reached unprecedented levels in July.[53] The gold backed note issue fell from its all time pre-war record level of 419 000 contos in February by 107 000 contos in the six-month period to the end of August, causing a 9.8 per cent contraction in the monetary base.

This sudden shrinkage of domestic liquidity was the final blow to the pre-war boom. Quotations of federal *apólices* started a headlong fall in the second half of the year as illiquid holders tried to unload them, and the fact that the national banking portfolio was saturated with these securities may account for the speed with which this reduction in high-powered money was translated into a contraction of credit and a reversal of expectations. Government payment arrears in Rio began to accumulate and in August there were reports that the banks were refusing to grant advances on government orders.[54]

In this same month, amidst a panic atmosphere, several proposals for a federal paper money issue began to be canvassed.[55] However in a last-ditch effort to maintain the confidence of private Conversion Office deposit holders and preserve the gold standard, the new Finance Minister refused to accept these proposals. Instead he presented a balanced budget proposal for 1914 embodying tougher cuts in public works programmes and announced the placement of another £2 million short-term loan in London, to be used to try and reverse the gold outflow from the Office. This loan, he argued wishfully, together with the expenditure of other non-federal loans raised during the first half-year would bridge the gap until the recently started coffee export season got into full swing.[56]

The decision not to abandon the gold standard at that stage, in spite of the fundamental balance of payments disequilibrium, as well as the disproportionate emphasis placed on budgetary discipline by the government, merits some comment, as these attitudes were maintained until the outbreak of the war.

It must be noted from the outset that the decision to stick to gold implied some optimism in relation to the future development of the balance of payments position since it was generally recognized that uncontrollable deflationary spurts caused by recurrent large gold outflows from the Conversion Office would have disastrous consequences for the economy. Up to a certain point the authorities were justified in expecting that the deterioration in the balance of payments position could be reversed at any moment, as its chief immediate causes were the diminution of foreign capital inflows stemming from the very tight credit conditions in Europe and the abnormal circumstances affecting coffee prices. If this is accepted, it is not unreasonable to suppose that they would view the current pressures on the exchanges as a temporary phenomenon that could be overcome if additional foreign financing could be secured by the federal government in the meantime. Indeed there are grounds for believing that the government still entertained serious hopes of being able to get further financial accommodation abroad as the twelve months preceding the outbreak of the war were monotonously marked by negotiations for a large federal loan in Europe. Thus the efforts to preserve exchange rate stability and the stress put on the need for budgetary equilibrium in official pronouncements during the crisis period should not be seen just as reflecting the strength of orthodox opinion on economic policy at home, but as directed fundamentally at preserving the confidence of foreign creditors, given the importance that the attainment of these two objectives had for the maintenance of the federal government's credit standing abroad.

In September a financial mission sent by Rothschilds arrived in Rio to assess Brazil's debt service capacity so as to provide the basis for the negotiation of a new large public loan. Although no decision came out immediately from this visit, there is indirect evidence to show that the bankers were not made optimistic by what they saw and to suggest that if financial assistance was to be provided it would have very tough strings attached to it.[57] The difficulties were increased further by the consequences of the rubber crisis for the debt-servicing capacity of some states which had borrowed heavily during the boom and based their revenue mainly on export taxes. In January, Pará, the richest rubber state, defaulted on a French loan and, even though the federal government had on several occasions publicly denied any responsibility in relation to state foreign liabilities,[58] their default affected Brazilian foreign bond prices and made it even more difficult to float a federal loan.

In March the Banco do Brasil could not keep the market exchange rate above the gold export point any longer and another period of violent monetary contraction began.[59] But even then the government did not give up its hopes of being able to muddle through the crisis with the help of a large foreign loan. At the end of the month it was reported that negotiations with Rothschilds were going on for the issue of a record £20 million and in April the London bankers enlisted the help of two large French banks with interests in Brazil, and later of a German bank, to support the operation.[60] In May, the Brazilians decided to send a special representative to conduct the talks in London.

The conclusion of an agreement, however, was delayed on two accounts. First, there was strong reaction in Brazil to the extremely hard terms imposed by the European bankers. The loan was made conditional, among other things, upon the transformation of the Banco do Brasil into an issuing bank under foreign administration and the leasing of the government-owned Central (Rio-São Paulo) Railway and of the large public shipping company, conditions that were not to be taken lightly by large sectors of Brazilian opinion.[61] Secondly, there was the problem of determining the way the government would disburse the loan proceeds. The creditor countries brought strong pressure to bear on Brazil to pre-empt the payment of federal and state arrears as well as long-standing claims to their nationals out of the funds to be raised with the loan.[62] The individual members of the banking consortium had also an obvious interest in the loan being used to meet Brazil's liabilities to them and their clients. On the other hand, the federal government naturally wanted to maximise the net foreign exchange receipts from the loan and disclaimed all responsibility with regard to local governments' liabilities.

Although political resistance in Brazil was overcome and in mid-June Congress authorised the loan, the talks continued as no *modus-vivendi* was found between the government and all the foreign pressure groups involved. As late as 23 July, Rothschilds were still telegraphing the Brazilian Finance Minister urging him to accept some German claims and stressing the importance of the continental bond markets for the success of the loan.[63] A few days later the Paris, and then the London, stock exchange closed with the approach of World War I.

3 The World War

3.1 THE EARLY RESPONSE TO THE DISRUPTION OF WORLD TRADE AND PAYMENTS

The British declaration of war against the Central Powers had two immediate economic consequences for Brazil. On the one hand, there was a break in the credit lines between Brazilian banks and their London correspondents: the former were unable to discount trade bills bearing German endorsements or drawn against goods shipped in non-Allied vessels in London, where the bulk of German-Brazilian trade was financed. On the other hand, there was the temporary but almost complete halt of transatlantic shipping.[1] This sudden disruption of foreign trade and payments immediately affected the foreign exchange market, the federal government's tariff revenue and the coffee industry, just as the period for marketing the 1914 crop was approaching its peak financial demand.

The government's impervious attitude towards the private sector's complaints throughout the 1913–14 depression changed as the problem posed by the outbreak of generalised warfare in Europe narrowed its policy options and shook it free of the morass of the loan negotiations. As with every trading nation, the Brazilian government's first reaction was to try and create a breathing-space with the issue of a series of emergency regulations, including the abandonment of gold convertibility, in the hope that it could later devise more permanent measures to deal with the abnormal situation. On 4 August it was decided to close the Conversion Office, restricting to the Banco do Brasil the right to convert its notes into gold, and to declare a ten-day bank holiday (later extended to 17 August), and a thirty-day moratorium on all debts following the resumption of banking operations.[2]

These first emergency measures, however, did nothing to relieve the coffee sector's financial problems and only postponed those of the cash-pressed government's creditors. Through their influence,[3] a Bill was introduced on 11 August, under government instructions, for the issue of 300 000 contos of inconvertible Treasury notes; two-thirds of this issue was to be earmarked to meet urgent federal obligations and one-third to be lent at low interest rates to national banks to relieve the liquidity squeeze and to be repaid by the end of 1915.[4] The terms

33

of this Bill were clearly influenced by the widespread belief that the war would not last long and was seen as a temporary expedient to overcome an abnormal situation.[5] Nevertheless, even though rushed through both Houses so as to become law on 24 August, the Bill met some doctrinaire opposition against the abandonment of the gold standard and had the limit allowed for Treasury expenditure reduced to 150 000 contos.[6]

The note issue fulfilled its immediate objectives and helped the Banco do Brasil to build up, through the increase in official gold reserves, a stronger line of defence to meet the Treasury's foreign obligations.[7] However, although the banks drawing on the new credit facilities were contractually bound to manage their foreign exchange operations under government instructions,[8] the temporary halt in exports, the closure of the Conversion Office and the inability of the Banco do Brasil to draw abroad to protect the exchange rate, caused an immediate exchange rate fall after the resumption of trading.[9] Fears that an exchange rate collapse would adversely affect the already critical budget position, on account of the debt service obligations and pending payments to foreign suppliers and contractors, led to a government agreement with Rothschilds, on 7 September, to discuss the basis of a new funding loan[10] and to extend the moratorium, allegedly at the incoming President's request, for a further three months.[11]

In October the funding agreement was signed. It provided for a total suspension of payments on all but one of the federal foreign loans – including French loans – not funded in 1898 until July 1917, and of amortisation payments until 1927;[12] during the period of total suspension of payments the service of the loans would be met by the proceeds of a new £15 million loan to be issued in London.[13] As similar agreements were made by other public authorities with their foreign creditors, total public foreign debt payments fell from £14.5 million in 1913 to £9.0 million in 1914, £7.5 million in 1915 and £6.8 million in 1916,[14] providing a substantial relief to the balance of payments position. This was crucial for the maintenance of approximate exchange rate stability at between 20 and 25 per cent below the pre-war parity experienced during the war.

Following the emergency measures described above, taken in the closing months of the Hermes da Fonseca presidency, the framework within which international trade would operate during the war began to take shape. The war had no adverse effect upon exports during 1915 and the widespread view that the Allied measures of economic warfare, in particular the economic blockade of overseas supplies to Germany – which accounted for about 15 per cent of Brazilian exports before the war – affected export earnings from early on in the war, is mistaken.[15] Although Britain was able to conclude a round of agreements with Germany's neutral neighbours before the end of 1914 to prevent their handling goods destined for the Central Powers classified as contraband by the blockade regulations, these initial 'restricted blockade' measures were not effective except in the case of Holland.[16] As far as Brazilian exports were concerned, goods continued to a large extent to reach Germany through her neutral Scandinavian neighbours, as shown in Table 3.1, and the quantity of total exports grew by not less than 33 per cent in 1915.[17] Only when the first German submarine raids against enemy merchant vessels led the Allies to retaliate by tightening the economic blockade and to introduce the blacklisting of firms from neutral countries trading with the enemy and the *navicert* system, did Brazil lose her German export markets.[18]

Table 3.1 Brazilian exports to selected countries: 1913–16 (in £ millions)

Year	Germany	Scandinavian neutrals			
		Sweden	Norway	Denmark	Total
1913	9.16	0.16	0.66	0.10	0.92
1914	4.64	1.07	0.31	0.29	1.67
1915	–	4.77	1.57	1.22	7.56
1916	–	1.53	0.29	0.41	2.23

Source: Brazil: IBGE, *Anuário Estatístico do Brasil*, 1939/40, op. cit., pp. 1366 ff.

In fact the sharp pre-war fall in milréis prices of staple exports was halted by the late 1914 exchange depreciation and for almost all export commodities 1915 was a favourable year.[19] The main economic policy problem posed by the outbreak of the war stemmed from the fiscal consequences of the stagnation in the volume of imports after the resumption of trade. This stagnation partially reflected the still depressed level of domestic activity, but was also a result of economic warfare measures such as the effective Allied blockade of enemy exports – which accounted for about 19 per cent of Brazilian imports before the war and some of which, such as dyestuffs, had no alternative supplier – and the mobilisation of industries for war by most of Brazil's other traditional European trade partners.[20] The sudden shrinkage of tariff revenue in 1914, superimposed on the halt of foreign lending and the large growth in public expenditure on extensive public works started during the pre-war boom, had already produced a serious budget disequilibrium.[21] The effect of war conditions upon the volume of imports threatened to transform this into a permanent fiscal crisis.

When President Wenceslau Braz took office on 15 November 1914, his government received an unenviable legacy of accumulated arrears and short-term obligations estimated at 311 000 contos, plus some £4 million immediately due abroad. Half of this was owed by the Banco do Brasil for overdrafts on government account before the outbreak of the war.[22] Besides this, the August note issue was proving to fall short of the federal government's financial requirements: by then the Treasury had already issued 82 per cent of the 150 000 contos authorised for government expenditure.[23]

The early measures of the new administration would be almost solely related to strengthening the federal financial position. They were conditioned by the political impossibility of proposing another note issue and were still strongly influenced by optimism as to the duration of the war.[24] Thus, although the new government kept budgeted expenditure for 1915 at the low figures that followed the 1914 cuts, it decided to buy time by rolling over the mounting federal obligations.

The budget law for 1915 authorised the issue of unspecified amounts of special one-year Treasury Bills – including gold-indexed bills – for the settlement of arrears and the expiry of the general moratorium scheduled for 15 December was again postponed by three months. Although these measures finally set the conditions for the gradual liquidation of the suspended obligations,[25] they provoked strong protests on behalf of the government's creditors from the Rio Commercial Association.[26] Nevertheless from February to May successive issues of the new Treasury bills were made at par value in partial settlement of federal debts.[27]

As the first half of 1915 progressed it became increasingly clear that this stopgap policy could not be sustained for long. Not only were the expectations of an early termination of the European conflict proving to be ill-founded, but the banking system's appraisal of the weakness of the federal government's financial position made the *Sabinas* – as the short-term bills were jokingly called, after Sabino Barroso, the new Finance Minister – almost unnegotiable as a financial asset as their issue grew.[28]

Moreover discontent was growing as the domestic economic outlook showed no signs of recovery. The August 1914 increase in high-powered money had failed to bring anything but a temporary relief to the credit squeeze which had gone on since 1913 and monetary conditions positively deteriorated during the first half of 1915 for, from December 1914, the Banco do Brasil shipped Conversion Office gold to settle its overdrafts in order to relieve the pressure on the Rio foreign exchange market and avoid a further fall in the exchange rate.[29] The reduction in the monetary base caused by the gold losses and the extremely bearish attitude of the private banking system – which went on increasing its cash reserves and drastically curtailing trade credit – wiped out the temporarily expansionary effect of the emergency note issue of late 1914 and the money supply resumed its falling trend during the first half of 1915.[30]

Manufacturing output had fallen by 8.7 per cent in 1914 after the rapid growth of production and investment up to 1912 and the levelling out of 1913, and activity levels were still depressed. Wholesalers and other large trading interests were the most vocal group against economic policy in early 1915, since the depression and credit restriction had considerably diminished the volume of their operations. Besides, they were the sector immediately affected by the government's failure to meet its commitments to suppliers and by the illiquidity of the new Treasury IOUs.[31]

On 1 June, the aged Finance Minister was replaced, allegedly for health reasons, by J.P. Calógeras, then at the Ministry of Agriculture. This cabinet reshuffle, much influenced by party political issues,[32] did not point to any marked shift in economic policy, as new and old ministers held similar orthodox views on inflationary deficit financing. However, as the war moved towards stalemate the government slowly came to realise the necessity of making a serious effort to adjust the economy to the effects of a prolonged European war superimposed on the already extremely depressed domestic economic position. It also came to realise that the first steps were to try and break the paper shackles created by the state of disarray of federal finances and to provide some relief to the extremely tight domestic monetary conditions.

3.2   READJUSTMENT TO CHANGED INTERNATIONAL ECONOMIC CONDITIONS

The shift of economic policy was signalled by a special presidential address delivered to Congress on 30 June 1915 which defined the two basic lines of action to be followed in fiscal and monetary policy during the next two years. On the fiscal front, the problems ahead posed by the probably long-lasting reduction of revenue were now clearly visible.[33] They were magnified by the possibility of having to face the resumption of full debt servicing – which was to rise to almost 40 per cent of total expenditure in 1916 in spite of the funding arrangement[34] – under war conditions. The strictest discipline over expenditure was to be maintained together with new attempts to raise and diversify the sources of indirect tax revenues. To deal with the pending debt accumulated since 1914 and presented as the result of the 'hurry to carry out a programme of public works beyond the economic possibilities of the country,'[35] the President still attempted to preserve the possibility of resorting to further Treasury Bill issues by proposing some alternative uses for them such as, for instance, the settlement of tax payments.[36] However, as the Finance Minister himself admitted, 'it was evidenced by the discussions [with the government's creditors] that part, at least, of these obligations should be compensated in cash since the [reduced] capacity of the domestic market to absorb the government IOUs would not allow . . . their complete liquidation through bills or bonds.'[37]

The second problem was the relief of domestic monetary stringency. The settlement of government debts in cash would, of course, go a long way in that direction. However, the determination to ease credit was not independent of the government's willingness to provide financial help to the staple export industries, especially coffee, whose prices were still low after the 1913–14 collapse and had fallen sharply since April 1915.[38] With the European capital markets closed, the coffee interests had been canvassing for direct federal financial help for coffee valorisation since the end of 1914[39] and by mid-1915, with a new crop about to arrive at the ports,[40] their demands coalesced with the government's fears that further wartime restrictions on world demand would adversely affect prices and, consequently, Brazil's external position.[41]

It is important to note in this connection that, at this stage, government's views began to reflect the growing complaints about what contemporaries referred to as the private banking system's 'inelasticity,' i.e., its limited capacity for credit creation resulting from high reserve ratios and its inadequate response to the financial needs of the real sector. Although private banks' reserve ratios were usually high indeed,[42] it was the seasonal variation in their ability to lend that proved to be the greatest source of the real sector's problems. Complaints about tight credit conditions always became louder during the third quarter of the year in urban financial centres, and especially in Rio, when the cash settlement of the farmers' accounts following the harvesting season involved 'a massive reshuffling of liquidity from the financial centres to the interior.'[43] Given the farmers' and agricultural workers' preference for holding money in the form of currency instead of banking deposits as compared with the urban population, due to the under-development of the banking network in the rural areas, the harvest season provoked a substantial drain in high-powered money away from the financial centres. This drain not only immediately reduced the banks' ability to lend, but eventually forced them to seek to reduce their liabilities by a substantial amount (given the usually high reserve ratios with which they operated), thus causing a contraction in the money supply which directly affected urban trade and industry.

The legacy of these complaints, from 1915 onwards, was the notion that the Banco do Brasil could play an important part in minimising the inadequacies of the private banking system by implementing the still unused central banking powers conferred by its 1905 statutes – especially those concerning rediscount operations[44] – and by spreading its branch network. These ideas were embodied in the June 1915 presidential address. However, the more radical step of granting issuing rights to the Bank, although forcefully advocated by its president throughout the war, did not come until the twenties. Nevertheless, from the second half of 1915 the government gave continuous financial support for the expansion of the Bank's operation and the wartime period witnessed a great leap forward in its growth as a nationwide institution.[45]

The new government's appraisal of the economic position in mid-1915 broadly outlined above led to a series of readjustment measures in the following months. In August the government authorised a further issue of 350 000 contos of Treasury notes and of an unlimited amount of federal *apólices* to liquidate milréis-denominated obligations incurred prior to 1915 and to meet current expenditure, to support 'national production,' and to provide 50 000 contos to the Banco do Brasil to develop its operations and open branches in all states of the Union.[46]

By far the largest part of the note issue went to meet government obligations, as the expected export restrictions did not materialise during the marketing of the relatively small 1915 crop and the Bank's rediscount operations and the gradual liquidation of federal debts increased the private bank's capacity to finance it.[47] Since, by the third quarter of 1915, the improvement in the balance of payments position already allowed the Bank to settle its remittances without resorting to gold sales, the withdrawals of Conversion Office notes stopped and the money supply finally regained a steadily rising tendency.[48]

In an attempt to adjust federal revenue to the changed economic conditions, the government decided to unify the different gold-tariff quotas created in 1905 into a single 40 per cent rate from January 1916 and broaden the range of products subject to the internal consumption tax. It did this in the budgets for 1916 and 1917, substantially increasing the share of this tax in total revenue, as Table 3.2 shows. Expenditure was kept at very low nominal levels and actually fell in real terms with the acceleration of inflation after 1915, largely as a result of cuts in consumption expenditure and although budget estimates proved far off the mark the real deficit fell substantially.[49]

The government's attempts to restore financial equilibrium and to make effective a more expansionary monetary policy in the second half of 1915 were helped by the start of a process of readjustment of the productive sector to wartime changes in world demand and to the sudden gap created between domestic demand and supply by the restrictions on imports, which boosted domestic activity in several tradeable goods industries.

The overall effects of the war upon Brazilian foreign trade, underlying the pressures for this readjustment of the real sector is visible in the aggregate data presented in Table A.4. The outstanding fact was the continuous fall in the barter terms of trade after their collapse during the pre-war crisis, largely as a result of the effects of world wartime inflation on import prices and the very slow recovery of export prices towards pre-war levels.[50]

The evolution of the export price index resulted from unfavourable

Table 3.2   Brazil: 1913–17, revenue from import and consumption duties
(in thousand contos)

	Import duties		Consumption tax	
	Revenue	Share in total tax revenue (%)	Revenue	Share in total tax revenue (%)
1913	367.7	76.0	65.1	13.5
1914	209.1	69.0	52.2	17.2
1915	165.0	55.9	67.9	23.0
1916	198.9	56.8	83.8	23.9
1917	169.4	46.4	117.7	32.3

Source: Villela, A.V. and Suzigan, W. (1973). *Política do Governo e Crescimento da Economia Brasileira*. (IPEA/INPES, Rio de Janeiro), table
A.13.

factors, discussed below, affecting coffee and, to a lesser extent,
rubber prices, and, in spite of substantial changes occurring in the
structure of exports during the war, was the basic cause of the
sluggish recovery of the value of exports.[51] It is important to note in
this connection that the volume of exports increased substantially.
Although shipping tonnage restrictions were a continual threat to the
further growth of Brazilian exports, they were not a binding constraint until 1917 and even then, as shown below, were successfully
overcome. Nevertheless the rise in the volume of exports relative to
pre-war levels was more than offset by the deterioration in the terms
of trade and Brazil's capacity to import continued to fall from the
already low levels that resulted from the collapse of 1913–14.

The most important change occurring in the structure of Brazilian
trade was the transformation of the commodity composition of exports. On the one hand the explosive increase in world rubber
supplies shown in Table 2.3 and the war-induced adverse changes in
the world demand for coffee from 1916 – such as the effective
blockade of Brazil's roundabout access to the German market and
the low priority given to coffee imports by Allied procurement
agencies – kept the prices of both commodities very depressed
throughout the war[52]. On the other hand, the curtailment of some
European sources of strategic industrial raw materials and foodstuffs,
which Brazil could supply at the high prices then prevailing, allowed
a rapid expansion of non-traditional exports and stimulated the
growth of production in several primary and food-processing industries. Such was the case with sugar, where the fall in beet sugar

supplies allowed a sustained increase in exports to Brazil's southern neighbours, with cereals, beef and other animal products increasingly exported to Europe, and with manganese ore, as the halt in Russian exports made Brazil the chief supplier to the United States.[53] The growth of the more dynamic of these exports is shown in Table 3.3. The importance of the growth of these non-traditonal exports to the maintenance of Brazil's foreign exchange earnings can be seen by comparing the behaviour over time of the share of Brazil's traditional staples in total exports, shown in Table A.5.

Table 3.3   Brazil: 1913–17, net export quantity of selected non-traditional exports (in thousand tons)

	Sugar	Manganese	Refrigerated Beef	Rice	Kidney Beans	Maize
1913	5.3	122.3	–	−7.7	−8.5	−8.8
1914	31.8	183.6	–	−6.5	−5.3	−1.1
1915	59.0	288.6	8.5	−6.9	1.0	−2.0
1916	53.8	503.1	33.6	0.4	44.5	3.5
1917	131.5	532.8	66.4	44.6	93.4	23.8

Sources: Williams, J.H., (1919). Latin American Foreign Exchange and International Balances During the War, in *The Quarterly Journal of Economics*, volume XXXIII, May, p. 451; Villela, A. V. and Suzigan, W., (1973). *Política do Governo e Crescimento da Economia Brasileira* (IPEA/INPES, Rio de Janeiro), p. 145 and *RC-JC*, 1917, p. 20.

The structure of imports did not show large changes as a result of the war, as can be seen in Table 3.4. Besides the marked fall in capital goods imports, basically stemming from the 1913–15 recession and from foreign supply restrictions affecting the importation of transport equipment, the main changes were the growth in the share of fuels and the fall in consumer goods. These changes reflected the different domestic supply elasticities between the two classes of goods, and the federal government's efforts to maintain the level of foreign coal supplies – whose prices increased enormously during the war[54] – to avoid the disruption of essential transportation facilities.

However, the real growth rates of different classes of imports shown in Table 3.5 help us to assess how strongly the wartime supply restrictions affected Brazil, inducing the growth of output and import substitution in different sectors – especially in non-durable consumer goods – as well as the small but sustained recovery of investment levels from 1916.

Table 3.4   Brazil: 1913–17, structure of imports by classes of use
(in percentage of total volume of imports)

	1913	1914	1915	1916	1917
Consumer goods	30.05	33.97	27.46	24.20	22.39
Non-durable	20.74	23.16	23.50	20.02	16.37
Durable	9.31	10.81	3.96	4.18	6.02
Fuels and lubricants	9.65	12.28	15.36	16.24	17.29
Raw Materials	45.22	42.87	52.12	53.95	53.41
Capital goods	15.03	10.84	5.04	5.59	6.88
To industry	4.18	3.34	1.65	1.88	2.21
Transport equipment	5.92	2.88	1.33	1.43	1.89
Other	4.93	4.62	2.06	2.28	2.78
Unclassified	0.05	0.04	0.02	0.03	0.03

Source: Villela, A.V. and Suzigan, W. (1973). Política do Governo e Crescimento da Economia Brasileira. (IPEA/INPES. Rio de Janeiro), p. 436.

Table 3.5   Brazil: 1913–17, annual percentage rates of real growth of
imports by classes of use

	1913	1914	1915	1916	1917
Consumer goods	−1.93	−37.18	−31.96	−3.75	−10.90
Non-durable	−3.25	−40.32	−12.45	−8.36	−20.44
Durable	−0.64	−30.57	−71.31	24.00	34.63
Fuels and lubricants	10.37	6.21	−11.97	−3.55	−22.21
Raw materials	1.84	−50.20	−10.51	17.60	−26.67
Capital goods	−17.87	−60.68	−62.01	29.19	8.41
To industry	−25.66	−58.45	−60.25	27.77	−0.06
Transport equipment	−18.79	−71.91	−60.93	52.77	2.34

Source: Villela, A.V. and Suzigan, W. (1973). Política do Governo e Crescimento da Economia Brasileira. (IPEA/INPES. Rio de Janeiro), p. 436.

Given the large margins of unutilised capacity prevailing at the beginning of the war, the import restrictions brought about a remarkable output recovery from 1915. However, the classical thesis of the dramatic impact of these wartime restrictions on the industrialization of Brazil[55] has been correctly qualified by several authors.[56] The behaviour of capital goods imports to industry during the war shown above and the still very limited technological capability of domestic suppliers of industrial equipment make it very unlikely that the war had a substantial effect on the expansion of industrial capacity.[57]

Despite the fact that some important sectors like building remained depressed throughout the war,[58] business in the tradeable goods sectors underwent a significant overall recovery after 1916. The government's gradual settlement of its compromises and the easing of monetary conditions it brought about was widely recognised as a crucial factor in the revival of trade.[59]

Of course the basic federal budget imbalance could not easily be redressed, particularly since further expenditure cuts were regarded as an unworkable proposition by the Treasury by the end of 1916.[60] The possibility of domestic borrowing was limited, as the Minister of Finance put it, 'by prudency'[61] as the long-term federal *apólices* were selling at a 20 per cent discount. The natural outcome was a further increase in indirect taxation and the budget for 1917 embodied a rise in the gold tariff quota to 55 per cent and a further widening of the incidence of the domestic consumption tax.[62]

Although the balancing of the federal government's accounts remained a source of permanent worry, the central issue of economic policy in 1916 became increasingly the government's ability to honour its foreign obligations and, expecially, the possibly damaging effects of the Treasury's foreign exchange payments on exchange rate stability. Worries on that score began to grow because the £5 million of one-year gold-indexed Treasury Bills, issued to European and American creditors as settlement of government arrears from the end of the first quarter of 1915 and renewed in 1916 in accordance with a contractual option for a one-year extension, would become due from March 1917[63] – only months before the full resumption of interest payments on the long-term foreign debt in August. Even though the Banco do Brasil had regained a reasonable control over the foreign exchange market by the end of 1915 and had kept the milréis exchange rate within narrow margins around 12d, the Treasury had refrained from liquidating its gold-indexed bills during 1916 in order not to 'weigh on the [foreign exchange] market'[64] and to avoid the budgetary consequences of a rise in the milréis equivalent of its current foreign payments.[65]

In fact the task of exchange rate management had been made more difficult in 1916. On the one hand there was a deterioration of the trade balance after its 1915 improvement, as a result of the rise in both import unit values and their quantities following the beginning of domestic recovery.[66] On the other hand there were the adverse psychological effects of recurrent news about the requisitioning of Allied ships employed in ocean routes between Brazil and Europe.[67]

With the London capital market blocked by the firm stand taken by the British Capital Issues Committee against foreign issues,[68] the

Brazilian government entertained during 1916 the new possibility of borrowing in New York signalled by the American wartime drive for financial supremacy in Latin America through the expansion of branch banking and long-term lending.[69]

On the occasion of the Pan-American Conference of Buenos Aires in 1916, during which United States Treasury Secretary McAdoo publicly dwelt on the dangers to the American Republics arising from their excessive economic reliance on European connections,[70] the American delegation visited Brazil and started negotiations for a loan which would relieve Brazil's pressing foreign exchange needs and possibly even allow the resumption of full debt servicing before 1917.[71] The brief Rio negotiations were followed up by a visit of the Brazilian Foreign Minister to the United States in July for talks with private banking interests, but nothing came of these efforts.[72]

The government made new attempts to raise US$25million to fund the federal short-term obligations in September, when representatives of the United States International Financial Corporation visited Rio, again with no success. In view of the possible political dividends afforded by the loan the Department of State took the matter up again in Washington with the International Financial Corporation and, on 20 October, the Department was informed that although the bankers could not see a way to grant the loan requested by Brazil, they 'would have great interest in a general reorganization of the finances of Brazil if such was desired by that Government.[73] However, Rothschilds were bound to oppose any such radical schemes and the Brazilian government did not desire to engender their hostility. Therefore, the Finance Minister's reaction to the American counter proposal was cool, to the great chagrin of the American Ambassador, who predicted:

> the main difficulty in arranging a loan in New York would come from the opposition of the Rothschilds who have so mortgaged Brazil's financial future that . . . they will place every obstacle in the way of her entering into banking relations with any other house than their own or with any other nation than England.[74]

3.3 THE END OF BRAZILIAN NEUTRALITY

As mentioned above, the Brazilian government's worries over the external position and its ability to start servicing its increased foreign obligations in 1917 were aggravated by the stepping up of the restrictive

Allied measures affecting coffee exports to Europe during 1916. The tightening of the blockade virtually closed the Scandinavian route to the German and Austrian markets and, in March, the French government told the Comité des Transports Maritimes to prohibit coffee imports from May to September. Although the French decision was not carried through owing to strong protests from Brazil, rumours remained that other Allies would eventually do so, since the level of existing stocks in Europe was too high in relation to their war procurement necessities.[75]

The prospect of a drastic reduction in coffee exports represented a far worse threat to Brazil's external equilibrium than the impending increase in federal foreign debt payments since, if the worst came to the worst, she could roll over the latter, but coffee still represented over 50 per cent of the country's current export earnings. Moreover the Allied restrictions on the trade in a commodity so crucial to Brazilian economic stability would have an important bearing upon the government's success in maintaining its settled policy of neutrality, in view of the diplomatic problems the war created for German–Brazilian relations.

When the war broke out the large superiority of British sea power led the German naval authorities to order the internment of her merchant fleet in neutral habours and, as a result, 46 German and Austrian ocean-going ships had taken refuge and were lying idle in Brazilian ports.[76] At the same time there were still about 3.2 million bags of valorisation coffee belonging to Brazil stored in European ports, serving as a guarantee for the 1908 coffee loan. Over 1.8 million bags of these stocks were in Hamburg, Bremen and Antwerp and, after the occupation of Belgium, the German authorities ordered the sale of this coffee without the production of the warrants held by the London Valorisation Committee and deposited the proceeds of their sales – amounting to the Reichsmark equivalent of £6 million – at the Berlin bank of Bleichröder to the São Paulo government's account. However, as the release of these funds would benefit the British and French bondholders to whom the coffee was hypothecated, the German government forbade their remittance and the proceeds of the sales remained frozen in Berlin.[77]

When the German sales ended in March 1916, the large depreciation of the Reichsmark against sterling – in which São Paulo's debt on account of coffee valorisation was denominated – led to a *Paulista* attempt to arrange with the German bankers that the payments should be made at the pre-war gold parity, but no firm commitment was forthcoming.[78] Even though the German attitude provoked great discontent in São Paulo, the federal government strongly denied the rumours that Brazil, following Portugal's example, would abandon neutrality and take over the German ships.[79] In fact, following the lead of the United States, Brazilian foreign policy since the outbreak of the war had been one of strict neutrality, and even when the pro-Ally campaign led by influential politicians like Senator Ruy Barbosa increased the opposition to the neutrality policy in mid-1916, the government took the very clear course of dissociating itself from any involvement in it.[80] The federal authorities would only go so far as to attempt to charter part of the German fleet held in Brazil against the funds blocked in Berlin. The proposal, however, was not accepted by the German government.[81]

Against this background, the tightening of Allied restrictions over Brazilian trade in 1916 provoked strong ill-feelings in official circles in Brazil who saw it as a high-handed interference with the country's neutral rights which could force São Paulo to act against the federal government's policy of neutrality.[82] There is no evidence, however, of any official communication between the Allies and Brazil relating to the use of the German ships during 1916.[83]

The outlook for the external position in Brazil was, however, completely transformed in the first half of 1917 by the German decision to initiate unrestricted submarine warfare, sinking without warning all merchant ships engaged in trade with the enemy. In spite of the neutrals' strong protests, an all-out U-boat offensive was launched in February, with devastating effectiveness. Allied and neutral losses soared. One out of every four ships that left the United Kingdom did not return.[84] Defeat was feared in Britain, failing the discovery of an effective deterrent to the German submarines. If losses continued at the level of the first few months' by the end of the year the carrying capacity of the British merchant fleet would fall to between to 1.6 and 2.0 million tons a month, against needs of 1.4 million tons for basic food supplies alone.[85]

The immediate consequence for Brazil of the German submarine offensive was the prohibition of imports of coffee into the United Kingdom in the second half of February 1917, as part of a comprehensive stepping-up of import restrictions by the British government. Although Britain was a minor importer of coffee, the Brazilian government feared the spread of the prohibition to other Allied countries such as France and Italy, both substantial consumers.[86] If the British decision were to be followed by other Allies it would leave the government no alternative but to protect the coffee industry by domestic purchases and to default on the foreign debt so as to maintain the level of imports, already compressed almost to the bare essentials.

On 3 March the Minister of Finance, who at the beginning of the year was declaring that 'the sole preoccupation, the sole objective of the present administration is to take up again the payment of the Funding Loan,'[87] telegraphed to Rothschilds disclaiming 'all responsibility for the financial consequences of the restrictions which must rest with those who have caused the said situation,' and threatening that 'resources intended for our European payments may even be applied here to acquire stocks of goods which, remitted opportunely when free navigation is re-established may allow us to pay our creditors,' unless some form of foreign financial assistance was forthcoming.[88] However, although the London bankers immediately put the matter before the British authorities,[89] the latter took a long time in interdepartmental deliberations over whether financial help to Brazil might be conditional on the seizure of the German ships.[90]

The position was further complicated by the prospect of a large coffee crop in 1917 – some 25 per cent above the previous year's figure[91] – when domestic credit conditions were again worsening in the second quarter of 1917 as the private banks, foreseeing the problems ahead, again started restricting credit and increasing their reserves,[92] thus aggravating the effects of the erosion of real cash balances cause by the acceleration of inflation.[93]

This bleak outlook and the possibility of obtaining a substantial *quid pro quo* from the takeover of the German ships were already sufficient to push the Government slowly but irreversibly, under the pressure of São Paulo, towards accepting inflationary coffee financing and the end of neutrality as justifiable policy propositions. These steps were made immensely easier on 4 April when, following President Wilson's request to the American Congress for a declaration of war against Germany, a Brazilian steamer was sunk by a German raider off the Brittany coast.

On 10 April Brazil broke off relations with Germany. On 15 May, the Brazilian Ambassador in Washington delivered official proposals to the American government, stating that 'Brazil was prepared to abandon its position of neutrality towards Germany' in exchange for United States 'guarantees'. The latter related to the 'necessary supplies, particularly wheat and coal, and that shipping used in trade with Brazil would not be withdrawn for use in transatlantic trade to a degree which would seriously embarrass Brazil' and also to military aid in case of an attack by Germany.[94]

On 18 May the Americans informed Brazil of the acceptance of its proposals '*en principe*'[95] and the sinking of another Brazilian merchant ship on May 20[96] washed away all opposition and completely freed the hands of the government to take a tougher line against Germany. On 22 May the President asked Congress to reconsider Brazil's neutrality in the war between Germany and the United States and, on May 28, a final decision was taken on this issue and on the takeover of the German ships.[97]

However, although the takeover of the German ships could be instrumental in avoiding an almost certain bottleneck in carrying capacity for Brazilian exports, it did nothing to relieve the foreign exchange constraint. Moreover the larger 1917 cofee crop was now coming to the ports and, as the world shipping crisis menaced exports with import prohibitions which could cut off important European markets at short notice, international prices had been falling.[98] Thus, when Santos stocks rose to the alarming figure of 6 million bags in July 1917, as compared to 1 million in July 1916[99], against an increasingly bearish attitude on the part of the banking system towards financing the stocks' retention in the difficult credit conditions then prevailing, Congress approved a new issue of 300 000 contos of Treasury notes to be lent to the São Paulo government for coffee purchases and to the Banco do Brasil for rediscount operations.[100]

The decision to end Brazilian neutrality opened up the opportunity of individual negotiations with the Allies for the chartering of the ships. Although an Inter-Allied Shipping Committee was set up at the beginning of the war, the experience failed and shipping control was still conducted on a national basis;[101] thus, given the dearth of shipping space and their strategic necessities, the Allies indulged in a veritable *sauve qui peut* to gain possession of the vessels held by Brazil. Eventually, by the end of November, Brazil concluded an agreement with France.

The main points of the agreement provided for the chartering under the Brazilian flag, until March 1919, of 30 out of 46 German and Austrian ships for a sum of 110 million francs – that is, over £4 million at the ruling exchange rate – and the opening of a credit line in France to the account of the Brazilian government for the purchase of two million bags of coffee from the 1917 crop, valued at 110 million francs, plus an equal sum for other Brazilian produce as required by

France.[102] The agreement did not come immediately into force, for its ratification was still dependent on the French Parliament's approval, but the more than £12 million involved promised a definite relief to the Brazilian government's preoccupation with the effects of its foreign exchange transfers upon the external value of milréis.

However, when the tension surrounding the 1917 decisions subsided, it could be seen that the 1918 outlook differed little from the past few years' and that, failing an early termination of the war, the government would still have to face a struggle against the fiscal and the balance of payments problems, while keeping a watchful eye on every new development on the coffee front.

The only new problems stemmed from the renewed acceleration of inflation. By the end of 1917 the acceleration in the growth of the cost of living given impetus by food price rises[103] was becoming a central issue in economic policy. The erosion of real wages with the rise in the cost of living provoked a wave of labour unrest in the main urban centres during 1917[104] leading to the creation of a federal food prices control authority in June 1918. This, in spite of the complaints of urban traders,[105] proved to be an effective countermeasure, while a police clampdown on the 'alien anarchist' labour leaders prevented the development of more serious political consequences.[106]

The conduct of fiscal policy gave rise to a clash between the government and the increasingly powerful industrial and commercial associations during the discussion of the 1918 budget in Congress. The proposal presented by the Finance Minister in the second half of 1917 was in keeping with the previous year's directives, according to which, as mentioned above, further nominal expenditure cuts were found impracticable and general increases in indirect taxation coupled with a spread of the incidence of the excise tax were made to compensate for the loss in tariff revenue.[107] However the government's proposal for a further rise in taxes met strong opposition and was radically altered in the Chamber Finance Committee under the influence of its Chairman, Deputy Antonio Carlos.[108] The clash led to Calógeras's resignation in September 1917 and the nomination of Antonio Carlos to the Finance portfolio and no radical alterations in taxation were made for 1918.[109]

Although the change in the Finance Ministry also foreshadowed changes affecting monetary policy, given Antonio Carlos's strong feelings against paper money issues,[110] in early 1918 the most pressing problems still remained the balance of payments weakness and the risk of a crisis in the coffee industry, failing an early termination of the war. Anxiety over the coffee and external position reappeared at the beginning of 1918 on account of delays in getting the French Parliament's approval of the expenditures relating the German ships chartering agreement, due to the opposition of a lobby led by deputies from Le Havre linked with the coffee business.[111] Moreover the São Paulo government had bought six million bags of coffee at the beginning of 1918,[112] with funds provided by the federal Treasury, on the understanding that a third of them would be released with the French purchases. With the approach of the 1918 crop, estimated at between 10.5 and 12.0 million bags – while total exports from the 1917 crop had just amounted to slightly over 7.3 million bags by April 1918[113] – and prices that were not firm, both the state government and the Santos coffee trade became increasingly apprehensive. Following the yearly meeting of the influential Santos Commercial Association in March, delegates pressed the state government for a further purchase of two million bags from the 1917 crop as being necessary to avoid a serious effect on prices.[114] However, the position was further complicated since the pre-war practice in the world coffee market was that stocks were held at the consuming centres and Santos' warehousing capacity was insufficient to hold the surplus stocks.[115]

Although the French Parliament finally approved the credits agreed with Brazil by a very small majority at the end of February[116] they failed to bring about the expected relief to the foreign exchange market. As late as October the Brazilian Finance Minister was complaining that 'there is much discontent with the French ship convention as the French government has only purchased half of the coffee agreed and is very backward with its payments'.[117] Furthermore the trade surplus continued to shrink because of the continued rise in import prices, the balance of payments position became critically weak and, in July, the exchange rate fell suddenly by almost 6 per cent. The somewhat loose exchange control measures enforced for the first time in Brazil after the declaration of war[118] were tightened by making foreign exchange remittances – restricted to import and foreign debt payments and the maintenance of non-enemy aliens abroad – subject to prior approval by the Banco do Brasil.[119]

The chronic wartime dilemma of maintaining external equilibrium with a substantially reduced market for coffee was, however, to be suddenly solved by a dramatic change in the coffee supply outlook when two days of unprecedentedly severe frosts in late June 1918 hit several coffee producing districts of São Paulo. In a matter of hours hundreds of millions of coffee trees were either entirely destroyed or had their productivity severely impaired, at a time when harvesting of the 1918 crop had just begun.[120] The market's prospects of a coffee glut in Brazil from August at the latest were suddenly reversed and, as expectations of an early end to the war grew and were confirmed, the importers' scramble to rebuild their stocks sent New York spot prices for the Santos 4 grade – which averaged 10.8 cents per pound in June – rocketing to over 22 cents per pound in December.[121]

The long term consequences of the great frost of 1918 to the world coffee market will be analysed in detail in the following chapter. It is worth pointing out, however, that, even though it put an end to the continued balance of payments weakness the Brazilian authorities had to live with throughout the war – as the value of exports more than doubled in the first half of 1919 as compared with the same period in 1918 – the frost had immediate and not unimportant adverse consequences on the level of economic activity in Brazil. The harsh weather affected not only the coffee trees but also other crops in which São Paulo supplied a substantial share of the market, such as sugar cane and cotton[122] and, as it occurred at the start of the harvesting season, its effects on current income levels in the agricultural sector of São Paulo were bound to be substantial. Given the importance of the level of São Paulo's agricultural incomes for the effective demand for industrial production and the supply shock caused by the failure of several industrial raw material crops, the frost would, by itself, be enough to deal a serious blow to domestic activity levels. Its depressive effects were perhaps aggravated by the recessive tendencies already present as a result of the sharp erosion of the trade surplus during the year[123] and industrial output stagnated in 1918 after two years of remarkable recovery.[124] Nevertheless, on 11 November, four days before the end of President Braz's terms of office, the Armistice was signed, ushering in a period in which the debate over financial reconstruction and monetary reform and the need for a stronger Brazilian control over world coffee markets would almost completely overshadow all other economic policy issues.

4 The Impact of the World Postwar Boom and Slump: 1919–22

4.1 THE POSTWAR BOOM AND AGITATION FOR BANKING REFORM

Brazil's macroeconomic instability in the three years following the return to peace as well as the difficult economic policy problems she faced until the mid-twenties have their roots in the violent worldwide postwar economic fluctuations and the 'trail of devastation' which, in the words of the late Professor Joslin, it left throughout Latin America.[1]

The boom experienced from early 1919 by the industrialized Allied economies – especially the United States and the United Kingdom – while Central and Eastern Europe still suffered from famine and stagnation, was shared by most primary producing export economies and is one of the sharpest on record.[2] Although output recovered quickly in the leading industrial countries after the mild and short-lived recession following the Armistice, this 'boom of astonishing dimensions'[3] was more impressive for its effects on prices.

The causes of the 1919 world price explosion are many, and some of them specifically national in character.[4] As far as the behaviour of the Brazilian economy is concerned, the most important feature of the world boom is the uncontroversial fact that it was accompanied by a frantic speculative drive towards accumulation of commodity stocks in the central countries.[5] Especially in the United States – which absorbed over 40 per cent of Brazilian exports in 1919 and 1920 – where the abolition of economic controls proceeded faster, but also in the United Kingdom and in France, the anticipation of higher commodity prices with the unleashing of pent-up wartime demand was supported by the easy money policy followed from early 1919 to help demobilisation (as well as for debt management reasons), and by the huge amounts of financial assets accumulated during the war.[6] During 1919 controls were dismantled, income recovered, and demand was redirected to peace-time needs against short-term inelastic supplies and a worn-out world transport system. The resulting

53

commodity price increases led to windfall profits from stock-holding which justified the speculative positions then being taken and maintained a bullish atmosphere in world commodity markets lasting until the second quarter of 1920.[7]

The positive effects of the sudden recovery of international trade upon primary producers' exports and income caused by the boom were amplified in the case of Brazil by the severe supply restrictions affecting the world coffee market since the frost of 1918. As mentioned in Chapter 3 coffee prices had already shot up during the second half of 1918, well before the acceleration in the growth of world commodity prices. The damaging effect of the frost was felt even more strongly in 1919, when a great reduction in the yield of the affected areas of São Paulo resulted in a 50 per cent fall in Brazilian output relative to the wartime average crop, and production reached its lowest point on record in the period under study. In spite of the partial compensation afforded by the very large crop of 1919 in other countries,[8] the booming world demand carried international coffee prices to new record levels in the second half of the year.

Favourable demand conditions also prevailed for other Brazilian primary export products and the boom caused an explosive increase in the value of exports in 1919. The release of pent-up demand for all classes of industrial goods after the long import starvation since 1914 in Brazil, also led to a sharp recovery in the value of imports. However, the growth of imports – even gathering an increasing momentum as the domestic boom progressed[9] did not prevent there being a large trade surplus in 1919.

The sudden improvement in the external position created great difficulties for exchange rate management. As early as the third quarter of 1918 the Bank was fighting against a sharp appreciation tendency in the milréis-sterling rate.[10] These efforts were abandoned after the 'unpegging' of the European exchanges in March 1919 and the target became the dollar rate, which was kept roughly stable, while the milréis substantially appreciated against all European currencies,[11] giving an additional boost to imports in spite of the still abnormal supply conditions in European industrial countries.[12] However, as export prices were booming, while domestic import-competing industries were more concerned about their investment plans and were momentarily protected by the sharp rise in world prices, this rapid exchange rate appreciation was not much felt by the private sector.

In 1919, reflecting the extremely tight monetary policy then being followed,[13] the economic policy debate would be dominated by the revival of complaints raised during the war about the inadequacies of the national banking system and the 'inelasticity' of the money supply. As mentioned in Chapter 3, the debate on banking reform had grown during the war. After the abandonment of the gold standard, the operation of the seasonal credit-tightening caused periodic demands from banking and business circles for an increase in high powered money to compensate for the harvest drain – particularly when the additional problem of financing a larger coffee crop was in sight – which, given the chronic financial needs of the Treasury, resulted in the large note issues of August 1915 and August 1917. Although inflationary deficit financing provided some relief to recurrent credit squeezes during the war, this was not considered an acceptable expedient except under the abnormal conditions then prevailing, for unbalanced budgets were not regarded with approval by any sector of Brazilian opinion and were not expected to continue after the end of the war. After the return to peace-time trading conditions, there appeared a growing consensus among bankers and businessmen that the fundamental point of reform should be to abolish Treasury issuing rights and to endow the Banco do Brasil with instruments – particularly with powers to pursue an active rediscount policy – which would enable it to vary the stock of high powered money at its own discretion so as to smooth out the seasonal credit problems as well as to act as a lender of last resort in times of crisis. This idea had, in fact, been forcefully defended throughout the war by Homero Batista, the president of the Banco do Brasil,[14] when it 'merited the applause of many commercial institutions and of notable personalities in trade, industry and finance'.[15] This agitation, as noted by Neuhaus, also reflected the worldwide growing influence of the real-bills doctrine among Brazilian banking and business circles, which saw in the granting of certain central banking powers to the Banco do Brasil the solution to the problem of adjusting the supply of money to the seasonally variable 'needs of trade.'[16]

The idea of reforming the Bank on these lines, endowing it with powers to issue inconvertible notes on a fractional gold reserve basis as proposed by its president had, however, encountered strong opposition during the war from a group of influential politicians who held orthodox views on monetary policy, men such as ex-Ministers of Finance Antonio Carlos and Leopoldo de Bulhões, and was opposed by the President himself. As Antonio Carlos recalled, wartime finance Ministers, without exception, 'have never hidden their radically opposed views to new experiments of banks issuing inconvertible notes, living only from the *cours forcé* [and] all attempts and efforts to create institutions of this kind foundered against [the President's] notorious unwillingness.'[17] However, this orthodox opposition to the proposed banking reform did not object in principle to the transformation of the Banco do Brasil into a central bank, but was utterly against taking any step in that direction before full convertibility was achieved at a revalued exchange rate. Most of all, they wanted to divest the monetary authority of all discretionary power to vary the monetary base, preferring a 1:1 gold backing on the lines of the pre-war Conversion Office. For that reason, the debate at the end of the war was fought not only on the issue of whether to grant some central banking powers to the Banco do Brasil before covertibility was again achieved but also on whether to allow the Bank to operate with a fractional reserve backing.[18]

The change in government in November 1918, and the appointment of Amaro Cavalcanti – a notorious defender of managed money[19] – to the Ministry of Finance indicated that the pendulum was about to a swing in the direction of reform. However, the serious illness of President-elect Rodrigues Alves just before he was due to take office resulted in his replacement by Delfim Moreira, the Vice-President and former Governor of Minas Gerais, a state from which came most of the supporters of the 'bullionist' view. Following the death of Rodrigues Alves in January 1919, Amaro Cavalcanti resigned the finance portfolio, being replaced by João Ribeiro, a *Mineiro* banker who shared the views of the orthodox opposition to immediate banking reform.[20]

However, according to the Constitution of 1891, new presidential elections were called and the provisional government was dissolved in July 1919, when Epitácio Pessoa, a prestigious lawyer and the political leader of one of the small north-eastern states, assumed the presidency as a compromise cadidate chosen by an alliance between São Paulo, Minas Gerais and Rio Grande do Sul oligarchies.[21] President Pessoa's nomination of Homero Batista, the ex-president of the Bank and the champion of the wartime banking reform campaign, to the Ministry of Finance was a clear indication that the orthodox party was again losing ground.

In the following August, the usual seasonal strain on the banking system's liquid resources was made worse by the slow growth of the money stock against a background of accelerating inflation and domestic boom,[22] leading several business associations to press the government for an early implementation of the Bank's rediscount operations.[23] Although opinion as to details of the reform still diverged widely and there was as yet no fully-fledged government plan which could command broad political support, the government reassured business interests of its intentions to reform the Banco do Brasil.[24] Finally, in May 1920, definite steps were taken when the Bank's yearly shareholders meeting approved a resolution – obviously reflecting a government decision as majority shareholder – to amend its statutes.[25] A committee of emminent Brazilian bankers and academic economists, chaired by the president of the Bank, was set up to report on the reform and a final draft to be submitted to Congress was published in August.[26] The basic lines of the report reproduced the proposals put forward by Homero Batista during the war, suggesting an increase in the Bank's capital to build up a gold or foreign exchange reserve against which inconvertible bank notes could be issued up to three times its value through rediscount of short-term bills.

However, in the second quarter of 1920, activity levels and consumer demand were already falling in the United States and United Kingdom.[27] From the middle of the year recession spread slowly in the United States and restrictive monetary policies adopted in both the world's financial centres triggered a deep worldwide depression and a precipituous fall in world prices from the second half of the year.[28] The world price slump had a shattering effect on the value of Brazilian exports.[29] After the explosive postwar increase, world coffee prices had already fallen from their abnormally high levels during the last quarter of 1919, when the flowering of the 1920 crop showed a remarkable recovery in the vitality of São Paulo coffee trees.[30] Although this fall was halted in the first months of 1920, when the world price boom broke in the second quarter and credit was tightened in the United States, American coffee imports almost ground to a halt:[31] New York coffee prices collapsed in July – just when the new crop was arriving at the ports – and a headlong fall continued through to the early months of 1921 for, in the prevailing bearish expectations in consuming centres, 'nobody was prepared to make even the smallest speculative purchases of the momentarily unwanted supplies and so the price fell and continued to fall in a way which suggested that no one would be tempted to buy even if it reached zero.[32]

On the other hand there was a great rise in Brazilian import orders following the end of the war, induced by the extremely good profit expectations afforded by the domestic boom and the large postwar exchange rate appreciation.[33] The growth of imports had already caused a trade deficit in May 1920 but after that, the perverse scissor movement of exports and imports opened a yawning deficit in the second half of the year and the exchange rate suffered a heavy and drawn-out depreciation. The problems created by the exchange rate collapse of 1920–1 for the management of the already unbalanced federal budget position plus the severe blow delivered by the world price slump to the coffee industry – as international coffee prices fell considerably faster than the external value of the milréis in 1920 – would profoundly alter the conduct of economic policy in Brazil.

4.2 WORLD SLUMP AND THE SUPPORT OF COFFEE PRICES IN 1921–2

When coffee prices collapsed in 1920, the government of São Paulo immediately came to the rescue of the industry for, after the undeniable success of the 1917 valorisation,[34] there was not a single voice in the state to deny the wisdom of price support schemes, particularly as the crisis was correctly seen as the result of temporarily abnormal demand conditions. Credits for spot purchases were granted in August but the state's disposable resources soon proved insufficient to produce a substantial effect on prices, given the magnitude of the disequilibrium.[35]

Meantime, as described above, the new government was earnestly moving towards the reform of the Banco do Brasil. However, in the panic developing during the third quarter of 1920 the *Paulistas* could not afford tying the urgent question of financial help for coffee to the successful completion of the necessarily drawn-out deliberations still needed before the reform could take place. Thus, in early September, Carlos de Campos, the *Paulista* leader of the government majority in the federal Chamber proposed a Bill to allow the issue of Treasury notes on the lines of the October 1918 issue, clearly with the intention of helping the coffee sector.[36]

Even though this proposal was put forward as an emergency measure, its debate in the Chamber brought about intense pressures from coffee interests to obtain federal government financial help to organise coffee price support on a more permanent basis. The arguments advanced in that respect by Sampaio Vidal and Cincinato Braga, two leading Deputies from São Paulo, is probably the best summary of the *Paulistas* position on the issue. They denounced the heavy losses that short-term demand fluctuations recurrently inflicted on the industry and the large speculative profits made by importers, given the much greater stability of roast coffee prices in consuming centres, criticised the behaviour of the foreign-controlled leading export houses, and urged the creation of a permanent scheme to regulate world supplies.[37]

The course taken by the debates in the Chamber was bound to cause considerable uneasiness in the government. Firstly, there is evidence that, at this stage, the government was not yet convinced of the necessity of sponsoring a price support scheme at all.[38] Furthermore, the institutionalisation of coffee valorisation under a federal umbrella was not the only issue at stake. There was also the fundamental question of the monetary consequences of federal government help to the coffee industry. At that moment to finance coffee price support through a new *ad hoc* issue of Treasury notes would probably have a demoralising effect on the government's carefully conducted banking reform plan. Accordingly, through the direct intervention of President Pessoa, who preferred to go ahead with the reform of the Banco do Brasil,[39] the Bill was withdrawn before being voted in the Senate.

However, in a protest against the President's interference Carlos de Campos resigned his position as leader of the majority in the Chamber, pushing the government to the brink of a political crisis. The prospect of an open clash with São Paulo and the growing realisation that the recessive tendencies following the collapse of the boom, coming on top of the prolonged liquidity squeeze since 1919[40] – which was aggravated by delays in payments to government suppliers[41] – could lead to a crisis of serious consequences unless immediate relief was provided for the banking sector,[42] induced the President to retreat towards a more conciliatory position. In October, he went to São Paulo[43] and, after brief negotiations, Carlos de Campos resumed his functions at the Chamber and a compromise solution was drafted in the Senate, proposing an 'emergency'issue of 50 000 contos of Treasury notes and creating a provisional Rediscount Department at the Banco do Brasil with powers to issue *fiat* bank notes against short-term trade bills up to a limit of 100 000 contos – which could exceptionally be lifted by the President of the Republic – 'until the creation of a special bank for this purpose'.[44]

This solution was a fine example of political compromise, for it avoided a confrontation between the government and the coffee interests while still preserving the former's position against direct involvement in a price support scheme, since the creation of a rediscount window was a solution dear to the coffee industry and this temporarily defused their pressures for direct federal support. In fact, during the September debates in the Chamber, the weakest point in the organisation of the coffee sector was singled out by Sampaio Vidal as the lack of a 'proper banking organisation' to finance the retention of large excess supplies.[45] This view reflects a relation seen for many years past by national coffee interests between banking reform – i.e., the creation of a rediscount window which could act as lender of last resort – and the stability of the industry which can be easily understood by looking into some basic features of the financing mechanisms prevailing in the coffee industry.

Since the first half of the nineteenth century, when coffee plantations moved from the outskirts of the city of Rio de Janeiro to the uplands of the states of Rio de Janeiro and São Paulo along the banks of the Paraíba river, the coffee industry developed a system of commercial and financial intermediation based on commission agents known as *comissários*. These men formed the basic link between the planters and exporting houses and were responsible for providing the planters with the funds needed to finance production until the marketing of the crop. As soon as the farmer had picked, dried, cleaned and sacked his coffee, he would send it to his *comissário* who usually would grant him cash advances to the extent of 60 per cent of the expected value of the crop. This cash would meet the planter's requirements during the period when his coffee had not been sold to an exporter in the Brazilian coffee exchanges, which period, in a normal year, usually did not exceed six months, the bulk of one year's crop being sold by the end of December.[46] To grant these loans, the *comissário* would simply overdraw his current account or borrow against a simple promissory note from his banker in Rio or Santos and even with the growth of a reasonably well developed system of branch banking in the southern coffee-producing region during the twenties, the position of the *comissários* as immediate suppliers of the bulk of the working capital needed by the planters did remain basically unchanged.[47]

The system of private and, increasingly, national banking engaged in financing the marketing of the coffee crop did not, however, have enough financial muscle effectively to help protect prices in case of adverse market conditions. In order to do that the money centre banks would have to assume the risk of taking illiquid positions by carrying large amounts of coffee bills during an unpredictably long period, a policy they were in no position to afford, particularly since the competing demands for short-term credit from other agricultural sectors also grew in the second half of the year. The notion that the existence of a lender of last resort would allow an increase in the credit creation capacity of domestic banks, strengthening the ability of national commercial intermediaries to carry larger stocks at times of unfavourable market conditions was, indeed, what led the politically influential large farmers and *comissários* to lend their strong support to the campaign for banking reform.

On the other hand the creation of the Rediscount Department could provide the necessary relief to the current credit squeeze while still allowing the government to avoid proclaiming the abandonment of its banking reform plan. The essential feature of the government's plan was – as the debates on monetary reform since the war illustrate – to grant powers to the Banco do Brasil so that it could control the monetary based through rediscount operations, an instrument of monetary policy which was considered fundamental to a more 'elastic' and 'self-liquidating' currency. The new proposal drafted after the political crisis of September 1920 only diverged from the government's 'ideal' reform as expressed in the August expert committee's recommendations in that, in the latter, the Bank notes issued through rediscount operations would have a fractional gold or foreign exchange backing, while now Rediscount Department notes would be totally fiduciary. However, as the President himself admitted, the old plan had, in any case, to be abandoned because of the effects of the acute balance of payments disequilibrium on the level of official reserves.[48]

The impending crisis accelerated parliamentary deliberations over the new government proposal but deep divergencies remained over important details relating to the operations of the new Rediscount Department.[49] Some of its features were criticised by banking circles and it was not implemented at once, leading to strained relations between President Pessoa – who endorsed some of the criticisms voiced against the law – and the president of the Banco do Brasil.[50] As a result, J.M. Whitaker, a São Paulo banker, was appointed in December to the presidency of the Bank and authorised to draft new operational regulations for the Rediscount Department.[51] On 30 December, he presented his draft project of new regulations which, in spite of an unfavourable report by the Senate Finance Committee, became law the following day.[52] These provided that the Rediscount Department would finance its operations through Treasury notes supplied at the request of the Bank's president and limited eligibility for the Department's portfolio to 'legitimate' trade bills with less than 120 days to maturity at the time of rediscount, explicitly forbidding the rediscount of Treasury Bills. Some by-laws were still issued in January and, in early February, the Rediscount Department began its normal operations.[53]

In the early months of 1921 the depression which had started in mid-1920 was reaching a critical stage. The greatest worries came from the persistence of the trade deficit in spite of a large exchange rate depreciation, and from the expected damaging effects of the exchange rate collapse on federal government financial equilibrium and domestic price stability. In January, the government announced a decision to establish 'official supervision' over foreign exchange operations on a permanent basis to curb speculative transactions which, although considerably modified after a flurry of protests from foreign bankers,[54] was eventually implemented in March, while negotiations for a large federal loan in New York were progressing towards a successful completion.[55]

The government's increasing anxiety over the balance of payments position did not, however, affect its uncompromising stance against coffee price support during the first two months of 1921, in spite of renewed pressure from the coffee trade.[56] In fact, the relief provided to the banks by the emergency issue of Treasury notes at the end of 1920, plus further purchases made by the São Paulo government in early 1921, had a slight beneficial effect on prices and, in February, after the end of the marketing of other suppliers' crops, New York prices stopped falling.[57] However, when the effect of a 'heavy bear raid'[58] in March sent coffee prices to new record lows[59] the federal authorities finally came to realise that direct intervention in coffee markets was an essential complement to its chief objective of redressing external balance.

There can be no doubt that the federal government decision to support coffee prices in late March 1921 was taken on exchange rate policy grounds. Since the re-establishment of peace-time world trade conditions, non-traditional products were progressively vanishing from the list of Brazilian exports while coffee regained its prominent place – accounting, in 1920, for about 50 per cent of the value of exports in spite of the heavy fall in prices. President Pessoa later publicly justified this step:

Coffee represents the biggest share in the global value of our exports and is, therefore, the product which provides more gold to the settlement of our foreign obligations . . . the defense of coffee thus constitutes a national problem, the solution to which is vital for a sound economic and financial policy in Brazil.[60]

Furthermore the decision solved a fundamental conflict in government policy objectives for, without supporting prices, the efforts to halt the headlong fall in the external value of the milréis would submit the coffee industry to an unbearable strain.[61] However the March 1921 valorisation decision implied no explicit permanent commitment to the protection of coffee prices as canvassed by São Paulo. Federal government action was limited to authorising the Treasury to endorse coffee bills drawn by a large private São Paulo coffee broking firm – which would act as government agents for spot purchases in Brazil – and to instructing the Banco do Brasil to discount them, with the help of the newly created Rediscount Department, if necessary.

Direct federal intervention helped prevent a further fall in prices from April on but failed to bring about an early recovery and balance of payments difficulties continued in the second quarter. In early May a panic almost developed in the Rio foreign exchange market when the Bank abandoned its attempts to hold the rate and a proposal appeared in the Senate, pressed by importers, for the declaration of a moratorium.[62] However, the New York loan negotiations were nearing completion and the proposal was withdrawn on government instructions. In fact, later in May, the first of two US$25 million tranches was issued in New York and, with the issue of the second tranche in August and the reappearance of a trade surplus in the third quarter, the Bank was able temporarily to regain control over the exchanges.[63]

By that time, however, the great federal budget disequilibrium was becoming almost unmanageable.[64] Although the incomplete data available on federal government credit operations[65] do not allow an adequate assessment of the ways in which the large postwar budget disequilibrium was financed, there is evidence that since early in 1921 it was becoming difficult to finance the federal cash deficits and, in spite of having recourse to the issue of domestic bonds on an unprecedented scale,[66] the Treasury had to rely increasingly on short-term advances from the Banco do Brasil.[67]

The immediate consequence of the growth of government short-term indebtedness to the Bank was to reduce the latter's ability to finance the coffee price support scheme by causing a quicker exhaustion of the Rediscount Department's issuing capacity. In fact, as mentioned above, Treasury drafts, issued against the Bank as guarantee when the former went beyond the legal borrowing limit on ways and means advances, could not statutorily be accepted by the Rediscount Department.[68] However the Department, although controlled by the Banco do Brasil, was created as a legally independent institution and the Bank itself had access to its rediscount window. Thus provided that the Banco do Brasil had enough eligible bills in its discount portfolio, it could, if necessary, take them to rediscount, thus making room to accommodate the Treasury's financial demands. The use of this expedient to finance the current budget deficit had, however, important constraints. One was the amount of eligible bills in the Bank's portfolio relative to Treasury needs. Another was the loss to the Bank's income caused by having to pay a penalty rate for money it was lending to the government at a lower interest.[69] The third and most important was the need to maintain the relation between the value of the Rediscount Department outstanding note issues and its legally fixed upper limit below a safe figure so as not to affect the confidence of the banks which now had large voluntary deposits with the Banco do Brasil.[70] Even though the Department's legal issuing limit could be raised by Executive action, it was a politically costly decision. Thus the Bank fought to avoid a dangerous reduction in the slack of unused Rediscount Department's issuing rights.

In March a menacing rise of Treasury drafts on the Bank was halted by protests from Whitaker, who went as far as to send his resignation to President Pessoa, but was convinced to stay on by assurances from Homero Batista that the Treasury would use the proceeds of the 1920 New York loan, then in the final stages of negotiation, to make good its debt to the Bank.[71] However, federal government financial demands remained high. On June 20 the government had no alternative but to raise the legal issuing limit, doubling it to 200 000 contos[72] and, in the first half of July only, the amount of outstanding Rediscount Department issues rocketed from 82 000 to over 150 000 contos.[73] In mid-July, when the total value of coffee bills endorsed by the Treasury and accepted by the Bank reached 270 000 contos,[74] the president of the Banco do Brasil – who had never been a wholehearted supporter of the valorisation scheme[75] and had insistently warned the Minister of Finance of the dangers of the situation – informed President Pessoa that 'the Treasury drafts continue to be very large and, for that reason, I [can] not see the way to fulfilling the insistent requests for cash that [the official coffee brokers] make to me.'[76]

To complicate matters further, Brazil's external position was still very vulnerable. The authorities had not yet halted the continuous exchange depreciation begun in early 1920 which, by July 1921, brought the exchange rate to 60 per cent of its February 1920 peak. The government feared that a fall in the volume of exports caused by official coffee purchases might have an adverse short-term effect on the balance of trade and this would lead it into attempting to get financial accommodation abroad to go on with the purchases.[77] Thus, in early August, the international financial press was already mentioning rumours of a large London coffee loan to Brazil[78] and an emergency Bill was rushed through Congress, authorising the Treasury to warrant its coffee stocks in foreign currency operations, as would be necessary to guarantee an eventual coffee loan.[79]

In the meantime, however, market intervention by the Brazilian government began to bear fruit. World coffee prices began a sustained recovery from August and the trade balance went back into surplus in the third quarter of 1921.[80] If these early signs of a brighter outlook for coffee prices could not be counted upon as a clear indication of the eventual success of the valorisation scheme by those aware of its financial difficulties, for the sake of propaganda they came as a blessing to the government as, indeed, did the simultaneous improvement in exchange markets,[81] since redressing external balance was, after all, the *leitmotif* of the March 1921 decision to support coffee prices.

President Pessoa used these first positive results with great political skill. In the second half of August he went on a tour through São Paulo, campaigning to boost confidence in the maintenance of the existing valorisation programme and to revive the old *Paulista* idea of a 'permanent', Brazilian controlled institution to thwart the vagaries of world coffee markets.[82] As far as coffee policy was concerned, the aims of this move were twofold.[83] First, there was an obvious intention to affect price expectations by reaffirming the federal government's determination not to abandon market intervention. Secondly, it was a reinsurance policy, since indicating the possibility of government sponsorship to a scheme placing the control of coffee markets on a permanent basis could be vital in the winning of political support if arranging foreign credits proved difficult and the government had to finance additional purchases through inflationary means.

Thus in October, as no foreign financial aid was forthcoming, the President sent a special message to Congress proposing the creation of a permanent council to manage coffee valorisation operations, suggesting that it should be presided over by the Minister of Finance – with the Minister of Agriculture as vice-president, plus three other members chosen from among persons linked with the coffee trade – and endowed with a capital of 300 000 contos made up of an *ad hoc* issue of Treasury notes plus eventual profits from its operations.[84]

The government was not, of course, unaware that its proposal to finance the holding of excess supplies of coffee through *fiat* note issues would not be taken lightly by orthodox opinion in the Chamber. When the draft Bill came out of the Finance Committee on 29 October, it already had ex-Finance Minister Antonio Carlos' minority vote against it[85] and during the debates it encountered fierce opposition led by Mario Brant, also a deputy from Minas Gerais.[86]

These debates, mostly between São Paulo and Minas Gerais representatives, are probably the best summary available of the diverging views then existing on the monetary and balance of payments effects of alternative ways of financing coffee prices support schemes, a division which would last until the mid-twenties. At this stage, the *Paulistas* feared that to raise a foreign loan backed by the existing government stocks could lead to the loss of control over coffee price policy to foreign creditors as happened in 1908, and thus they preferred to finance the scheme with domestic means. This, however, could only be done in Brazil through increases in high-powered money. Accordingly they tried to minimise the effects of the proposed note issue on internal and external equilibrium by pointing to its 'self-liquidating' nature, since the Bill provided that the Treasury notes issued should be withdrawn from circulation when the coffee stocks were sold. On the other hand the orthodox opposition to the Bill favoured financing the scheme through foreign loans and argued that even a 'transitory' increase in the monetary base could be destabilising, given the large note issues which might be needed to make price support effective and the long period possibly required to liquidate the stocks bought.[87]

Debates dragged on throughout November. By this time, however, estimates of a short crop for 1922 and the sustained recovery of coffee prices had immensely increased the chances of raising abroad the funds needed to relieve the Banco do Brasil of its glut of coffee bills. A renewed weakening of the exchanges after the brief recovery in August and September made it even more attractive from the federal government's point of view and, in late November, through the agency of the Brazilian Warrant Co., a British-owned Brazilian coffee exporting firm,[88] and Schroeders, the São Paulo London bankers, the Brazilian Treasury obtained short-term credit lines in a pool made up predominantly of London discount banks, against which it could issue three-months finance bills warranted by its coffee stocks.[89] These short-term drafts were issued to the tune of £5.5 million – the equivalent of 170 000 contos at the ruling exchange rate – and the proceeds were credited by the Treasury to the Banco do Brasil, partly to buy almost the whole of the still existing excess supplies,[90] partly to redeem a fraction of the coffee bills arising from previous purchases. This enabled the Bank to bring down to very small figures the outstanding Rediscount Department note issue during the first quarter of 1922[91] and provided it with enough foreign exchange reserves so as temporarily to regain control over the exchange market.

When the last purchases ended in December 1921, valorisation stocks amounted to 4.5 million bags, while estimates for the 1922 crop were at least 11 million bags.[92] Since Brazilian coffee exports in 1921 totalled 12.4 million bags the government could not – barring an unlikely sharp recovery in world demand – dispose of its stocks early in 1922 so as to repay the short-term sterling advances without an adverse effect on prices. So although the London credits came as manna from heaven to the government, they could not be counted upon as a final solution to the coffee problem unless they could be funded.

The Brazilian authorities were, of course, well aware of that and negotiations for a longer coffee loan were started with Schroeders, Rothschilds and Barings as soon as possible.[93] In early May, after protracted negotiations, a £9 million loan, secured by the whole 4.5 million bags of coffee held by the Brazilian government, was floated in London and New York.[94] The money thus raided in excess of the Treasury's short-term foreign liabilities would be used to liquidate the remainder of coffee bills still held by the Banco do Brasil, giving a definitive solution to the problem of an orderly disposal of the huge valorisation stocks accumulated during 1921.

However, as feared by important sectors of the Brazilian coffee trade, the strings attached by the bankers involved a substantial loss of national control over the future of world coffee markets. As happened in 1908, the loan was made conditional to entrusting the management of the sales of valorisation stocks – the receipts from which would be used to serve the loan – to a five-member committee based in London, in which the Brazilian government would have one representative, the other four being appointed by each of the three houses involved in the operation and by the Brazilian Warrant Company, which was placed in charge of effecting all the sales on behalf of the committee.[95] Furthermore the Brazilian government agreed 'to employ its good offices to avoid the creation of a new coffee valorisation plan' during the term of the loan.[96] This clause was the more restrictive since, as British Treasury regulations then in force forbade the issue of foreign loans shorter than ten years, the Brazilian loan could not be redeemed before 1932.[97] Even if this constraint could be circumvented, the speeding up of sales to shorten the redemption period could have an adverse effect on prices and authority for doing that was, in any case, in the hands of the London committee.

The federal government's decision to place the future of the coffee industry in the hands of foreign bankers and to give the monopoly of sales from the large valorisation stocks to a British firm aroused the anger of *comissários* and exporters in Brazil.[98] Moreover the government's pledge to the bankers of denying its approval to further price support schemes made a mockery of a Permanent Coffee Defence Bill, which had produced so much heat in the Chamber in 1921 and had been shelved in the Senate at the end of December to await the beginning of the 1922 congressional session.[99] Congress took the matter up again in 1922 and a slightly modified version of the 1921 Bill became law on June 19, creating the Institute for the Permanent Defence of Coffee as an independent federal government agency.[100]

The Institute, however, was not to be formally founded. Besides being against the express dispositions of the 1922 contract with the London bankers, it was also quite unnecessary for President Pessoa to do anything in the last five months of his term of office. Coffee prices were now rising strongly, helped by the recovery in world demand and by the effect of the successful consolidation of the 1921 valorisation stocks on importers' expectations.[101] Furthermore, by mid-1922 the Brazilian economy was clearly coming out of the severe shock caused by the postwar slump and the private interests in the coffee trade could well manage to finance the marketing of the small 1922 crop with their own resources.

4.3 DOMESTIC RECOVERY AND THE FISCAL CRISIS OF 1922

The recovery of domestic activity levels in 1922 after the brief but severe recession of 1921 marks the beginning of a second short period of rapid economic growth after the war, lasting until 1924. According to Haddad's estimates, total output growth, which had fallen to just 1.9 per cent in 1921 after reaching 10.1 per cent in 1920, rose again to 7.8 per cent in 1922.

The larger number of real output estimates available for the post-1920 period, although showing wide divergencies in some years, indicate that the manufacturing sector experienced wider fluctuations than the rest of the economy in the postwar cycle, rising much faster in 1922.[102] The behaviour of the volume of imports of fuels, raw materials and capital goods to industry, shown in Table A.2, illlustrates the pattern of the 1920–2 fluctuations in industrial activity and investment, if the usual lagged response of the capital goods imports series to changes in current output levels is taken into account. Although the 1922 expansion in industrial production basically stemmed from utilisation of idle margins and industrial investment did not fully recover until 1923,[103] construction activity did not fall as sharply as industrial production in 1921 and boomed in 1922, when it grew by almost 45 per cent,[104] almost certainly reflecting the large public works projects then being carried out.

It is interesting to note, however, that the basic causes of the impressive upturn of 1922 resulted both from the unintentional effect of the 1921 coffee valorisation in stimulating effective demand by helping to maintain real income levels in the coffee industry, and from the huge exchange rate depreciation from early 1920 and the persistence of high levels of public expenditure and budget deficits up to 1922, which were both clearly undesired by policy-makers.[105]

The success of government intervention to support coffee prices had an undeniable influence in attenuating the effects of the world slump in Brazil. Not only did the value of exports recover and the terms of trade improve earlier than would otherwise have been the case, but it also had the extremely important effect of maintaining real incomes in the coffee sector which had been rapidly eroded since mid-1920 when coffee prices were falling more rapidly than the rate of exchange.

However it should be stressed that the decision to support coffee prices was motivated to a large extent by balance of payments considerations and taken on exchange rate policy grounds. Even so, the long period of indecision by the Federal government before taking this course of action allowed a very large exchange rate depreciation until mid-1921 which, in fact, continued at a reduced speed throughout 1922 after a slight recovery in the third quarter of 1921.[106] The importance of the collapse of the milréis – by the end of 1922 it was down to a third of its early 1920 value against sterling – in isolating the economy from the deflationary impact of the world price slump, thus protecting it from the devastating effects it would otherwise have had on exporters' incomes and on domestic import-competing activities must not be under-estimated. This was the fundamental reason why Brazil experienced a far more modest fall in domestic prices than did the central countries during the recession.[107] The index of Brazilian import prices shown in Table A.4, actually *rose* during 1921 and only fell in 1922 when the speed of exchange rate depreciation slowed down while prices were still falling heavily among Brazil's main suppliers. The volume of imports, which was recovering fast during the short-lived postwar boom fell in 1921 to about half its pre-war level and, in spite of the strong recovery in domestic activity from 1922, pre-war import levels were not attained again until 1924.[108] Moreover the exchange rate collapse was an important contributory factor to the large fall in imports in 1921 which explains the bulk of the trade balance readjustment in the period 1920–2.[109] The stimulus given to domestic producers by the exchange rate collapse as well as its inflationary effects were, as in the experience of the early 1890s, reinforced by high budget deficits maintained throughout the postwar cycle and the related shift to much higher rates of monetary expansion in 1921–2.

The return to easy money dates from the 'emergency' Treasury note issue eventually made in late 1920, but the large growth rate of the money stock sustained throughout 1921 and 1922 was the result of Rediscount Department operations.[110] The influence of the creation of the Department on the growth of the money stock was not simply due to the increase in high-powered money it brought about, but also relates to the structural changes it provoked in Brazilian banking: the powers it gave to the Banco do Brasil effectively to act as a lender of last resort, commanding the confidence of the domestic banking

Table 4.1   Brazil: 1919–22, quarterly monetary ratios

End of Quarter	Currency Ratio (c)	Reserve Ratio (r)	Coefficient of expansion $\left(\frac{1}{c+r}\right)$
1919 IV	0.98	0.50	0.67
1920 IV	0.72	0.58	0.76
1921 I	0.77	0.61	0.72
II	0.70	0.55	0.80
III	0.67	0.50	0.85
IV	0.62	0.46	0.92
1922 I	0.55	0.44	1.01
II	0.51	0.40	1.09
III	0.50	0.38	1.13
IV	0.55	0.37	1.08

Source: Table A.16.

system, allowed a sharp decrease in the banks' usually high reserve ratios, which prior to 1921 fluctuated around 0.5 in normal money market conditions. As shown in Table 4.1 the fall in the reserve ratio coupled with the secular falling trend of the currency ratio stemming from the continuous spread of banking services and the widening use of bank deposits by the public[111] caused a 50 per cent rise in the marginal coefficient of deposit expansion between the end of the first quarter of 1921, when rediscount operations started, and the end of 1922.[112]

With this remarkable increase in the banking multiplier, the 19.7 per cent increase in the value of Treasury notes outstanding coming from Rediscount Department issues during 1921 and 1922 – of which just a small fraction went into the vaults of the Banco do Brasil – caused an increase of 67.1 per cent in sight deposits and a 51.7 per cent growth in the money stock.[113]

It is worth mentioning in passing that the creation of the Rediscount Department enabled the Bank to pursue with great success a policy of attracting voluntary deposits from other national banks[114] and immensely expand its operations.[115] The expansion of the Banco do Brasil coupled with the preferential treatment afforded to national banks in rediscount operations, placed foreign banks at a competitive disadvantage, ending what the President of the Bank saw as 'the lack of confidence by the public, shown by the humiliating preference towards the foreign banks' in times of crisis[116] and substantially

Table 4.2   Brazil: 1919–22, share of national and foreign banks in total
sight deposits (in percentages of total deposits)

	1919	1920	1921	1922
National banks	49.13	45.20	60.05	72.72
Foreign banks	50.87	54.80	39.95	27.28

Source: Movimento Bancário, in Brazil. Ministério da Fazenda, Diretoria de
Estaística Commerical, *Comércio Exterior do Brasil*, Oficinas da Estatística
Commercial, Rio de Janeiro, several issues.

reducing their share in Brazilian banking business (see Table 4.2).[117]

The growth of the money stock during 1921–2 to the extent
described was not, however, the result of a conscious monetary
policy objective. The growth of Rediscount Department issues,
which was the ultimate cause of the return to high rates of monetary
expansion in 1921–2, resulted from large random financial needs of
the Treasury during the period, coming from two different sources:
the first, effective up to the third quarter of 1921, were the financial
needs of coffee valorisation as described above; the second, effective
to a minor extent in 1921 but the sole cause of the large expansion
from the second quarter of 1922, was the spill over to the Rediscount
Department of unplanned federal deficits which then rose to unprecedented levels, as Table A.12 shows.

The causes of the large stepwise growth of the federal deficit from
1919, in spite of wide yearly fluctuations verified both in revenue and
in expenditure are manifold. Its basic underlying reason was the lax
conduct of taxation and expenditure policy, despite the Executive's
frequent public pledges to fiscal discipline. It cannot be overlooked,
however, that, given the sensitiveness of both federal revenue and
expenditure to exchange rate fluctuations, the unstable behaviour of
Brazil's external position during the postwar boom and slump had
also very important budgetary consequences.

The effect of the large postwar federal budget deficits was not
restricted to its direct expansionary impact on effective demand. As
mentioned above, government fiscal imbalances had an important
influence in allowing the high rates of monetary expansion obtained
in 1921 and 1922, when even the large long-term credit operations
then undertaken both in domestic and foreign capital markets proved
insufficient to cover the excess expenditures and the Treasury had to
rely heavily on advances from the Banco do Brasil.

As described above, the Bank was instrumental in financing Treasury needs in 1921 on occasion. However, in 1922, the government's budget problems became acute on account of the authorities' failure to reduce the level of current expenditure and the need to settle a large volume of arrears accumulated in 1921. During the first half of 1922 the Treasury financed its payments imbalance through the usual issues of one-year bills but, in July, the amount of Treasury bills outstanding already reached not less than 428 000 contos, 82 per cent of which was accepted by the Banco do Brasil.[118]

Under the pressure of the growth of government debt on the Bank's portfolio on such a large scale, Rediscount Department note issues began to rise sharply again towards the middle of the year and it became increasingly dangerous for the Bank to go on financing the government's cash flow imbalance.[119] However there was no indication that federal excess expenditures would fall in the short run and to raise finance through the issue of long dated *apólices* was out of the question since these fixed nominal interest Treasury consols, issued in very large amounts after the war, were then accepted only at a heavy discount if sold to the extent required. The only alternative left was to resort to Treasury note issues but, after the creation of the Rediscount Department, this would only be possible if its statutory prohibition to rediscount government paper could be altered.

The government certainly knew that it could not count on getting parliamentary support to definitely change the law which had created the Rediscount Department in that direction. If Treasury access to rediscount facilities was to be proposed, some upper limit had to be placed upon it to make the proposal more palatable. Thus, on 31 July, the Treasury arranged a credit with the Banco do Brasil for the issue of up to 500 000 contos of special promissory notes and in August the government asked Congress for authorisation to rediscount these notes.[120] In October, after ill-informed debates in the Senate amidst claims of impending disaster, given the dangerous position of the Banco do Brasil, permission was granted.[121]

Since federal government financial demands remained high and the Treasury had to draw heavily on the new line of credit,[122] the decision to authorise the Bank to rediscount the promissory notes had an immediate impact on monetary equilibrium. Rediscount Department issues soared – the legal limit being raised to 300 000 contos in October and to 400 000 in November – causing a large increase in the money stock in the last quarter of 1922.[123]

The way in which the very large budget disequilibrium of 1922 was financed had, moreover, lasting consequences. On the one hand the sharp monetary expansion caused by inflationary deficit financing in the second half of 1922 increased the strong inflationary pressures already present in the 1922 upturn and was to aggravate the still vulnerable external position. On the other hand it gave rise to a huge federal floating debt to the Banco do Brasil, in the shape of Treasury bills held by the Bank and promissory notes of the 1922 special loan accepted by the Rediscount Department, officially estimated at the beginning of 1923 as being over 800 000 contos.[124] The need to settle this debt, which had a paralysing effect on the Bank's operations, as well as the growing pressures on external and internal equilibrium would decisively influence the priorities and the conduct of monetary and fiscal policies during the next few years.

5 Attempts at Financial Reconstruction

5.1 PRESIDENT BERNARDES' ECONOMIC POLICY PROGRAMME AND THE CONSTRAINTS ON ITS EARLY ENFORCEMENT

The political tensions generated by the dissent over the 1922 presidential succession between Brazilian regional groups marked the beginning of recurrent strains on the political stability of the First Republic during the twenties. As early as the beginning of 1921, São Paulo and Minas Gerais politicians had opened informal talks aimed at placing Arthur Bernardes, then governor of Minas Gerais, at the head of the Brazilian government. Although Bernardes' candidacy did not find overt opposition from other regional interests, a confrontation over the choice of the vice-president developed between the two leading north-eastern states of Bahia and Pernambuco. When even Pessoa's direct intervention could not settle the dispute and a third name had to be put forward as the government's official candidate, ex-President Nilo Peçanha of Rio de Janeiro succeeded in obtaining the support of the now disaffected political cliques of Bahia and Pernambuco plus that of the strong southern state of Rio Grande do Sul in his bid for the presidency, standing as an independent 'opposition' candidate.[1]

This alliance between four large states, holding a substantial share of the voting population, represented in itself a serious threat to the São Paulo-Minas Gerais traditional pre-eminence. Moreover the opposition to Bernardes' candidacy had a free hand to manipulate the growing urban middle-class discontent with the regime and openly attempted to amass the support of politically active sectors of the Army behind its candidate.[2] Even after the March 1921 elections had given Bernardes a small majority, accusations of electoral fraud and growing anti-Bernardes feeling within the Army created such uneasiness in government circles that the President-elect's resignation was not pressed by Pessoa only because of the uncompromising support given to him by the leading political groups of São Paulo and Minas Gerais.[3] Even after the ruthless suppression of anti-government armed risings by loyalist troops in July 1922, the political

75

situation remained very tense and Bernardes took office in November under states of siege declared in several states, which were maintained throughout his term of office.

The resolution with which São Paulo and Minas Gerais politicians closed ranks in defence of Bernardes' candidacy was not fortuitous, since his government programme, as shown below, had resulted from negotiations between controlling groups in these states. This programme, put forward officially in October 1921 following his nomination as the government's candidate and addressed 'mainly to financial questions and to the economic situation,'[4] defined three major objectives. The first was to re-establish external balance, a goal which stemmed basically from the postwar experience of great exchange rate instability and the current weak external position. Measures addressed to improving the trade balance would be directed at obtaining 'a reasonable rate of exchange which will satisfy the interests of the Treasury, industry and commerce and render exchange as stable as possible.'[5] Among the proposals to achieve this the 'urgent necessity of a permanent measure' to support coffee prices figured prominently, and special attention would also be given to the development of other agricultural exports such as raw cotton and to the provision of 'proper and stable customs assistance to national products, so as to increase and develop products similar to those imported;'[6] the import substitution programme laid special emphasis on developing Brazilian coal-mining – whose output, although still a small fraction of domestic consumption, had substantially increased during the war – and in building up a domestic iron and steel industry based on the large iron ore deposits of Minas Gerais.[7]

Secondly the programme emphasised the necessity of reducing the chronic federal budget deficit. Trying to minimise the painful effects of a tight fiscal policy, the candidate ruled out extensive expenditure cuts both because incompressible expenditure items such as the salary bill and public debt service formed the largest share and because of the depressing effects of discontinuing the vast programme of public works started by President Pessoa.[8] Alternatively it was proposed to hold the growth of expenditure and to increase revenue without raising the tax burden but rather through a thorough reform of Treasury operational mechanisms of budget management and control aimed specifically at curbing tax evasion and unauthorised expenditure, both considered chronic problems.

Last but not least a 'definitive solution' would be established to the long-standing problem of banking and credit organisation, with the creation of a fully-fledged central bank. This was, in fact, the main item in Bernardes' platform, seen as a 'fundamental condition' to the achievement of economic stability, as was almost universally believed in the twenties.[9] Even though the operational features of the proposed central bank were not precisely defined, it was clear that in contrast with the previous debates on central banking reform, convertibility was only considered as a long run objective and that the bank should be as independent as possible from the government, as was thought necessary to enforce fiscal discipline.[10]

The stated aims of Bernardes' 1921 platform were not affected by the political turmoil of the presidential campaign. On the eve of his inauguration he reaffirmed the basic items of his programme[11] and, almost certainly owing to the crucial support given by São Paulo to his candidacy, the *Paulista* Sampaio Vidal – one of the leading proponents of permanent coffee defence and banking reform since 1920 – was appointed Minister of Finance, and Whitaker was invited to stay at the head of the Banco do Brasil.

However, in spite of the great measure of continuity in government economic policies implicit in Bernardes' platform, the incoming administration was quite unaware of the developments which occurred in 1920 and which seriously constrained the implementation of some of its chief policy objectives. It was unaware both that the conditions accepted by Pessoa's administration in the 1922 coffee loan contract temporarily restricted new federal valorisation operations[12] and that official foreign exchange reserves had been totally depleted in attempts to support the exchange rate during the second half of 1922.[13] Moreover, the extent of the acute fiscal problems appearing in 1922 was only properly gauged when, after a fortnight in office, the new Minister of Finance produced a gloomy report on the criticial budget position.[14]

This situation posed not insignificant obstacles to the fulfilment of Bernardes' platform objectives. On the one hand, the idea of putting permanent coffee defence into effect was virtually blocked unless some working agreement could be made with the London bankers on the question of freedom of coffee policy. On the other hand, the government plan for central banking reform was put in jeopardy by the critical budget position, since an 'independent' central bank would block the more or less usual process of deficit financing through Treasury note issues existing since the war. It is not surprising, therefore, that the early months of Bernardes' administration were almost exclusively dedicated to solving these problems.

The acute financial problems of the federal government – both on account of its current budget position and of the large Treasury short-term debt accumulated with the Banco do Brasil during 1922 – and central banking reform, were tackled first and the solutions found were closely interrelated.

To enforce a substantial reduction in the large deficit forecast in the budget estimates for 1923, presupposed a much tighter fiscal policy than had been suggested by Bernardes' programme and, backed by government parliamentary spokesmen, he began to advocate drastic expenditure cuts, such as the suspension of public works and a reduction in the public sector's salary bill.[15] These cuts were resolutely enforced – those on investment being particularly severe[16] – causing a sharp contraction in the growth of real expenditure.[17] This, together with the increase in the gold tariff quota from 55 to 60 per cent and the sustained recovery in activity levels maintained during 1923, resulted in a reduction of the real budget deficit to about a fourth of its 1922 level.[18] Finally, the government's proposed reform of Treasury operational procedures and public accounting methods was implemented in 1923, apparently with some measure of success.[19]

However the Treasury's financial problems were greatly complicated by the need to settle its huge floating debt to the Banco do Brasil which, due to its paralysing effect on the Bank's operations[20] and high interest charges, came to be seen by the government as the most urgent priority in economic policy.[21] Since it was clearly impossible to liquidate this enormous debt in the short run through budget surpluses and a funding operation on this vast scale was nowhere near possible in domestic capital markets, the alternative of issuing a long-term loan abroad had to be contemplated. However the Minister of Finance argued that this problem 'should be solved without emissions or foreign loans, at least for the present [for] it would be preferable for Brazil to show that she has the capacity to solve her difficulties through her own economic life.'[22] This view reflected the government feeling – explicitly admitted by the Brazilian authorities in December – that, in the present circumstances, foreign financial assistance would not be forthcoming without a previous show of fiscal discipline.[23]

Nevertheless the government was not at a loss in facing this problem and, as Vidal cryptically mentioned in his report, a 'general plan' to reduce the floating debt, resting upon 'a permanent foundation to be cemented by the utilisation of the [Treasury] gold reserve' was being studied.[24] This 'general plan' was, oddly enough, the government project for central banking reform. However the reasons leading the authorities to deal jointly with these seemingly unrelated problems are not difficult to understand.

In order to create a central bank according to the broad principles defined in Bernardes' electoral platform in favour of inconvertible notes issued on a fractional gold reserve basis, the government had to find a way to amass a substantial amount of gold or convertible foreign exchange. Given the low level of official foreign exchange reserves and the fact that the government ruled out on political grounds the possibility of 'contracting with foreign bankers' the foundation of the new central bank,[25] the only alternative left was to mobilise the £10 million worth of gold the federal government had accumulated as a war chest. There were legal constraints binding on the use of these gold reserves: although held idle in the Treasury vaults, they could not be exported without express legislative authorisation, and the Minister of Finance feared that 'Congress would never consent in letting the golden calf to part'.[26] However the new government did not fail to notice that by granting central banking powers to the Banco do Brasil and transferring the Treasury gold to it, they could not only obviate their promised banking reform but also settle a part, but nevertheless a substantial part, of the federal liabilities to the Bank against the value of the gold transferred.[27]

Thus the basic lines of the Bernardes government's banking reform bill, presented to Congress in late December, consisted in transferring the Treasury gold reserves and granting the monopoly of issue to the Banco do Brasil, without curbing its usual functions as a large commercial bank. This would be done through the creation of an Issue Department at the Bank which would issue inconvertible banknotes, up to three times its gold or foreign exchange reserves, against rediscount of commercial bills. Fiscal considerations other than the wish to reduce the Treasury floating debt also influenced the project: with the purpose of defining the note issuing ceiling to be granted to the new Issue Department in terms of domestic currency, the government proposed that the gold reserves backing the Bank's issues should be valued at 12 pence per milréis and that this rate should be taken as a target for eventual full convertibility of the new notes, which should be automatically declared as long as this exchange rate had prevailed in the market for three consecutive years. Since the current exchange rate was around 6.3d, the 90 per cent appreciation implicitly defined by the government project could have a sizeable medium-term impact on public expenditure, especially as amortisation payments on the foreign debt funded in 1914 would be due again from 1927.

It must be stressed, moreover, that although the mentors of banking reform paid lip-service to postwar fashion in monetary policy,[28] the basic operational features of the reform had very little to do with contemporary central banking orthodoxy, a point which recent writers have misunderstood.[29] Although a limit of 25 per cent of annually voted revenue was placed on the usual Banco do Brasil current account advances to the Treasury within each fiscal year, the reform embodied clauses explicitly reaffirming the federal government's majority control over the Bank. Thus the new central banking regulations enforced no greater restraint on inflationary deficit financing than the previously existing arrangements, since the new Issue Department stood in relation to the Bank in exactly the same position as the Rediscount Department which, in fact, the former only replaced. Furthermore, and this is perhaps the most important aspect of the reform, in spite of the deflationary bias implicit in its express objective of exchange rate appreciation, it gave the Executive ample ammunition to pursue an expansionary monetary policy: at the 12d valuation rate, the initial £10 million gold reserves transferred to the Bank alone defined a ceiling of not less than 600 000 contos for its note issues, and the powers to vary its outstanding volume within this ample limit were left at the sole discretion of the Bank's board of directors, whose members were appointed by the government. One can say, indeed, that, far from being influenced by contemporary doctrinaire principles,[30] the operational regulations of the new Brazilian central bank were shaped by the government's wish to preserve its currency-issuing powers because of the uncertainty still surrounding the evolution of its budget position as well as the likely possibility of having to support coffee prices with domestic resources.

The process of reforming the Banco do Brasil gave Bernardes the opportunity of forcing the resignation of Whitaker, whose goodwill in government circles had been damaged by the heated public debate between new and former top-ranking government officials following the disclosure of the problems inherited from Pcssoa's period. The President of the Banco do Brasil was not even consulted during the drafting of the reform and resigned on 27 December,[31] being replaced by Cincinato Braga, a man closely linked with the Minister of Finance in the coffee valorisation-credit reform debates of 1920 and the author of the government central bank project.[32] Congress approval of the proposed banking reform Bill did not present difficulties and it became law on 8 January 1923. Having ensured the approval of its basic fiscal and monetary policy proposals within the short time left of the 1922 congressional session, the new government had still to face the difficult problem of defining its new coffee policy.

As mentioned above, the main difficulties in defining any independent coffee policy stemmed from the clauses of the 1922 London coffee loan restricting the federal government's ability to support prices before the end of the loan's 10-year redemption term. In this connection, the need to achieve a negotiated agreement with the bankers was of paramount importance for keeping open federal government access to London for at least two cogent reasons. Firstly it was urgently necessary to arrange the re-scheduling of the short-term credits advanced by Rothschilds in the second half of 1922 and the government hoped to fund part of the federal floating debt through a foreign loan.[33] In the second place, as early as mid-1922, strong protests from American roasters against coffee valorisation were endorsed by the United States Secretary of Commerce, under whose influence access to loans destined to finance it in the New York capital markets would be denied as a means of fighting the 'Brazilian monopoly'.[34] Since Department of Commerce views against Brazilian coffee valorisation were not secret[35] and, given Rothschilds' customary aversion to lend on coffee, London would certainly be wary of lending new money before the liquidation of the 1922 loan, financing the retention of the 1923 crop abroad was out of the question. However, if the government had eventually to finance coffee price support with domestic resources, it could only do it through domestic inflationary means and the additional expansionary effects this would entail could have serious balance of payments consequences. If that happened, as was likely, the goodwill of the London bankers could eventually be decisive in lending credibility to the government exchange rate policy, given the low level of foreign exchange reserves.

Thus, in the second half of January 1923, the Brazilian government approached its London bankers to try and negotiate the settlement of the 1922 sterling short-term credits and the abolition of the restrictive clauses of the 1922 coffee loan.[36] The impression caused by the Brazilian government's fiscal and monetary policy measures and the firm recovery of international coffee prices opened the way towards a solution. It was agreed that the credits would be renewed, to be liquidated with the net proceeds of the sales of the coffee stocks guaranteeing the 1922 loan. Furthermore as the 1923 crop estimates pointed to a larger output and a less favourable outlook for prices, the bankers accepted Brazilian demands for a shortening of the coffee loan redemption period[37] and, to ensure the prompt repayment of Rothschilds' short-term credits, the committee agreed to speed up the sales.[38] However, the London agreement overestimated the absorptive capacity of world coffee markets in 1923. The stocks guaranteeing the 1922 loan were still at the high mark of 3.4 million bags[39] – some 22 per cent of world production in the 1922–3 crop year – and as soon as these stocks began to be disposed of in February, the upward price trend was reversed[40] and sales had to be spread more thinly.

Nevertheless the government was finally free to define its new coffee price stabilisation policy. The new scheme introduced a basic innovation in relation to the usual method of price support through direct intervention in the market: price control would now be effected by the regulation of the quantity of coffee flowing from the producing areas to the main ports of embarkation in Santos and Rio. The new mechanism of crop retention up-country and control of port entries was to be enforced with the construction of special public warehouses at the main railway junctions, to which all the coffee produced would have to be shipped by the planters to be released in quantities defined by the federal government according to a first in – first out schedule.

The new system differed radically from previous valorisations also because the government now assumed no responsibility for purchasing the coffee delivered by the farmers to the official regulating warehouses, whose action would be limited to issuing negotiable certificates of deposit against which the farmers or their *commissários* should procure the cash needed to cover the farms' working capital requirements during the retention period. Now it was the farmer, as the ultimate holder of the stocks, and not the public authority as heretofore, who would bear the risks of the operations and reap the profits resulting therefrom. In the prevailing optimism regarding the effectivenesss of artificial price control following the success of the 1922 valorisation, this was a perspective which appealed to the private interests in the coffee trade. The crucial question was, once more, how to finance the planters' cash needs during the period of retention of stocks for, under the new system, in a bumper crop year the average length of the advances needed by the planters would be considerably increased by the longer average period between the shipping of the coffee to the regulating warehouses and its final sales to an exporter. In such a situation, if no additional liquid resources were forthcoming to strengthen the lending capacity of the city commercial banks, they would be unwilling to freeze a large share of their assets in a commodity lacking short-term liquidity, given their heavy seasonal demands for credit from other branches of activity.

In spite of the worries voiced on this score by sectors of the coffee trade[41] no special provision was formally made by the government to help finance the retention of stocks. However, even considering that the current official estimates for the coming crop placed it at 13.2 million bags, which was not an alarmingly large figure, it is unlikely that the federal authorities simply overlooked this problem 'trusting', as suggested by Rowe, 'that the ordinary banks would be able to discount the planters' bills.'[42] As later events would demonstrate, the government knew that, if necesssary, the large and still unused issuing powers granted to the Banco do Brasil could be used to back the private banking system through rediscount of their coffee bills and that this could be done by straightforward Executive decision.

What the government seems to have underestimated was the size of the 1923 bumper crop, which amounted to not less than 19.5 million bags for Brazil as a whole (almost twice the previous year's figures[43]), 14.9 million bags coming from São Paulo alone. Thus, in June, when the extent of the supply disequilibrium became clear, prices began to slump in Brazil, causing what was described as a panic in the chief export markets.[44] Although the London coffee stocks had not yet been liquidated, before the end of the month Washington Luis, the Governor of São Paulo, went to Rio to discuss the position with Bernardes and it was decided to enforce at once the control of daily entries at the ports. However, the government still refrained from creating an institution responsible for permanent valorisation as authorised by Congress in 1922, promised by Bernardes and enthusiastically supported by the present Minister of Finance since the early twenties, and not even an official communiqué was issued on this occasion to signal the beginning of the new retention policy.[45]

Given the ample ammunition held by the Banco do Brasil, as a result of its new central bank status, from the strict point of view of price control the new Brazilian system was bound to be effective. In fact the falling price trend in the second quarter of 1923 was reversed in August and a mild but sustained recovery maintained until the end of the year.[46] The policy dilemma was, however, how to maintain roughly stable coffee prices without a large impact on monetary equilibrium, as would be unavoidable if the demands on the Banco do Brasil happened to be large. This was to depend not only on world supply and demand conditions but also, crucially, on domestic credit conditions which influenced the private banking system's capacity to play its part in finacing the retention of stocks.

However the conduct of monetary policy during the first half of 1923 had been extremely restrictive. Moreover, as inflation began to accelerate during 1923, it is probable that the slow growth of the money stock implied a fall in real cash balances at a time of strong recovery in economic activity.[47] So when, in July, to the financial needs of coffee valorisation was added the usual seasonal increase in demand for loans connected with the harvest of other agricultural crops,[48] the rapid drain of other banks' deposits at the Banco do Brasil and the government's failure to reduce its frozen floating debt to the Bank so as to relieve its cash position left no option but to turn on the Issue Department's tap.[49]

These domestic monetary management problems and the return to easy money from the beginning of the second half of 1923[50] coincided with increased difficulties in controlling the exchange rate. During 1923 the balance of trade surplus had not improved and foreign capital flows dried up[51] while, owing to the need to settle the federal coffee loan in London, 'the gold bills resulting from the sale of the government's coffee . . . passed straight from the hands of the committee controlling valorisation in London to the hands of the bankers.'[52] The Treasury was unable to rebuild its foreign reserve position, the Banco do Brasil almost abandoned the foreign exchange market[53] and, in the second half of August only, the milréis fell by 12 per cent.

The events at the beginning of the second half of 1923 had a profound influence on the future course of economic policy during Bernardes' government. Having lost control over the Banco do Brasil note issues and fearing recurrent exchange rate crises,[54] the authorities came to consider raising a large foreign loan as the only way of avoiding the premature failure and demoralisation of its reformist economic programme. Such a loan, if employed to settle the Treasury floating debt to the Banco do Brasil, would re-establish the latter's control over the foreign exchange market, while the parallel growth of its liquid domestic assets could increase its lending capacity, thus reducing the need to resort to the Issue Department.

Accordingly, in September, to avoid the painful alternative of deflationary readjustment which might not only cut short the recovery in activity levels begun in 1922 but seriously impair the political feasibility of its coffee price support programme, the Brazilian government approached Rothschilds for a £25 million long-term loan to 'liquidate the [Treasury] floating debt and set Brazilian finances in order.'[55] The bankers, taking advantage of their very strong bargaining position and arguing that the federal government's foreign debt was already very large and that the current low quotations of Brazilian bonds in international capital markets would render the operation difficult, adopted the firm position that the loan should be made conditional upon their appraisal of the recommendations of a mission of financial experts which would visit Brazil to assess *in loco* the actual state of federal finances.[56] As will be shown below, the bankers' intention was to try and make the granting of financial accommodation dependent upon the Brazilian government's enforcement of the mission's recommendations on whatever changes should be made in the institutional and operational framework of monetary, fiscal and coffee policy in Brazil, so as to strengthen the country's capacity to pay, particularly with a view to the resumption, in 1927, of amortisation payments on the foreign debt as agreed in the funding scheme of 1914.[57]

Following the Brazilian government's acceptance of these general terms, the bankers began to recruit their team of experts. Their choice of the senior members of the financial mission fell upon men with no particular competence on Brazilian affairs but who came from highly influential circles within the City. The Mission was to be led by Edwin Samuel Montagu, former Liberal M.P., Financial Secretary to the Treasury and famous for the co-authorship of the Indian post-war constitutional reforms while Secretary of State for India.[58] The other four senior members were Sir Charles Addis, a Director and member of the Committee of Treasury of the Bank of England and Chairman of the Hong-Kong and Shanghai Bank; Lord Lovat, a man with large interests in real estate and cotton plantations overseas; Hartley Withers, former editor of the London *Economist*; and Sir William McLintock, partner of one of the largest British accounting and auditing firms. Sir Henry Lynch, a British manufacturer and Rothschilds' permanent representative in Rio was to serve as liaison between the mission and the Brazilian government, acting as interpreter during the negotiations.

Until November the secrecy with which the real purposes of the financial mission were surrounded worked to perfection. By late November, however, as 'exaggerated gossip' was growing in the City,[59] Rothschilds notified the British Foreign office of their intentions and, at the Brazilian government's request, issued an evasive statement to the press concerning the mission's purposes.[60] Though this version for public consumption was not generally taken at face value in Brazil,[61] the reaction of informed opinion was not altogether hostile to the mission, probably because the loan was seen as the only painless solution to the current economic policy problem in the short run. However, there certainly were fears that the mission might put forward unpalatable proposals to the government as condition for granting financial accommodation and for those who took a less orthodox or a more nationalistic view on economic policy the latter's extremely weak negotiating position was a cause for concern. For, in fact, as the British Ambassador bluntly summed up the position to London: ' . . . if [Bernardes] is forced to beg for money he may have to swallow the pill of foreign advice.'[62]

5.2   THE MONTAGU MISSION[63]

The mission left Britain in the second half of December. Although none of its members had any close acquaintance with Brazilian affairs, the preparatory discussions they had on board, based on information provided by the bankers, served to cement general opinions already held in London that budgetary discipline was of the essence and that some means through which the bankers could in the future influence financial policy in Brazil would have to be devised.[64] On 30 December they finally arrived in Rio, but formal negotiations were not to start until three weeks later.

The nearest approach to business the mission had in their first month in Rio, before going to São Paulo, were interviews with President Bernardes and a first formal negotiation with Vidal, the Finance Minister, on 17 January. In their first interview with Bernardes they were asked whether they proposed to make any recommendations to the government. Although the British had not settled this point, Montagu answered that they would do so after ending the investigations. The President stressed that he 'wanted any recommendations to be made to him and verbally discussed with him.'[65]

The first formal meeting with the Finance Minister was arranged as soon as rough up-to-date figures on the floating debt had been compiled. The government short-term liabilities were put at over 800 000 contos – around £25 million[66] – and the exploratory discussion on this occasion centered on the net amount required from the bankers and the security to be offered. Although this meeting marked the beginning of formal talks, it would not be followed up until after Montagu's return from São Paulo in mid-February. The evidence from the mission's records clearly shows, however, that by the end of this first fact-finding and exploratory spell in Rio the mission's views on the various issues they were to tackle had already taken shape.

Firstly the mission found it essential to reform federal budgeting techniques so as to allow the government effectively to implement a more restrictive fiscal policy. Even though Montagu fully endorsed what he thought was a general acknowledgment that 'the government is trying to get its financial house in order [and] has certainly improved tax-collection and accountancy beyond belief,'[67] the mission was very critical of budgetary procedures themselves. In their opinion, in the prevailing circumstances 'what is called a Budget is an *olla podrida* of votes of supply, authorizations for expenditure and for borrowing, and taxation proposals . . . [which moreover] jumbled up capital expenditure and revenue expenditure.'[68]

This judgement was far from inaccurate. Indeed in Brazilian budgetary procedures there was no mechanism – except the political muscle of the government of the day – to guarantee that expenditure in a given year could be kept in line with voted revenue and credit operations, or to ensure the expenditure of borrowed funds to the ends for which they had been earmarked. The main reason for this, quite apart from errors in the estimates, was the authority traditionally granted in the budget for the opening of 'Additional Credits' – over and above budgeted expenditures, for which either inadequate provision had been made or no revenue at all provided and often without indication of their amount – which were usually voted at a late stage of the budget's passage in Congress and hurriedly approved, often for petty political reasons.[69]

Besides, still on the budget front, it was thought important to achieve some once-and-for-all reduction in public expenditure. Not surprisingly the mission struck upon the idea of advising the creation of a committee of eminent persons from outside public service which would investigate the various departmental expenditure proposals and advise on possible cuts, especialy the reduction of personnel, on the lines of the British Geddes Committee.[70]

Thus, on fiscal policy issues, the mission had two aims: to introduce a new system of budgetary procedures – basically aimed at eliminating the 'budget tail,' restricting current expenditure to the limit set by approved revenue and limiting borrowing except for capital expenditure items – and to ensure the creation of the expenditure watchdog committee.

The second problem the British were concerned with was how to curb excessive foreign borrowing by the states and municipalities. The reason for this concern was the depressing effect the default by some states, which had borrowed freely during the pre-war boom, was having on the quotations of federal bonds issued throught Rothschilds and held in London. It was a long-standing desire of the bankers that the Brazilian government should submit non-federal public foreign borrowing to some form of control and, as noted in Chapter 2, the federal authorities had in 1912 unsuccessfully attempted to pass legislation to that effect. Since then the government had resigned itself to issuing public warnings from time to time – usually at the bankers' instance – denying any responsibility in relation to non-federal obligations. However the mission was committed to finding a final solution to this problem even though it would require the ammendment of the Constitution of 1891 and meet fierce opposition from state governments.[71]

The third point at issue was Brazilian coffee policy. Rothschilds had traditionally been no sympathisers of government price support schemes except in very special circumstances and would certainly not approve of any commitment of federal resources to a permanent scheme now, given the government's shaky financial position and with the beginning of the amortisation payments to the 1914 funding loan looming just three years ahead. Montagu was soon to learn that the new coffee price support system, based on the retention of surplus stocks in the recently built government regulating warehouses and successfully tried in the second half of 1923, was to be made permanent.[72] To finance the new scheme the government proposed to raise a foreign loan to be repaid out of the proceeds of a gold-indexed tax, charged on each bag carried by the railways collecting the coffee for delivery to the government's warehouses, to be paid by the farmers into a special account at the Banco do Brasil. Although Montagu's initial impression was that the new scheme 'was dear to the heart of Vidal'[73] and that 'the government will not, and perhaps cannot, keep out of coffee transactions owing to the enormous influence of São Paulo,'[74] he was convinced that 'these coffee transactions . . . run definite risks of inflation and stock accumulation'[75] and these fears would lead him to press the Brazilian authorities to avoid any involvement with the Coffee Institute. Moreover his negotiating position on this issue was very strong for some details of the plan were still not settled, as opinion in Brazil was divided on the question of whether the new Institute should be controlled by the federal government or by the coffee interests themselves and, as Brazilian loans for coffee valorisation could not be raised in New York at the time owing to Department of Commerce opposition, its financial feasibility depended upon support from London, which the mission could decisively influence.

The fourth issue the mission was to deal with was the possibility of an Anglo-Brazilian most-favoured-nation commercial treaty, consistently refused by Brazil and dear to the British Foreign Office. Although this question led Montagu to a little soul-searching,[76] the classic City view prevailed in the end and the issue was not pressed.[77]

The fifth problem was how to minimise the total sum of the proposed London bond issue, given the amount required by the Brazilian government. The answer to that was, naturally, to induce the government to raise what it could both by a concurrent internal issue of milréis bonds, and by disposing of some of its marketable assets. These two possibilities were to be pursued, though not without serious obstacles. The former would be restricted by the size of the Brazilian capital markets. The latter would be resisted since the government could not sell, or lease for a long period, the two public companies to which the mission's attention was attracted – the Lloyd Railway – without surmounting a not inconsiderable political opposition.[78]

The sixth point of concern to the mission arose from its endorsement of the British railway's complaints that the government control of freight rates had not allowed them to rise to the extent required to compensate for the squeeze in their sterling profits caused by the large postwar exchange rate depreciation.[79] The solution envisaged here was to propose the creation of an 'independent' Railway Tribunal, with British representation on it, to frame and control federal railway policy. To sweeten the proposal, Montagu persuaded other members of the mission to back the issue of a special £5 million railway development loan in London[80]

The penultimate problem the mission had to face was how to dissuade the President from going ahead with the iron and steel development plan which, as mentioned above, was part of his electoral platform.[81] Montagu strongly objected to the government's plan from the outset. However, it should be stressed that his objections resulted from apprehensions that its implementation would cause an undesirable expansion of the public sector and require an unwarranted increase in public expenditure, and apparently not from any intention to curb the development of a steel industry in Brazil.[82]

Last but not least, there was the delicate task of securing what Montagu called 'some palatable form of foreign financial control.'[83] This matter had been raised in London and before their arrival in Rio the British were unanimous that some form of control by the bankers over Brazilian financial policy should be devised. Even though the bankers' view (and, by implication, the early views of the mission) tended to favour 'the employment of a representative of the bankers by the government for the purpose of watching the progress of the proposed reforms . . . and of using his influence to prevent a recurrence of the present situation,'[84] towards the end of January the mission's attention started to be drawn instead towards the possibility of securing British influence over the Banco do Brasil.

Ironically, the idea of proposing the sale of the government's 52 per cent stake in the Bank had been conceived early in January on the consideration that this was just another public asset eligible for sale or, as Montagu then put it, 'another method of finding money for the Brazilian Government.'[85] However, as their understanding of Brazilian Government institutions and instruments of economic policy grew, it did not escape their attention that the 1923 monetary reform had formally transferred the control over monetary policy to the Banco do Brasil and that if the influence still exerted by the government over the Bank's policies could be eliminated, the Bank could effectively be used to impose budgetary discipline. Besides, the mission had been explicitly instructed by the London bankers to try and devise means to prevent further exchange rate depreciation[86] and since the Bank was, in normal times, the controlling influence on the Brazilian foreign exchange market, it was the natural instrument through which this aim could be realized. Furthermore a large part of the liabilities the Brazilian government wished to fund were due to the Bank, and it could easily be suggested that the proceeds of the sale of the government shares should be used to settle these liabilities,[87] so that if London had an interest in acquiring the shares it could be done without increasing the total amount of the proposed London issue, for the government liabilities would be reduced *pro tanto*.[88] Finally, the mission may not have overlooked the fact that

the Bank had in recent years distributed dividends of 20 per cent –
the maximum allowed by the statutes – on top of sizeable increases in
its reserves.[89]

So when these considerations had matured Montagu telegraphed
to London, saying that the mission was considering including the sale
of the government shares at the Bank as one of their proposals and
asked whether Rothschilds 'or their friends' would be interested in
buying them.[90] The bankers' answer was as realistic as it was prompt:

> We have discussed the question of the Banco do Brasil with our
> friends and we have unnanimously [sic] come to the conclusion that
> while we agree with you that it would be an excellent thing for the
> Banco do Brasil to be independent of the Brazilian Government
> we think it would be most unpopular in Brazil for the national bank
> to be owned by foreigners, nor do we think it would be advisable
> for us to control such an institution as it might lead to grave
> difficulties between the government and ourselves. Under these
> conditions we think that if you advise the Brazilian Government to
> dispose of its shares it should do so to its own nationals.'[91]

Montagu was surprised by this reply and in a strong defence of his
position immediately reminded them that their views when he left
London, and the only firm conviction the mission had formed, was
that the sole guarantee of a sound financial policy in Brazil 'is that
there would be some foreign, that is British, element in [the] financial
system,' and concluded unambiguously that the 'best places for this
element would be first in the Board of Directors [of the] Bank of
Brazil and secondly in the Tribunal of Accounts.'[92] Rothschilds
answered back, making it clear that they concurred with the point
that the implementation of the mission's recommendations would
require 'British supervision,' but reaffirmed their opinion that the
Bank should be sold to Brazilians.[93] Montagu, however, was already
strongly attached to his own alternative which he was to pursue even
against the bankers' advice, though not altogether abandoning attempts to include London's representation in the Brazilian executive
as preferred by them.

Broadly this was how the mission's views stood at the end of their
first month in Rio. Summing up his own feelings on the all-embracing
question of the loan, Montagu, though expressing irritation with
what he called the 'peculiar and precarious' Brazilian government
personnel, would conclude that he himself was 'fast inclining to the

idea to give them what they ask on conditions.'[94] On 31 January, two days after a short interview with the President, in which the mission handed in an *aide-mémoire* containing a summary of what they proposed to recommend on most of the issues, they left for São Paulo. 'After this interview,' Montagu wrote optimistically, 'we have no secrets except the one on financial influence and we shall be able to peg away.'[95]

The visit to São Paulo consisted solely of public appearances, visits to coffee plantations and the like and was of no consequence for the issues being discussed.[96] On 12 February they were back in Rio and the memorandum left with the government on their departure had already been digested by the cabinet. From then on the pace of the negotiations quickened. On 19 February, the first of a series of meetings with Vidal took place. The first point to be touched on was the iron and steel plan. The Minister reaffirmed that the government project would not lead to any large expenditure, and that Bernardes thought that for defence reasons he must have steel in Brazil. However, when Montagu proposed delaying action on the project until his return to London, when he would try and get financial support for it and couple it with Vidal's request for long-term coal supply contracts, the Minister agreed and they passed to the sensitive issue of coffee policy.[97]

Vidal considered Montagu's suggestion of turning the management of the price support scheme into some sort of planters' association to be utterly unrealistic, on the grounds that the planters lacked both the organisation and the skills needed and dismissed as unwarranted the usual criticisms that valorisation would encourage foreign competition and lead to over-planting in Brazil. After a long debate it became clear that Brazil would not leave coffee prices at the mercy of market forces, but Montagu was satisfied by the assurances the Minister gave as to the limited role the federal government was planning to play in their control.

From coffee they moved on to the possibility of sale of public assets. The Finance Minister said that the government would sell Lloyd, with the proviso that it would have to keep the coastal lines under Brazilian flag, but that the sale of the Central was 'politically impossible.'[98] Montagu did not press the point of the Central but carefully mentioned for the first time the sale of Banco do Brasil shares as another possibility.[99] The Minister took no offence at this suggestion, saying however:

the government was very anxious to separate the Banco do Brasil from the State . . . but they did not consider that the present was an opportune time for accomplishing that change. Opinion in Brazil was very divided as to whether there should be a Banco do Brasil at all as a central bank of emission, and until they had firmly established their view that it should so act they ought to be in a position to protect the Bank. After all the President of the Federal Reserve Board was the Secretary to the [U.S.] Treasury, the President of the Bank of France was appointed by the Government, the President of the Reichsbank before the war was appointed by the Government.[100]

Vidal's argument did not fail to impress Montagu. However, after some admittedly feeble remarks the latter expressed his disgust with what he considered was the government's non-committal attitude during the negotiations,[101] and these stronger words led the Minister as far as to say:

he was not at all averse to the sale of the Banco do Brasil shares; he was quite prepared to do it if [the mission] pressed it. All he asked [them] to consider was whether . . . it ought to be done now – at once. Was it wise in a new country like this to leave to private bankers in this country the total control of the bank of issue and of the money?[102]

Montagu gave no answer to this question; they agreed to pursue the matter further and the meeting adjourned.

Negotiations between Vidal and Montagu continued the following day but there is no evidence that the question of the sale of the Bank was raised again on this occasion. This meeting was entirely devoted to the debate of the proposed budgetary reform and the question of federal control of non-federal public foreign loans. Again, on these issues, there was little opposition to the British proposals. The government had nothing in principle against a tight fiscal policy and in fact the pledge to pursue one figured prominently in Bernardes' electoral platform. So, although the proposed budgetary reform was probably more radical than the government would have undertaken on its own initiative,[103] the Finance Minister agreed to try and implement it, implying however that this was understood as guaranteeing that the loan would be floated.[104] The 'Geddes Committee' recommendation was also firmly supported by Vidal[105] and on the question of the state and municipal loans he assured Montagu that the government was 'negotiating with the new Presidents of all States with a view to seeing if they could not arrange outside the Constitution that any attempts by the States and Municipalities to borrow should be approved by the Federal Government.'[106]

On Monday 18 February the negotiations continued and Braga, the President of the Banco do Brasil joined in to discuss technical details of the Bank-Treasury agreement of 1923 and exchange rate policy. Montagu did not hide his appreciation of the 1923 monetary reform but after comments from the Brazilians on the difficulties they were still having in passing it into law,[107] he hinted at having heard rumours that these difficulties were in fact due to fears that the agreement as it stood would not suffice to make the Bank independent from the Treasury. Whether this remark was meant to be provocative or not, it led the President of the Bank to make a long – and, in the circumstances, quite untimely – statement that he and Vidal shared these misgivings and 'were very anxious as soon as may be to assure the complete independence of the Bank of Brazil from the Government' and that the solution he personally favoured 'if the elections produced a result which would make it possible to get through such a law, was the selling of the shares of the Government in the Bank of Brazil to the other banks in Brazil, both national and foreign, and to model the bank of issue on the lines of the Federal Reserve Bank in New York,' with the President of the Bank still appointed by the government but with no powers to overrule the directors as it had now.[108]

Montagu could not have wished to hear a statement more in line with his own views and after telling Braga that this was 'exactly the scheme we would recommend,' asked whether it would help him if the mission said so in their report to Bernardes.[109] At this point, according to Montagu, Braga 'appeared to be afraid he had gone too far' and backed down by saying that the question had not been discussed with Vidal and that he hoped that if the mission wanted to recommend anything it would do so 'on general lines.'[110] His slip, however, renewed Montagu's hopes – somewhat shattered since the Finance Minister's reaction a few days before – that it could be feasible to secure the Bank's control.[111]

On the following day Vidal and Montagu met again to settle the final point, viz., the net amount of financial assistance immediately required by the government. The Minister brought definitive estimates of the floating debt and again emphasised that there was no alternative to a foreign loan as 'the issue of even 500 *apólices* upsets the market.'[112] However, it was finally agreed that 100 000 to 150 000 contos could be raised internally, not in *apólices* but in '7 or 7 $\frac{1}{2}$ per cent fairly long bonds.'[113]

Since this meeting concluded the discussion of all the issues raised by the mission, Vidal took the results of the negotiations to Bernardes for his consideration and on 21 February informally told Montagu that the President was in complete agreement with them: the railways and Lloyd, with the negotiated provisos, could be sold; an internal loan up to a limit of 150 000 contos should be raised; he would wait for Montagu's proposal on steel; constitutional amendments would be introduced to control non-federal foreign borrowing and meanwhile moral suasion would be used to curb it; the budget reform proposals were accepted and the President was 'enthusiastic' about the 'Geddes Committee' idea.[114]

With these assurances the mission sat down to draft their report to the President; it was meant to embody the proposals to which Bernardes' formal pledge would be requested in a final interview before their departure. It should be noted, however, that the acceptance of any of the two alternative ways envisaged by the mission as means to secure influence over Brazilian economic management had not up to now been guaranteed. On the two occasions the sale of the Banco do Brasil was mentioned, the Brazilian position – though in principle more favourable than one would have thought *a priori* – was eventually non-committal. Besides, the matter had not been clearly pressed by the British as an urgent or necessary condition for the loan, and neither was it among the proposals mentioned by Vidal as having had the President's approval; furthermore the alternative of arranging for the bankers' representation in some important government position had not even been mentioned to the Brazilians.

Thus, probably because of this, during the process of drafting the report, the mission agreed with Sir Henry Lynch's opinion that they should 'volunteer a proposal that the bankers should appoint a man who would be able to satisfy them that the reforms were being carried out and that the loan was being properly spent,'[115] and on 22 February he went to see Vidal to press a proposal for a Treasury 'advisor.'[116] Although the suggestion was put forward with great care and after a long preparation, it was strongly objected to by the Finance Minister. In Lynch's own words 'Vidal went every colour of the rainbow and completely out of his head'[117] and, as later reported to the bankers, 'went as far as to say that he would rather abandon all hope of restoring the financial position of Brazil than consent with fiscalization of the Treasury; that [the mission] had secured from him his consent, and he was hopeful that [they] should receive that of the President to [their] other proposals, but he could never put this proposal to the President: that if he did it would never be accepted, and no Government that consented to it could live.'[118]

Vidal's reaction was discussed by the members of the mission on the evening of the same day and they came to the conclusion that they 'were asking a great deal.'[119] Despite Lord Lovat's reminder that 'Rothschilds gave [this concession] great importance,' they agreed 'to leave it to them to raise it again from London.'[120] Montagu would, however, include the sale of the Banco do Brasil on the lines suggested by the Bank's president among the proposals in the report to the President and personally press Bernardes for a definition on the issue at their last meeting.

The draft report was signed by the British on Saturday 23 February copies handed to Bernardes and Vidal, and finally, on 2 March, two days before the mission was due to leave the country, the decisive meeting with the President took place.

Bernardes agreed, as expected, with the budget reform recommendations, with the simultaneous domestic bond issue, and emphatically assured the British that there would be no 'indiscriminate borrowing abroad' – a point which the report warned against in passing[121] – adding that Brazil 'was not going to borrow from any other source but them.'[122] However, when the proposal of the sale of the Banco do Brasil was reached, the President would only go as far as to state his agreement 'in principle', as he was not sure if it was the moment to do it.[123] His vagueness on this all-important issue was at once deprecated by Montagu who pressed for a clear definition, threatening that the bankers 'would not be happy with agreement in principle.'[124] Although the sharpness of this intervention shocked Bernardes,[125] Montagu remained deliberately impassive, trying to create the impression that a fundamental deadlock had been reached and to force the President to make the next move.[126] The bluff succeeded, and after a long conversation with Vidal, Bernardes put forward a compromise proposal to sell half of the public shareholding, arguing that he would not like to leave the Bank without government influence 'in case the Directors were making a mess of things.'[127]

The justification of this counterproposal was, however, in direct contradiction with the government's avowed intention to part with powers over the Bank and Montagu was not slow to complain that it showed that there was

not even an agreement in principle which the President alleged, for he desires to part with effective control and maintain a connection which meant that the Bank of Brazil's liberty might always be interfered with by the Government for political purposes . . . and now whilst pretending to agree with us in principle he was attempting to preserve the Government's influence

and feeling the strength of his position, he concluded by demanding unambiguously 'a definitive answer to our question: Did he intend or did he not intend to carry out our recommendations?.'[128] After another long consultation with his Finance Minister the President finally asked whether the mission 'had any objection to a President appointed by the government, provided that the President had no executive power and was merely there to preside at meetings.'[129] This question was unnecessary, however, for this was the very idea put forward to the British by the President of the Bank a few days before, and which they had included in the report.[130] Agreement having been reached, Bernardes solemnly declared that the mission 'could tell the bankers, and accept his assurance, that he would do everything in his power to persuade Congress to pass the necessary legislation to carry out [the] Report.'[131] Finally as the other recommendations came up for consideration they were all approved with little discussion.[132]

On the following morning the British party called for the last time on Vidal. The Minister, when reminded of the importance of implementing the proposed measures at once 'to influence opinion in London,' gave the additional assurance that the passage of legislation would not be difficult as the parliamentary elections had returned a large government majority in both houses.[133] Indeed, as Montagu's graphic record of this last encounter with Vidal shows, he was left in little doubt that the Finance Minister meant what he said:

We arrived at the Treasury . . . to find the usually crowded entrance empty. As we entered from the lift into Vidal's own room, I saw what really amounted to the most pathetic sight I have ever seen – poor Vidal alone and unattended (for the whole Treasury was Carnavalling), sitting at a typewriter laboriously thumping and fingering on the instrument his own answer to our Report. Can one want a more convincing picture of determination and earnestness?[134]

5.3   NARROWING OPTIONS AND DEFLATIONARY ADJUSTMENT

When the British mission left Brazil, the crucial decision regarding the loan came to depend solely on the bankers' reaction to its advice. By the end of March the main part of the *Report to the Bankers* was already finished.[135] Although dedicating about two-thirds of its length to superficial comments on Brazilian geography, institutions, public administration practices, and containing even references to the Brazilians' 'marked intelligence and great charm,'[136] the final section of this document is entirely devoted to discussing the central question facing the mission, that is, to give or not to give the financial assistance requested by the Brazilian government in the light of the concessions and assurances obtained during the negotiations in Rio. On this issue the report was unambiguous: after exhaustively pointing out the difficulties facing Brazil, the mission concluded that it was 'satisfied of the good intentions of the Government and that it intends to do everything in its power to effect economies in expenditure and carry out the other reforms that have been suggested and strongly recommend that a loan should be started with as little delay as possible.'[137]

However it was unlikely that a loan could be floated soon. Despite the rumours about a loan to Brazil which started appearing almost at once in the financial press,[138] there was a need to reassure investors that the government was really moving towards implementing fundamental financial reforms, a move which demanded a good deal of political skill as well as time to be carried through, for Congress – on which several of the proposed reforms ultimately depended – would not reconvene until early May.

The first concrete steps came with a series of government acts and declarations on the lines of the Rio agreements. They began in late April at the shareholders meeting of the Banco do Brasil. There was an announcement of the arrangement to cancel the 400 000 contos due to the Treasury on account of the Rediscount Department issue against the debt the Treasury owed the Bank and Braga's report ends with the cryptic suggestion that the Bank's internal organisation might be changed to make it less dependent on the government and for that purpose an extraordinary meeting could be called.[139] At the beginning of May, Bernardes opened the congressional session with a speech which brought up, at the start, the issue of Constitutional revision, stressing the necessity of making 'budget-tail' credits unconstitutional as a condition for balancing the federal budget and advocating, among other things, greater federal control over the states' financial affairs.[140] The need to balance the budget and cut the additional credits was further emphasised in the budget draft Bill, presented soon afterwards by Vidal, and the 'Geddes Committee' was appointed on 3 June. A few days later, a telegram from Rothschilds congratulating the government on the outlined reforms received great publicity in the Rio press and was, according to the British Ambassador, 'widely taken here as indicating that a loan is imminent.'[141]

Parallel to these manifestations of intent, the Brazilians also started negotiations with Montagu towards agreement on the terms of a final publishable version of the mission's report to the President.[142] As a result of these consultations many minor points and even some important safeguards were conceded by the bankers. However, where the Brazilian requests for changes in the draft touched on passages concerning possible monetary consequences of coffee valorisation policy, the British position was adamant. The Minister's proposal to delete a sentence pointing to the inflationary dangers of government participation in coffee price support schemes was not only rejected, but led Montagu to remark that 'unless the public in this country were satisfied that there had been a radical alteration in the government policy in regard to the valorisation of coffee it would be impossible to raise a loan in this country.'[143]

A mutually acceptable wording for the final draft of the report was finally ready before mid-June. Since the draft bill on the constitutional reform had already been sent to Congress it was now the moment to back it up by publishing the 'independent' report, as it was certainly to be read by informed opinion as a set of conditions upon the fulfilment of which the loan depended, thus softening the opposition to the reforms. This move tactfully placed the government in the position of mediator between the wishes of the foreign creditors and those of the Brazilian Congress, from which concessions could be induced from both sides. Indeed, in a much publicised interview to the pro-government newspaper *O Paíz* on 24 June, the President publicly linked the possibility of British financial assistance to the proposed constitutional reform, preparing the ground for the publication of the report.[144] Four days later the document was released to the press in Rio and London.[145]

As was to be expected, the report was praised by the pro-Bernardes and the British papers.[146] The opposition press, on the other hand, although starting from a position which, by and large, centered on superficial remarks on the 'humiliation' Brazil was being submitted to by the government and on the 'arrogant' tone of the report, rapidly evolved towards exploiting the sensitive issues with an attack on the proposals to sell the public companies and the Banco do Brasil, 'beginning', as the British Ambassador put it 'to take the line that [the report] is an attempt to turn Brazil into a British colony.'[147]

Ironically, however, it was at this stage – when its almost year-long efforts neared fruition – that the government's strategy received a mortal blow. And it was probably Bernardes' greatest misfortune that the loan was to be blocked not as a result of a political deadlock in Brazil over the issues at stake, but as an indirect consequence of a domestic policy decision taken by the British government, viz., the embargo on foreign government issues in London, imposed with a view to strengthening the paper pound towards the return to gold at pre-war parity.

The British embargo on foreign government loans was prompted by the rapid worsening of the United Kingdom's ˙ trade balance deficit[148] and by the alarm caused by the growth of overseas lending in the early part of 1924 following the substantial freedom regained by the London overseas issues market in January, in a situation in which to try and deal with the imbalance through a tightening of monetary conditions 'would have raised a political storm.'[149] Probably because the embargo was not a formal official act, it has been mistakenly dated as effective from November 1924, even by such an authority as Brown.[150] More recently, however, it has been suggested by Moggridge that 'it would seem that the Bank [of England] became much stricter in its treatment of applications for foreign government new issues from mid-1924,'[151] an assertion based on evidence from an extract from the private diary of the Bank of England's Governor, as published by Sir Henry Clay, showing the very poor opinion Lord Norman had of foreign loans by April 1924, as well as on the observation that 'after 24 May there were no non-League of Nations, non-Reparations loans for foreign governments or municipalities until January 1926.'[152] In fact the importance of Norman's opinion in the imposition of the embargo cannot be overestimated. The method of imposing the embargo was, according to Brown, 'quite unobstrusive, informal and characteristically English . . . It was merely made known to those considering such issues that they would not meet with the approval of the Bank of England. This was sufficient. Though it was without a shred of legal or legislative justification, the embargo was exceedingly effective,'[153] and it is suggestive that well informed British Treasury officials referred to the embargo as 'the Governor's polite blackmail against foreign issues.'[154]

In the light of these remarks, some documents recently published by Professor Sayers[155] lend further support to the notion that the embargo was enacted by mid-1924. In a minute of 9 April, Norman is quoted as informing the Bank's Committee of Treasury that 'he was strongly of the opinion that only applications on behalf of those countries which were in need of money for reconstruction purposes deserved consideration' and in a similar document dated 22 October he states that 'having been approached, since the closing of the German loan, as to the issue of foreign loans in London, he had *again* replied that all such issues were, and were likely to be, undesirable under present Exchange conditions . . .'[156] Indeed, as far as the Brazilian loan was concerned, the usually well-informed *South American Journal* was telling its readers as early as 5 July, in an editorial on the British mission to Brazil, that its issue 'seems to have been postponed for the moment'.[157]

To assess the consequences of the British decision on Brazil it is worth recalling that the joint achievement of the basic goals in the government's economic programme – namely, the funding of the floating debt and the creation of a central bank designed to drive the milréis back to gold at a substantially revalued exchange rate – had been made to depend crucially on the successful conclusion of the British loan, and that since the first contacts with Rothschilds were made the domestic economic outlook had shown little change.

The rise in the domestic price level, which accelerated sharply in the first year of Bernardes' government, showed no signs of slowing down, and a sentiment had been growing for some time that inflation had become a major social problem, as seen in the special measures to curb food price increases taken in March and July.[158] Though the origins of this inflationary outburst dated back to the 1921 exchange rate collapse and the easy money period of the Rediscount Department, the lax way the Banco do Brasil managed its note issuing rights – particularly during the second half of 1923 – was certainly not in tune with the government's avowed deflationary intentions. By the end of June 1924, the Bank had already issued over 400 000 contos, that is over two-thirds of the statutory limit set by the valuation of the gold reserve transferred from the Treasury, expanding the monetary base by almost a fifth.

Moreover the rather delicate external position remained very much the same. The beginning of the substantial export growth of 1924 brought about by a firm rise in coffee prices was compensated by a concomitant growth of imports as the economy recovered from the postwar slump under strong inflationary pressures relative to her main import suppliers, as shown in Table 5.1. As the trade balance

Table 5.1   Price indices: Brazil, US and UK, 1920–4 (1913 = 100)

Year	Brazil	US	UK
1920	181.1	220.5	307.3
1921	153.5	139.4	197.2
1922	167.5	138.1	158.8
1923	218.0	143.7	158.9
1924	242.0	140.1	166.2

Sources: Brazil: General (Agriculture, Industry and Transport and Communications) Deflator presented by Haddad, C. L. S., (1974) *Growth of Brazilian Real Output, 1900–47*, University of Chicago, unpublished Ph.D. dissertation, Table 76, p. 191.
United States: Bureau of Labour wholesale price index, *in* U.S. Department of Commerce, Bureau of the Census, *Historical Statistics of the United States*, 1789–1945; (USGPO, Washington), p. 233.
United Kingdom: Board of Trade wholesale price index, in Pigou, A. C. (1947). *Aspects of British Economic History*: 1918–1925, pp. 234–235.

failed to recover and no foreign loans were forthcoming, the exchange rate remained at about one-half of the planned stabilisation rate. In this situation, if the indefinite postponement of the loan caused by the embargo was to last for long, it was bound eventually to force the government to alter its tactics.

However, almost simultaneously with the failure of the London loan, the government's attention would be shifted away from economic policy towards more pressing problems, as a military revolt broke out in the city of São Paulo on 5 July. Concerted armed risings broke out simultaneously in some other states and, in São Paulo, the rebels were able to oust the state government from the capital on 9 July and effectively controlled it until 27 July when, with the port of Santos controlled by the loyalist Navy and the capital besieged and bombed, they withdrew.

These rebellions had very weak connections with organised political groups and in no way should they be seen as representing a reaction of São Paulo or of the coffee interests against Bernardes' economic policies. They were almost exclusively a sequel to the July 1922 military upheaval in Rio preceding Bernardes' inauguration and immediately motivated by the anti-Bernardist hatred still cultivated in some sectors of the Army as well as by a diffuse but growing discontent in certain quarters of the middle-class elite with what they considered as the abandonment of original republican ideals by an anti-democratic and power-centralising political regime.[159] However, the armed revolts had two indirect effects of major importance in shaping the course of economic policy in the later part of 1924.

The first was to enable Bernardes to strengthen his political support among the controlling regional oligarchies. This came as a natural outcome of the prompt and uncompromising way the revolts were quelled everywhere – except for the symbolic Coluna Prestes-Miguel Costa – due to the rather conservative outlook of the Brazilian political establishment startled at the potential for popular unrest which the revolts uncovered. Having received exceptional powers concerning law and order measures as well as wide support from the higher ranks in the armed forces at the start of the risings, the President would eventually publicly consolidate his authority with an impressive referendum from all state Governors in November.[160]

The second effect was to force the Banco do Brasil to cause a large monetary expansion during the third quarter of the year, as both the unforeseen and large military expenditures and the need to help the banking system out of liquidity problems (arising from the temporary blocking of transactions with São Paulo and other centres), had to be met with further issues by the Bank. Its 600 000 contos statutory limit was passed in mid-August when a further issue of 100 000 contos – the maximum allowed by law in emergency conditions – was authorised. However, though the Bank tried at this stage to restrict its rediscount operations[161], its note circulation rose to an all-time peak of almost 753 000 contos in early October, with no legal backing.

If the greater political support Bernardes was able to amass at this critical juncture gave him the necessary strength to enforce unpalatable economic measures, the Bank's behaviour would provide the motive for conservative groups to press for a radical redefinition of the conduct of economic policy, definitely resolving in their favour a division which had always existed within the government on central issues of financial policy.

The origins of this division can be traced to the contradictory basis on which Bernardes had gathered support for his economic policy programme. The initial support São Paulo had given to his candidacy, as noted above, led not only to the formal inclusion of coffee 'defence' in his programme, but also to the granting of the finance portfolio and the Bank's presidency to *Paulista* politicians. These were men bound to take a less orthodox view on monetary policy and to be particularly lenient on occasions on which the financing of coffee stock retention depended on the Banco do Brasil. On the other hand, because of the predominantly regional organisation of party political life in Brazil, the president was close to and bound to be influenced by the extremely orthodox opinions sustained by a group of influential politicians from Minas Gerais led by Deputy Antonio Carlos, the former Finance Minister and now appointed leader of the majority in the House, Mario Brant, former Deputy and now Financial Secretary of Minas Gerais, and Affonso Pena Jr., leader of the state lobby in the House.[162]

In these quarters, a name that could hardly arouse more suspicion was that of Vidal. In 1921, as a Congressman, the present Finance Minister had made a passionate defence of his Permanent Coffee Defence Bill providing for Treasury fiduciary issues to finance the retention of the coffee surplus, an idea which was scarcely less than anathema to this group. Indeed the Bill was defeated after a strong attack by Mario Brant and Antonio Carlos, apparently with the backing of Bernardes himself, then governor of Minas Gerais.[163]

Under the more conservative consensus regarding monetary management after the Rediscount Department's 'scandal,' the Minister could hardly afford to repeat his 1921 utterances in favour of paper money issues. However such consensus only existed to the extent of not letting Treasury needs influence the behaviour of the monetary base, a consensus against financing budget deficits with note issues beyond ways and means requirements.[164] The theoretical defense of Braga's central bank plan had been exclusively constructed on the basis of a real-bills doctrine argument[165] which, in essence, differed little from the more crude and explicit 'coffee bills' argument Vidal had used in 1921.[166] In fact the new central bank could, as was indeed feared by the British mission, become the source of unwarranted increases in the money supply under pressure from the random – and large – financial requirements of coffee valorisation, as had actually happened in 1923. Thus, the more conservative group led by the leader of the government's parliamentary majority had perforce to nurture great misgivings about the decision of having the Bank's rediscount operations at the discretion of men in whom they had no confidence and who, moreover, were likely to bow to pressures from the coffee interests. This point receives further support from the British mission's records: in fact, as early as January 1924, Antonio Carlos indiscreetly confided to Montagu that he did not approve of the coffee valorisation scheme, expressing the view that the exchange rate depreciation was 'entirely due to emission' and that

> he would deprive the Bank of Brazil of the right to issue for the next seven years and undertake a careful reduction of existing currency . . . that Vidal was a fanatic of figures of emission [sic] and that he represented united public opinion and the opinion of most ex-Ministers of Finance and that he had every reason to believe – he spoke confidentially – that Bernardes was wavering on the subject.[167]

Accordingly, it was quite natural that, after the formidable expansion of the Bank's issues during the military revolts, these men should bring strong pressure to bear upon the President for a contractionary monetary policy. Although, on this occasion, the Bank had not specifically issued to rediscount coffee bills[168] and had actually been instrumental in overcoming the emergency, the circumstances could hardly be more favourable to the deflationists' preaching. In face of the growing outcry against the rise in the cost of living and the still vulnerable external position, the certainty now existing that no early loan was forthcoming from London would, in itself, leave no other option besides some measure of deflationary adjustment. Moreover the government's recent public endorsement of the British mission's report counselling a rather cautious attitude regarding increases in the Bank's note liabilities,[169] made it extremely difficult to leave things as they were after the return of internal peace, for such a complacent view of the Bank's behaviour was bound to have a demoralising effect and probably block the way to an eventual — and certainly still entertained — reopening of negotiations with London. Not surprisingly, they were to succeed in bringing Bernardes over to their side.

The secretiveness with which the tactical details towards the enforcement of a contractionist monetary policy were worked out between the President and some of the leading deflationist politicians – a process which, as will be shown, kept both Vidal and Braga totally in the dark – makes it difficult to ascertain precisely when the decision to deflate was reached. However the fact that the decision would later be publicly justified as having been prompted by the desire to neutralise the effects on domestic and external equilibrium of the monetary expansion caused by the Bank during the third quarter of 1924, suggests that its immediate cause was present, at the latest, from the beginning of October.[170]

The existing institutional framework enabled the Executive to tighten monetary policy through the control of the Bank's rediscount policy and by enforcing a clause in the Treasury–Banco do Brasil 1923 contract relating to the retirement of the Treasury note issues with the resources of a special reserve fund for which some of the Bank's income was earmarked. Since the deflationists' immediate objective was to reduce high-powered money and the reserve fund mechanism provided an automatic way of doing it, their attention focused at first not only on pressing for the observance of this clause, but also on finding means of enlarging the resources for the fund. However, the latter called for a revision of the Treasury–Bank 1923 contract, which required Congress approval. So a Bill had to be drafted which only reached committee stage in mid-December, where it was to meet opposition from São Paulo members once it became clear that Vidal and Braga had been totally excluded from its making.[171]

Though eventually it was found impossible to debate the Bill during the final crowded days of the congressional session then remaining, this had little practical consequence since its fundamental aim could be secured by the existing legislation if only the Treasury and the Bank could be placed under the command of men in line with the new policy. So when the public demoralisation suffered by Vidal and Braga over the Bank's reform Bill affair led to their resignation on 27 December, Bernardes was left with a free hand to fill their posts with his new advisors: Anibal Freire, the author of the draft Bill became the new Finance Minister, and Braga was replaced by James Darcy, a legal advisor to the Bank, who was to follow faithfully the new directives. Before the end of the year the Bank was already stepping up the withdrawal of Treasury notes with the allocation of some 55 000 contos to the reserve fund. This process, coupled with a drastic cut in the Bank's rediscount facilities, which would bring the Bank's issue back within the legal limit during the first half of 1925, would be relentlessly pursued for the following twenty months. By November 1926, when this policy was finally abandoned, the monetary base had been reduced by 14 per cent, causing an 11 per cent contraction in the money stock.[172]

5.4 THE END OF FEDERAL COFFEE DEFENCE

The redefinition of Bernardes' economic policies in late 1924 was not to be limited, however, to this radical change in monetary policy. A no less radical turn occurred in November, when the federal government transferred all responsibility for the financing and control of coffee valorisation to the state of São Paulo.[173] Although the formal change in coffee policy in fact preceded the actual implementation of the decision to deflate, the two measures had a logical connection and were, in a sense, complementary. For a better grasp of this point it is necessary that some specific developments in the coffee industry during 1924 should first be described.

As Table A.8 shows, in 1924 world coffee prices were rapidly recovering from the stagnant levels of the previous two years, both on account of the effective implementation of the new coffee defence system with financial help from the Banco do Brasil and of the small crop of 1924 5 which amounted to only 11 million bags against 19.5 million in 1923–4.[174] However, paradoxical as it may seem, the very success of the government's coffee defence scheme reopened the debate about its merits. It should be remembered that under the new scheme the financial burden of carrying over the stock fell exclusively on the planters. With more than one-quarter of their 1923–4 crop still unsold by mid-1924,[175] the planters were finding it extremely difficult to meet their current expenses with the advances from the banking system which they received against the warrants furnished by the government warehouses.[176] They had welcomed the defence plan without much discussion when the prospects for the industry were rather bleak but now, after prices had nearly doubled and still hard-pressed for cash, they faced no alternative in the short-term but to wait for the release of their coffee for export. On the other hand, they were now more convinced than ever of the advantages of valorisation and certainly did not want to throw the baby out with the bath water. As an obvious outcome, the notion grew stronger that there was a pressing need for some *ad hoc* provision of funds to smooth the financing of the crop carry-over.

As a result, negotiations between São Paulo and the federal authorites in search of a new financial formula to appease the planters started during the winter.[177] It should be noted that São Paulo's negotiating position was much weaker, since the federal government had already finished the liquidation of its old stocks and, with the exceptional prices now ruling, it was free to take a more detached view. However this should be interpreted as meaning only that it was now politically easier for the federal government not to bow to pressures from the coffee lobby to commit additional resources to valorisation. It is wrong to construct, as Rowe does,[178] an explanation for the extreme measure Bernardes eventually took – disclaiming all federal responsibility towards coffee valorisation and selling the government's recently built warehouses to the state of São Paulo – solely on the relatively better bargaining position of the federal government. If it is clear that São Paulo politicians could not possibly think of abandoning coffee valorisation at this stage, it is also clear that they could not justifiably take it for granted that they could carry the baby without the nursing of the federal government, since no alternative sources of finance could be immediately envisaged: the private domestic banking system could not cope with a large crop; the market for internal state bonds was quite narrow; London was blocked, and New York was not likely to lend a cent to coffee valorisation as long as Herbert Hoover remained at the Commerce Department. Thus, if São Paulo could not get what she wanted from the federal government, the assurance that the *status quo* would be maintained – with the Banco do Brasil ready to step in, in case of trouble – was certainly the second-best alternative in the foreseeable future.

However the federal government's stand in the negotiations was not limited to resisting the planters' pressures for further financial assistance. The decision it eventually took to wash its hands of all responsibility towards coffee valorisation implied cutting the institutionalised ample access coffee bills had to the Bank's rediscount facilities. True, the promising prospects then enjoyed by the coffee industry made the decision politically easier, but one is left with no explanation of the motives which led the government actually to take advantage of the situation if the analysis of the change in coffee policy is made in isolation from the broader monetary policy decisions being shaped at the time.

In fact the link between the change in coffee policy and the decision to deflate should not be overlooked. The monetary consequences of the coffee defence scheme were already seriously worrying the federal government during the negotiations with São Paulo. As later stated by Bernardes himself, this was a central issue, since the substantial disagreement which then separated the government and the producers, and which was resolved by the change in federal coffee policy, revolved around the question of financing the defence scheme through Banco do Brasil note issues.[179] It is unlikely that worries of that sort would arise from Vidal or Braga's advice. This being so, there are strong reasons to believe that the President's action on coffee was already being taken under the influence of the deflationists and with a view to the change in monetary policy. As shown above, in their own minds, the federal government's compromise with coffee valorisation involved, under the prevailing system, a serious potential threat to monetary stability, since they feared that the scheme's financial requirements could lead to unwarranted increases in the Bank's note issues. Naturally, they also saw the maintenance of this compromise as a permanent menace to the continuity of the monetary policy they were pressing for, and strived to end it.

Besides the absolute need for foreign financial assistance to attain Bernardes' economic policy goals in the two years he still had left to govern suggests another, stronger motive for the change in coffee policy, because of the negative reactions of potential lenders towards federal involvement with coffee valorisation. The opinion the government's London bankers had of their clients' sponsoring the coffee defence scheme has already been pointed out and was quite unambiguous: they shared the deflationists' views on the inflationary dangers of the scheme and saw its abandonment as a necessary condition for a successful floating of a loan in London. Furthermore, given the size of the loan Brazil was asking for, it is likely that a New York tranche was already seen as being necessary: it is revealing that the Montagu mission's report had been cabled shortly before publication in July, to Dillon, Read & Co. – Brazil's New York bankers[180] – and that New York's participation, when the loan was finally raised in 1926, was crucial. However, given Secretary Hoover's fierce opposition to coffee valorisation, it was unlikely that a loan which could enlarge the Banco do Brasil's financial strength would be viewed with favour by the United States government under the existing *modus operandi* of coffee defence.[181]

Thus, if the arguments set out in the preceding two paragraphs are accepted, the end of federal support for coffee valorisation should not be seen as it has been up to now, as an isolated and opportunist decision. Strange as it may seem, it was a necessary outcome of both change and continuity in Bernardes' economic policy. Of change, because it was in the deflationists' logic necessary for the success of the new contractionist monetary policy. Of continuity, because it was seen as necessary for keeping open the access to the world's capital markets, since their assistance was still a necessary condition for the completion of Bernardes' financial policy programme within his term of office.

5.5 DOMESTIC RECESSION, WORLD RECOVERY AND THE POLITICS OF INTERNATIONAL FINANCE

The enforcement of the new directives on monetary policy started immediately after the dismissal of Vidal and Braga. The Banco do Brasil raised its rediscount rate, restricted the amount of rediscount operations, and set aside increasingly large sums for its Paper Money Redemption Fund, so as continuously to reduce the amount of the outstanding Treasury issue. This process of monetary contraction was to last for almost two years. From January 1925 to November 1926 Brazil experienced her severest deflation on record in times of managed (i.e., non-gold standard) currency since the turn of the century. The timing and magnitude of the contraction in the money supply and its components can be seen in Table A.16.

As noted above, in the minds of the policy makers the feasibility of pursuing a policy of monetary contraction at that time also presupposed a strong effort to attain budgetary equilibrium. This was so because they saw in the large financing requirements of the federal government a basic source of the growth in the money supply, which they identified as the cause of the twin problems of inflation and exchange rate depreciation which the new monetary policy was designed to solve. It followed that, after freeing itself from the financial requirements of coffee valorisation, the government had still to intensify its efforts to balance the budget, and the restrictive fiscal policy followed was to reinforce, particularly in 1925, the depressive effects of monetary policy.

As shown in Table A.12, the current budget deficit was substantially reduced in 1925, in spite of the Senate's rejection of a government Bill aimed at raising income-tax revenue on the lines proposed by the Montagu mission,[182] and in 1925 and 1926 domestic long-term credit operations continued to be undertaken well beyond current budget deficit requirements.[183] In 1926 the depressive impact of the financial – especially monetary – policy pursued in 1925 on the level of indirect tax revenue, substantially reduced federal revenue, partially frustrating the government's intentions.[184] It should be noted that the difficulties the Executive had in getting Congress's approval of its budget estimate for these years – neither the expenditures nor the revenue bills for 1925 were voted by the 31 December deadline and Congress failed to pass the expenditure bill for 1926[185] – made things easier for the government, since Brazilian legislation empowered the President to roll-over the past year's budget in these circumstances.

Coming on top of the depressing effects of the political crisis of the second half of 1924, and given the heavy reliance the private sector had on the banking sector in the absence of a developed financial market, the deflationary interregnum of the mid-twenties was bound to have a damaging effect on the economy. In fact references to an unusually large number of business failures abound in contemporary writings: bankruptcies were indeed abnormally high in the first half of 1926 and three large banks failed.[186]

The effects on current activity levels were particularly harmful. Industrial output, which had been recovering strongly since 1922 as a consequence of the easy money policy and the extra protection afforded by the exchange rate collapse of the early twenties, stagnated during 1925 and 1926 at the 1924 level, which had been abnormally low due to the revolution in São Paulo.[187] Industrial real investment, as measured by a quantity index of capital goods imports to industry, which had been rising continuously since 1923, fell by not less than 26 per cent in 1926![188]

The credit squeeze also had a strong influence upon the working of the recently created São Paulo Institute for the Permanent Defence of Coffee in its early days. The state law creating the Institute[189] framed its financial scheme on exactly the same lines as those of the still-born federal defence, maintaining that its requirements were to be met by a foreign loan. Nor did the price control mechanism differ from the former practices. Its basic principle still consisted, in the longer run, in regulating coffee entries at the port of Santos through retention at Institute-controlled warehouses up-country, so as to maintain a low visible stock at the marketing end of the trade, complemented, when necessary, in the very short run, by spot purchases of tenders in the market.[190] The need to strengthen public confidence in the new Institute by not letting prices drop, added to the awareness of its own extreme financial weakness until such a time as it was able to raise a foreign loan,[191] made its managers over-anxious not to let the stocks at Santos accumulate, since this could lead to larger financial requirements in the event of slack demand.

Thus, from the very beginning of its operations, the Institute relied heavily on a totally arbitrary day to day regulation of port entries,[192] keeping available market stocks at a very low level, which was also a very effective way of magnifying the impact of its market operations upon prices. Indeed, following the beginning of the Institute's operations, prices shot up, spot Santos 4 in New York reaching an all time high of over 28.3 cents per pound in average during January 1925, as against 26.6 cents per pound in December 1924.[193]

The immediate effect of this price rise at the time of the arrival of the Colombian crop was to prompt an all-out boycott by American roasters of Brazilian coffee. Under these circumstances the enforcement of the federal government's deflationary policy put the planters under a heavy strain: unable to get their warehouse deposit certificates discounted at the banks, in the words of the president of the Institute, they 'helped the downfall – which with great effort we were able to avoid – by ordering the sale of their product at any price.'[194] The situation was politically manageable this time only because it did not affect a large majority of the planters, since the relatively small 1924–5 crop had caused a substantial reduction in the valorisation stocks,[195] but it foreshadowed a kind of problem which would recurrently imperil the success of the price support programme until its collapse in 1930.

Notwithstanding its heavy costs, the deflationary policy attained its basic objectives. The exchange rate rose abruptly by over 40 per cent in the five months from May to October 1925[196] and the continuous rise in the domestic price level was brought to a halt – after a deceleration of inflation in 1925, prices actually fell by some 10 per cent during 1926.[197]

The causes of the 1925 exchange rate rise are not discernible from the available yearly balance of payment figures on trade and long-term capital account. It seems to have resulted from the very high trade surplus in the third quarter of the year[198] and probably also from short-term capital inflows induced by the domestic credit squeeze. What deserves attention is the fact that, after the 1925 appreciation, the Bank was able to peg the rate around the 7.5d level reached in October through to the end of Bernardes' government, owing to the marked improvement in the country's external position starting in 1926.[199]

The origins of the improvement in Brazil's balance of payments from 1926 cannot be properly understood without reference to the recovery of the world economy in the mid-twenties. In fact, emphasising the importance of this exogenous factor in the explanation of Brazil's economic revival in the second half of the decade helps one to avoid the mistaken view, not uncommon in contemporary writings, that the recovery from 1926 was due mainly to the retrenchment policy followed by the Bernardes administration during his last two years of government.

One should not underestimate the importance to the world economy of the sudden reversal of the pessimistic expectations characteristic of the early years of the decade, which came after the flotation of the Dawes reconstruction loan and the stabilisation of the German mark, followed by that of several other European currencies, including the pound sterling. As Clarke cogently puts it 'as Europe's political quarrels temporarily abated and the venerated symbols of normalcy and stability were re-established, investors began to look forward to a new era of international economic growth and prosperity.'[200]

The bases of this prosperity were the extremely good outlook for investments and the long repressed demand for foreign capital in the primary producing countries and in several areas of continental Europe, at a time when economic conditions in the United States and, particularly, in Britain, the two leading potential lender countries, were still depressed. This favourable conjuncture brought about a huge wave of American foreign investments and was followed by a concurrent outflow of British capital, as London fought to regain its pre-war role as the world's greatest market for long-term capital, after the complete lifting of the foreign loans embargo at the end of 1925.[201]

However, although Brazil was a relatively large primary producer and a traditional borrower in international capital markets, it is interesting to notice that she would not be able to satisfy her pressing and large demands for foreign financial assistance – on account of coffee valorisation and the federal government's necessity to fund its large domestic short-term debt – until 1926; and that this was possible because of the intense competition between London and New York prevailing at the time, which allowed Brazil to neutralise political constraints of all sorts imposed by the lender countries on her freedom to borrow in their markets.

As far as coffee loans were concerned it has already been mentioned that, before the transfer of responsibility for valorisation to São Paulo, the federal government had found it impossible to borrow abroad since 1922. London was out of the question because of the government bankers' opposition, and New York had proved impossible owing to Secretary Hoover's strong views on primary commodity price supporting schemes. It has also been shown above that, after the creation of the São Paulo Institute, floating a foreign loan was a matter of survival for coffee valorisation in the long-run and that by 1925, with the coming of a new crop in the second half of the year, it became increasingly evident that the foreign loan should be obtained as early as possible if disaster was to be avoided.

Since the foreign loans market was closed in London, attempts had to be made in New York. Accordingly, to try and weaken the U.S. Commerce Department's opposition, the Institute made an attempt to enlist support from American roasters. This proved far less difficult than one would have thought *a priori*. In July an agreement was drafted in which, in return for the roasters' help in floating a US$35 million loan in New York (with a view to forming a bank in São Paulo to finance the planters on reasonable terms while their coffee was being retained at the Institute's warehouses), the Institute promised (a) to maintain a minimum of 1.2 million bags in Santos at all times; (b) to keep away from buying directly on the market except in extreme circumstances, so as to keep FOB prices in Brazil as steady as possible and (c) to spend one million dollars in the United States over a two-year period on coffee propaganda.[202]

Negotiations for a loan began at once but, on 30 July, *The New York Times* was already announcing that a loan for coffee valorisation had been prevented by State Department action. Although throughout August and September the Roasters Association brought continuous pressure to bear on the relevant government departments for a change in their position[203] the former's arguments were invariably turned down with phrases such as that 'the ordinary free play of supply and demand could not operate' or that São Paulo 'could best show their good intentions . . . by throwing their coffee on the market.'[204]

With the arrival of the 1925–6 crop, with the tight credit conditions in Brazil remaining the same and, above all, after the substantial exchange rate appreciation of the second half of 1925, the situation in São Paulo became very tense. The American roasters, now backed by the bankers interested in the operation, made a renewed effort in late October, pressing the strong arguments that the Institute would look elsewhere for money in view of the shortly anticipated lifting of the London embargo on foreign loans.[205] This last representation seems to have impressed Secretary of State Kellogg, for he wrote to Hoover asking his opinions on the possibility of lending to São Paulo 'against some guarantees.'[206] Hoover's opinion, however, was quite clear. He thought the Institute Bank's idea 'merely a method of pouring credit into the coffee speculation' and suggested that the question should be taken up at a cabinet meeting.[207] The cabinet considered the question shortly afterwards and decided to block the loan.[208]

However the American government's opposition at that time was nothing more than a political gesture for, in January 1926, as anticipated by the American bankers, the Institute was able to float its first foreign loan in London. As will be shown in the next chapter, the issue of this loan would have important consequences for the organisation of the Institute, and the establishment of a more or less institutionalised access to financial assistance from London would define the form in which it would operate during the next four years.

As to the large loan the federal government had wished to float since 1923, this, as has already been discussed, was halted by the London embargo after the long and wearing negotiations with the British bankers in early 1924. However, even after President Bernardes had freed his hands of the coffee support scheme, recourse to New York assistance was blocked during the whole of 1925 by an arrangement which, according to the British Ambassador in Rio, was reported to exist 'between British and American bankers not to lend money to Brazil until her internal position has improved.'[209]

Eventually, at the beginning of 1926, with the lifting of the embargo and after twelve months of unrelenting monetary squeeze and budgetary discipline to show to its credit,[210] the government was at last able to reopen negotiations for the issue of the £20 million agreed in 1924. Arrangements for the loan proceeded without delay since it was now just a matter of setting the terms of the transaction and fixing the size of the New York tranche. However, by the end of 1925 the British Foreign Office had obtained the Treasury's agreement in making loan applications from South American governments subject to official scrutiny on political grounds, since, in their opinion, 'the raising of difficulties in regard to such [loan] schemes represents really the most potent means of pressure which we can exercise in the case of certain recalcitrant governments.'[211]

At the time, Brazil was involved in a rather sensitive diplomatic disagreement with Britain over the question of Brazilian permanent representation in the Council of the League of Nations. Brazil's long-standing claim to a permanent seat in the League's Council had in the past been deferred until the time had come to increase the number of its members, so as to admit Germany.[212] After being re-elected in the September 1925 League Assembly to a non-permanent seat on the Council, the Brazilian Ambassador in Geneva made a public statement saying that at the next Assembly, which would vote the question of German admittance to the League, Brazil would only accept permanent representation in the Council as America's representative, provided she had the approval of all American League members, and that she would resign in favour of the United States in case the latter decided to come into the League.[213]

Though Brazil's attitude is understandable in terms of the importance she attributed to the question as a step towards the attainment of diplomatic leadership in South America, the British Foreign Office became extremely worried lest Brazil's insistence on her claims prevented Poland from getting a seat on the Council, in view of the importance of German-Polish relations to European political stability. In early 1926 Anglo-Brazilian relations became extremely strained when agreement between the European powers was reached about Poland and Brazil vetoed the admission of Germany.[214] However, there was nothing the British government could do within the statutory framework of the League to eject Brazil from the Council.[215]

Aware of these events (and given the prevailing official surveillance on South American government loans in London), the bankers asked the Foreign Office in March whether 'in view of the attitude of Brazil at Geneva His Majesty's Government would have any objection to this loan' and were told that 'the loan would not be regarded with favour' and that the Foreign Office 'hoped, therefore, that the proposal should not be entertained.'[216] In view of the Foreign Office's opposition, Rothschilds told the Brazilian government that the loan should again be postponed and asked the American bank which was to participate in the operation 'to hold their hand.'[217]

Although Brazilian diplomatic representation in London proved ineffective,[218] the American bankers found Rothschilds' request unacceptable and affirmed their determination to go ahead and float the New York tranche.[219] Worried by the long-term political consequences of the affair, the British bankers pressed the Foreign Office for an 'unequivocal reply' on the question, arguing that 'it could be most unfortunate for the interests of this country if the American group were to go ahead alone. We have financed Brazil since her independence and to allow her to go to America would mean a great loss to this country.'[220] The Foreign Secretary's attitude was, however, adamant. Even though he would privately write to the British Ambassador in Rio saying he did 'not wish to appear as preventing a loan,'[221] he firmly instructed Foreign Office officials that the bankers should be told that 'the action of Brazil at Geneva was not conducive to the furtherance of peace which I take to be the first of British interests and especially the first interest of the City of London' and that he could 'give no encouragement' to the loan.[222] In view of Chamberlain's fairly unequivocal statement the bankers 'promised to respect his wishes loyally' and withdrew.[223]

However, as in the case of the American government in the coffee loan episode, the British government's intention to use the political muscle it derived from being one of the world's financial centres proved futile. Given the intensive Anglo-American financial competition then prevailing, the federal government was able to raise the US$60 million New York tranche in two issues in May and June 1926. With the help of this loan President Bernardes was finally able to go a step further towards solving the problem which occupied the attentions of economic policy from the beginning of his government, viz., to liquidate the Treasury's short-term debt to the Banco do Brasil and to provide the Bank with ample foreign exchange reserves so that it could reassert its command over the exchange market.

However by that time the very nature of the economic policy problem was again beginning to change. As had happened at the turn of the century, the pursuance of a strongly contractionary monetary policy against the background of a world business upturn was causing a sharp improvement in the country's external position. The issues this change was going to raise in 1926 and the policy response eventually given by the incoming administration would be strikingly similar to those of twenty years before.

6 The Postwar Gold Standard

6.1 THE POLITICS OF EXCHANGE RATE POLICY AND THE RETURN TO GOLD

The radical economic policy changes of 1924 did not affect the compromises implicit in the formal alliance made between the political establishments of São Paulo and Minas Gerais in 1922. In May 1925, Antonio Carlos went to São Paulo as the government's envoy and settled the terms of the presidential succession. As the natural outcome, Washington Luis, former Governor of São Paulo, was appointed as the government's – and the only – presidential candidate in the March 1926 elections, and this was confirmed without much ado at the regional parties' convention in September.[1]

As should be expected, his early, publicly expressed views on economic policy issues were in tune with the main orthodox opinions currently held by the government as far as fiscal policy, the advantages of the gold standard and the role of central banking were concerned.[2] However Washington Luis could not be unaware of the growing opposition from domestic producers against the protraction of deflation and exchange rate appreciation to the extent avowedly envisaged by the government. After the substantial exchange rate appreciation of the third quarter of 1925, protests against the established monetary policy grew stronger, coming not only from industrialists[3] but also from São Paulo coffee interests. In fact, exchange rate appreciation represented a serious threat to the political feasibility of the coffee defence scheme for, under its prevailing organisation, the planters suffered the effects of the fall in the milréis value of their coffee retained at the Institute's warehouses. Against this background, the candidate, being a *Paulista* politician could not fail to try to allay those fears by openly attributing to exchange rate stability around the current rate an urgency far greater than that given to it by the current government's policies.[4]

It should be noted that there was no divergence between him and Bernardes about the advantages of exchange rate stability in itself. The return to gold found few opponents throughout Latin America at that time.[5] Indeed this was the long-term aim of Bernardes' financial

119

reconstruction programme and, as shown above, figured prominently in Washington Luis's platform. However the urgency given to exchange stabilisation in the future President's economic programme foreshadowed a deep variance with Bernardes on exchange rate management which was to grow and become the core of the economic policy debate in the course of 1926.

In this debate differences of opinion can be noticed on two, not unrelated levels. On the one hand, on a more abstract plane, there were divergencies stemming from varying emphases put on different aspects of the consequences of exchange rate changes. Bernardes approached this question, pointing to the short and medium term distributive consequences of exchange fluctuations, from the point of view of their differential impact on the real income of different social groups.[6] Although Washington Luis agreed with Bernardes on this,[7] the emphasis of his analysis was put on the economically damaging and socially disruptive short-term consequences of exchange rate movements. Nothing can better illustrate his position than the phrase he coined to summarise it: 'the axiom', as he put it, 'that the fall of exchange ruins [loan] capital as the rise crushes production and, with both, labour is disorganised.'[8]

However, behind those doctrinaire and somewhat similar positions there was an essentially political question, viz., the rate at which to peg the exchanges and the timing of stabilisation. This was the really crucial issue and here positions diverged markedly. Bernardes, though conceding that the equilibrium rate could be 'perhaps below the 12d rate' which had been fixed as a target at the beginning of his government, would firmly assert 'that this point is still above the current rate, because the dearness of living still weighs heavily upon the shoulders of the population despite the fact that the wholesale price indices have fallen approximately 30 per cent in the course of one year.'[9]

It is not easy to trace the political rationality of this position, especially after the floating of the American loan. If the restrictive policies being followed had some meaning in 1925 in face of the acceleration of inflation, of the vulnerable external position and of the stance of the potential foreign lenders, by the first half of 1926 prices had stabilised and the external position was improving. The government was, of course, aware of the painful effects of deflation. Nevertheless it went on minimising the extent of the crisis caused by the credit stringency which its monetary policy was inducing and pointing to its positive effects on the rate of inflation.[10]

The source of Bernardes' resistance in the midst of a rapid erosion of his political prestige was, apparently, the weight that orthodox opinions current in financial circles, particularly the fears of a devaluation-induced inflation, carried within the deflationist group. For banks, and perhaps some other financial intermediaries such as insurance companies, were the principal holders of long-term fixed income domestic assets – of which, in federal *apólices* alone, there were over two million contos outstanding, following the large issues made after the war. They had suffered heavy losses with postwar inflation and were now trying to recover their position with the depressing effects of an exchange rate appreciation on the domestic price level.[11]

On the other hand the contours of Washington Luis's alternative position for an immediate stabilisation without revaluation became even more clear in the course of 1926. In a series of articles, published as coming from his pen by the official newspaper of the São Paulo Republican Party during April, the emphasis on the urgency of stabilisation was sharpened and turned into a frontal attack against the position defended by the government.[12] Furthermore he thought a lower rate necessary to allow a sustained increase in the trade balance which, coupled with the expected foreign capital inflows arising from exchange rate stability and the revival of international lending, would help to build up the reserves needed to make possible an early return to gold.[13] To Bernardes' argument that exchange appreciation would benefit labour, he opposed the view that its effect on employment could make it detrimental to the interests of wage earners and – in tune with the conservative mood of the Brazilian political establishment – that it was politically dangerous.[14]

One cannot fail to be struck by the similarities between these and the 1905–6 controversies on monetary and exchange rate policy. In fact the economic background of both debates was the same. The two occasions were, with minor differences of detail, moments of very tight monetary policy between a past of great exchange rate instability with a strong underlying depreciating trend and a future in which, according to the general expectation, there would be a favourable balance of payments position due, particularly, to the good prospects of foreign capital inflows. The deflation of the mid-twenties, like that of the turn of the century, had been imposed at a moment when widespread concern over the fragility of the external position enabled the government to present those policies almost as measures of national salvation. However now, as twenty years before, the protraction of deflation and orthodox rhetoric by the government after the disappearance of the external conditions which had led to their adoption was tantamount to political suicide in a system in which exporters and, increasingly, other domestic tradeable goods producers held decisive influence.[15] If, in 1905–6, the distorted but widespread view which attributed the early twentieth century recovery to Murtinho's policies as well as 'the mystical respect of 27d'[16] gave the deflationists some countervailing power, in 1926 the political strength of the two opposing positions was hardly comparable. Bernardes had become a very unpopular figure, while Washington Luis had the backing of the politically significant forces in Brazil.[17] Moreover Washington Luis's allegiance to fiscal orthodoxy and the return to gold gave him at least the qualified support of Brazil's London creditors, whose political muscle had, in any case, temporarily diminished since the 1926 loan and the growth of competition with New York.

Accordingly, as the end of Bernardes' government came closer, it became virtually certain that his successor was going to face very little opposition in carrying his proposals through. It only needed Washington Luis to publicly reaffirm his views on exchange rate policy in 6 October,[18] over a month before his inauguration, to trigger a bullish movement in the foreign exchange market which sent the milréis down 6 per cent in two days, falling below the 7d mark reached in April in spite of strong intervention by the Banco do Brasil.[19] So it came naturally, when, on 21 November, after less than two weeks in office, he introduced a currency reform Bill providing for the return to gold.

The Bill was formally a phased long-term plan for the eventual achievement of full convertibility of the total outstanding note issue at a new legal parity of 5.9d, breaking the 27d par of 1846.[20] The first phase of the plan would be an interim period of *de facto* stabilisation at the new parity. For that purpose, there was proposed the creation of a Stabilisation Office, under Treasury management, which was to issue special notes against gold deposited with it at the new par, these notes being convertible at sight at the Office on exactly the same lines as the pre-war Conversion Office. To avoid unwanted changes in the monetary base – i.e., in its component made up by the new Stabilisation Office notes issued – which could be induced by exchange rate fluctuations beyond the gold points determined by the new legal parity and arbitrage costs, the Treasury was empowered to operate in the exchange market through the Banco do Brasil.[21] The period during which the Office was to operate – that is to say, the first phase of the plan – was left open in the Bill. It was intended that it should do so until the time its gold deposits, accumulated either by government action or through arbitrage-induced private gold inflows, were considered adequate to guarantee the convertibility of the total note circulation. Then, through an Executive decree to be issued with six months notice, the government would announce the beginning of full convertibility at the new parity on conditions to be then specified. Finally, the Bill envisaged changing the name of the monetary unit after full convertibility was achieved, creating the *cruzeiro*, worth one milréis at the new parity, but without the clumsy notation of the milréis and with a subdivision of just up to a cent. The coinage of the *cruzeiro* was considered by Washington Luis as the third and crowning phase of the reform.[22]

Congressional reaction to the Bill was undeniable evidence of the appeal of Washington Luis's proposals and of the widespread feeling against Bernardes' untimely orthodox policies. The expected opposition from the Minas Gerais benches – the stronghold of the ex-President's supporters – did materialise at the beginning of the debates. However, when Antonio Carlos, the deflationists' leader and now Governor of Minas Gerais, came to Rio prepared to try and make the President reconsider his plans and met a strong reaction from Washington Luis, the initial parliamentary opposition was immediately dropped on instructions from Antonio Carlos himself.[23] The latter's reaction – classified as feeble or even immoral by the opposition press – was most probably informed by the fear of the consequences of an open confrontation with the federal government to his expectations of succeeding Washington Luis in the presidency, based on the unwritten practice of alternation between São Paulo and Minas Gerais politicians as heads of state. After this minor incident, the Bill was passed almost without debate in both houses and became law on 18 December.

A large body of the literature on the motivations of the 1926 monetary reform has placed an undue emphasis on alleged doctrinaire influences bearing upon Washington Luis, taken to be its only mentor.[24] According to these views, the President-elect had been influenced either by Cassel's ideas on the reconstruction of the postwar gold standard,[25] or by the recommendations of the Peret Committee's report, which served as a basis for the stabilisation of the French franc.[26] These voluntarist and subjectivist approaches, although instrumental in bringing home the old point that Brazilian monetary policies were usually an uncritical mimicry of European fashion in these matters,[27] besides being unconvincing on some points of fact, blur the real issues by overlooking the objective economic and political conditions which shaped the reforms.

The speculation about Cassel's influence is partly based on the assumed analogy between Washington Luis's frequent utterances to the effect that the stabilisation rate should reflect 'the relation of the cost of living' and the Swedish economist's purchasing-power-parity theory.[28] Firstly it should be said that nowhere in the President-elect's pronouncements is a single reference to Cassel to be found. What is more important, however, is to understand that what Washington Luis meant by his 'rate which represents the proportion of the cost of living' was simply 'that rate to which, after a certain length of time, the public have become accustomed, which the commercial and industrial transactions of the country are used to'[29] and that the value chosen for the stabilisation rate was justified on the grounds that it reflected the average exchange rate for the period 1921–6,[30] an altogether different thing from Cassel's purchasing-power-parities.

As to the alleged influence of the Peret Report, it should be recalled that Washington Luis was bent on exchange stabilisation from at least late 1925 and was all-out against deflation and further revaluation by April 1926. So, it is hardly likely that his opinions on the substantive aspects of the reform should have been shaped by the French experts' report, which was signed on 3 July 1926.[31]

There is, in fact, a formal resemblance between the Brazilian phased reform and the Peret Committee's recommendations of a stepwise way to the stabilisation of the franc, viz., managed fixed rates, *de facto* convertibility and convertibility at a new legal par. However, the Peret Committee did not contemplate anything like the Brazilian Stabilization Office. This is not a formal point. The creation of the Office is the central part of the Brazilian monetary reform since it defined the kind of monetary system which was to be immediately effective. In fact, it is the choice for this particular kind of institutional set-up which indicates – more than the authorities' possible allegiances to the fashion of financial thought of the times – the rationale of the reform of 1926.

Naturally the new government's policy objectives reflected Washington Luis's strong pledges to immediate exchange stabilisation and the end of dear money. However the attainment of exchange stabilisation, in particular, presupposed the solution of the pressing problems of how to prevent Brazil's participation in the international investment boom – including the Treasury's desire to consolidate abroad the still large part of its floating debt not funded by the 1926 loan – which was gathering momentum, together with the recovery in world trade, from exerting an unbearable upward pressure on the exchanges.

There was no need for new legislation to cope with this problem. Ideally a central bank operating, for instance, on the lines of the 1923 Banco do Brasil reform, still legally in force, could manage this. However, even a cursory glance at the contemporary debates on monetary policy will show that, because of the results of the recent experiments with the Rediscount Department of 1921–2 and the central bank of 1923–4, the proposal for any sort of monetary system with some margin of discretion by the monetary authority to alter the volume of high-powered money, but lacking full convertibility, was out of the question for the time being. And Washington Luis shared these views. Subsequently he would state:

A central bank has to assume the obligation to make all our fiduciary currency convertible and should only issue notes convertible into gold and rediscount bills which can be converted into gold . . . It is easy to establish a bank to issue paper money and to open rediscount portfolios with paper money . . . However, its economic and financial effects are harmful, as the formidable losses suffered by all of us demonstrate.[32]

Now, given that Brazil's international reserves were then only a small fraction of the outstanding note issue, the implementation of full convertibility in the short run with a modicum of public confidence had to be temporarily shelved. However, the idea of eventually having the Banco do Brasil operating as a central bank, under a fractional gold reserve system with full convertibility, was still envisaged. Although not explicit in the reform Bill, the President repeatedly proclaimed his intentions to devolve central banking powers to the Bank after full convertibility was achieved.[33]

Against this background, the creation of the Stabilisation Office appears in its right perspective. It was not original, since it was exactly the same sort of monetary contrivance which operated in pre-war days, or a copy of mainstream contemporary ideas on financial reform, as were the solutions adopted by several Latin American countries of the west coast on the advice of a Kemmerer Mission.[34] It was intended to be nothing more than a stop-gap device chosen because its characteristics were instrumental both to guarantee the fulfilment of the above mentioned short-term objectives of the incoming government and to pave the way towards full convertibility under a fully fledged central bank. It guaranteed the attainment of the immediate government policy objectives since it was, by design, an exchange stabilisation mechanism and, if the expectations of a favourable evolution of the balance of payments position materialised, would sharply reverse the deflationary trend of the last two years of Bernardes' government. Besides, it was also convenient as a transitional system towards full convertibility for its potential for (gold) reserve accumulation.

Moreover, it derived an additional advantage from the 'automatic', i.e., non discretionary, character of its operation, whose political importance should not be underestimated: it would take much of the heat out of the debates about the management of the monetary base and exchange rate policy – to the extent that prices and incomes adjusted to the new stable rate – which had been responsible for so much cacophony between policy makers and their critics since the war.

6.2   SÃO PAULO'S REORGANISATION OF COFFEE DEFENCE

As described in Chapter 5, the São Paulo Institute had been able to survive during its first year of operation only because the very small crop of 1924 – which together with federal intervention and the Institute's early policies had sent prices to levels never attained before – was followed by a crop of average size. Even so, the Institute was not able to prevent world prices from falling by some 20 per cent during 1925, the fall in milréis prices being even larger, due to the exchange rate appreciation brought about by the Bernardes administration.[35] The resources held by the Institute, coming from a railway transportation tax, and the additional funds reluctantly handed over by the state government, were utterly insufficient to provide any effective form of financial assistance to the trade and were mostly used for direct intervention in the market. As it happened, the planters had to bear the brunt of carrying over the stocks of the 1925 crop and were still far from being converted into wholehearted supporters of the Institute's policies.

The uncertainty about the future financial strength of the Institute, coupled with the São Paulo government's intention of having a decisive say over such an important issue as coffee policy, did cause some anxiety among planters and *comissários*, and it was the latter's unwillingness to relinquish their influence over the decisions to be taken by the Institute which led to the early organisation of its governing council as a collegiate body of five members with their strong representation in it.[36]

Quite apart from its shaky relations with the planters and *comissários*, the other crucial problem to be solved by the Institute was to bring the coffee marketing policy of the other producing states under some sort of common rule. Although São Paulo at that time was delivering some 50 to 60 per cent of Brazilian coffee output, the 8 million bags which could easily be farmed out by the other states in a bumper crop year would certainly put the success of São Paulo's price support scheme at risk, since at the current prices world demand was levelling out at a little over 20 million bags a year, with 7 million being supplied by Brazil's international competitors. It was quite clear to the *Paulistas* that if states such as Minas Gerais and Rio de Janeiro, which, respectively, accounted for approximately 20 and 8 per cent of Brazil's coffee output, were allowed to market their produce unconstrainedly at the prices guaranteed by the Institute's intervention, it would be hard to convince the planters of São Paulo that they were not being sacrified for the benefit of producers in other states.

The government of Minas Gerais, the second largest producer, had, in fact, already been forced to take measures similar to São Paulo's because of the characteristics of the railway network in the state, which obliged part of its exporters to ship their coffee to Santos – thus becoming liable to payment of the São Paulo transportation tax – while the other part, exported through Rio, derived an unfair advantage. In August 1925, Minas Gerais passed a law creating a transportation tax equivalent to São Paulo's and authorising a state bank to lend its proceeds to the planters.[37] The law, however, explicitly stated that the entire crop should be marketed within the agricultural year.

In November 1925, the Institute had made a move to bring Minas Gerais and Rio de Janeiro into an agreement for concerted action in marketing the crop. However, although the Rio de Janeiro government promised to organise a system of coffee support on the lines of São Paulo,[38] the *Mineiros* stuck to their position of marketing the whole crop in one year, in spite of the indignation it aroused from *Paulista* politicians who took a broader view on the issue.[39] It is against this background that one must judge the relief felt by the Institute's managers when they finally succeeded, as mentioned in Chapter 5, in raising a large long-term loan in London, after the lifting of the British foreign loans embargo.

The floating of the Lazards £10 million loan in January 1926 was the first turning point in the history of the Institute. This was so not just because it went a long way towards solving the crucial problem of how to finance its operations. It was also extremely important in changing the Institute's relation with the planters. This was possible because the London bankers made the loan conditional upon the state of São Paulo's guaranteeing it, [40] thus allowing the state government to play a stronger hand in solving the long-standing dispute between the government members and the planters' and *comissários'* representatives at the Council of the Institute as to who should have the last word about the Institute's policy. A few days before the loan was signed, the Institute was renamed the State of São Paulo Coffee Institute; in May, the São Paulo government replaced one of the planters' representatives at the Council without even consulting them[41] and, in October, supported by public statements by the Governor of São Paulo to the effect that the guarantees given to the foreign loan 'demanded unfettered control'[42] over the Institute's transactions, a law was passed transforming the Institute's governing Council into a merely consultative body, its three other members besides the president and vice-president – still both Secretaries of the state government – being now directly appointed by the Governor of São Paulo.[43]

The first three quarters of 1926 were times of growing confidence in the Institute's future. It was known that the year's crop was going to be of a quite manageable size and after the second part of the London loan was floated in June, the Institute started to implement the instruments and procedures which would regulate its operations on a more permanent basis. It bought the regulating warehouses which had been sold by the federal government to São Paulo in 1924 and, together with the state government, acquired the control of a bank, in which the latter already had an interest. This bank, renamed Banco do Estado de São Paulo, was to manage the Institute's financial operations, lending the proceeds of the loan on the security of warrants issued by the official warehouses against coffee delivered to them, at a fixed valuation of 60 milréis per bag, which was about 40 per cent of the current quotation of the grade 4 option at the Santos market.

Finally, in November 1926, the greater financial strength the Institute now possessed enabled it to abandon the previous practice of arbitrary day to day regulation of the amount of coffee which was permitted to flow out the *reguladores* towards Santos – a practice which, as noted above, had prompted complaints from the marketing end of the trade – for a new system of regular daily shipments based on the amounts exported in the previous month, so as to keep the visible stock at Santos more or less in line with the requirements of demand.[44]

However almost at the same time that the Institute was able to establish itself the market was shaken by the forecast of a crop of unprecedented proportions for 1927 which, when it did materialise, was to be an all-time record, rising some 30 per cent above the previous 1906 record. Although the level of world stocks prevailing in the last quarter of 1926 was low, a bear attack in New York caused prices to slide from 22.1 cents per pound in October to 20.1 in December and 16.8 in July 1927, in spite of heavy purchases by the Institute in the Santos terminal.[45]

If the Institute was to stick to its stated directives, the new outlook demanded that it should protect itself in two ways. The first was to try to negotiate some form of additional financial support from their London bankers so as not only to be able to finance the retention of the much larger crop at its peak, but also to allow for an extension of the advances to the more cash-pressed farmers over the longer period during which their coffee was likely to be retained up-country. The second, upon which the success of the first action would obviously depend, was to convince the other producing states to adopt the Institute's new policy of regular release of the crop to the ports.

The *Paulistas* moved swiftly and competently in both directions. Now that all producers were threatened with the prospect of a bumper crop, it was to prove easier to get the reluctant states under the Institute's umbrella, and an agreement in principle was reached according to which the other producing states agreed to follow the Institute's marketing procedures as from 10 June, and provisional quotas were fixed defining the shares of each state in the exports of each port. However, the other states would not sign a formal agreement before they were assured that the Institute had the funds to finance it and a further meeting was arranged to ratify it in September.

With this partial result to show to their credit, the Institute's managers turned to London and, in mid-1927, negotiations were held in Brazil with Sir Robert Kindersley of Lazards to draw up a financial plan to deal with the coming crop.[46] The plan turned out to be a pefect solution to the Institute's problems: a one-year £5 million loan was arranged, to tide over the financing of the peak stock, plus another £5 million long-term loan, to be issued in four series of equal amounts, upon which the Institute's Bank could draw to lend on long-term, sterling-indexed mortgages on very reasonable terms to planters.

This put an end to all the Institute's worries and the September conference, attended enthusiastically by all seven producing states, ratified the May resolutions and, by the end of 1927, the organisations with which coffee defence would be run in the foreseeable future was firmly established and the prospects looked brighter than ever before.

6.3   THE 1927–8 ECONOMIC RECOVERY

The political and economic outlook during the first year of Washington Luis' government showed a marked improvement from the troubled times of the mid-twenties. By the middle of 1927 all signs of the wave of political unrest started in 1922, as well as some long standing conflicts between competing regional oligarchies, had subsided. Last but not least, as was expected from the debates during the 1926 presidential campaign, by the second half of 1927 there would be a complete shift away from the previous two years of restrictive monetary policy, and towards the end of the year there would be every sign that a sustained recovery had begun.

The President chose his top economic advisors from Rio Grande do Sul, Brazil's southernmost state and the third largest bench in the Chamber of Deputies, not only to broaden its parliamentary support, but also because the *Gaúchos*, unlike the Minas Gerais politicians, looked with approval on his stabilisation programme.[47] Getúlio Vargas, then only 43 and a rising star in his state's politics, was nominated Finance Minister, and Mostardeiro Filho, a banker and Vargas' close friend[48] took the presidency of the Banco do Brasil.

True to its idea that a tight fiscal policy was one of the preconditions for the success of the exchange stabilisation programme, the new government continued Bernardes' efforts to balance the budget in spite of the depressed economic situation inherited from the previous administration. The deficit position of 1926 was progressively reversed into a substantial surplus in 1927 – a budget position not obtained since 1907.[49] This was brought about, on the one hand, by the increase in tariff revenue arising from the end of the period of grace, in 1927, of a 1925 law which abolished tariff exemption (granted since the times of the Imperial government) on inputs imported by some industrial, transportation, and public utility companies and which in 1925 had been valued at over 220 000 contos; that is, about a third of total collected federal revenue in that year.[50] On the other hand, public expenditure on social overhead investments was kept at the low levels the previous administration had reduced them to, except for a heavily publicised road building programme which was the cornerstone of the new government's transport policy.[51] The rise in overall public spending from 1927 is almost totally accounted for by expenditures relating to the public debt due to the re-starting of amortisation payments on the foreign debt funded in 1914.

The depressive effects of fiscal orthodoxy would, nevertheless, be far outweighed by the operation of two strongly expansionary influences from the second half of 1927. The first was the reversal in monetary policy which, however, would only become effective by the third quarter of 1927. Negotiations with the federal government's London and New York bankers, for a loan to provide the necessary ammunition to carry out Brazil's stabilisation programme, started as soon as the new government defined its monetary reconstruction plan,[52] but were suspended at the beginning of 1927, seemingly because of the uncertainty felt in relation to Brazil's capacity to pay, due to the worsening of the coffee outlook which followed the forecasts of the 1927 bumper crop, as described below, at the time of the increase in the federal government's debt repayment burden as agreed in 1914.[53]

Nevertheless, since Brazil's external position remained strong, the government decided to go ahead with the reform and, on 16 April, the Stabilisation Office began to operate, converting the proceeds of a small municipal loan to Rio de Janeiro raised in the United States.[54] This was essentially a formal act of inauguration, probably aimed at keeping confidence in the President's financial programme until there were new developments in the coffee and stabilisation loan negotiations, and the Office issues remained stagnant throughout the second quarter of the year.

By the middle of 1927, however, the wave of American and British investments, begun in 1926 and which had receded in the months around the end of the year, rose again.[55] These were mostly public loans[56] to states and municipalities and, though many of them were for the redemption of the outstanding foreign debt, by no means an insignificant amount was destined for public works or other forms of domestic expenditure and were converted through the Stabilisation Office.

Although the office issues started to rise in August, the government became anxious that credit stringency could affect financing the retention of the large coffee crop and spread to other sectors before the São Paulo Coffee Institute could get the additional funds to tide it over.[57] These fears prompted a confidential instruction from the Ministry of Finance to the Banco do Brasil in early September to allow the Office to issue as required against the £10 million Treasury gold reserve held by the Bank.[58] Although the measure raised a storm of unjustified protest as to its legality[59] and the Treasury did restore the reserve within a short period,[60] it was instrumental in providing a temporary help to the money market and to the Coffee Institute over a brief but crucial period. After September, with the successful completion of the coffee loan negotiations in London and the issue of the long awaited federal stabilisation loan in 11 October,[61] the office was flooded by a continuous stream of gold which continued unabated until April 1928.

It is the nine-month period from August 1927 to April 1928 which marks the strong inflationary interregnum due to the operation of the gold standard.[62] The monetary base rose steeply in the last quarter of 1927, sharply reversing its downward trend from January 1925 and that, in the atmosphere of growing confidence then prevailing,[63] resulted in a marked increase in the money supply until mid-1928.[64]

The way in which the federal government managed its domestic debt reinforced the expansionary effect of the increase in the monetary base. On the one hand, the government restricted the growth of the long-term domestic debt and not a single issue was made until 1928, reversing the trend of the first half of the twenties when annual increases of over 15 per cent in the total debt outstanding were not uncommon. On the other hand, the government used the proceeds of the stabilisation loan raised at the end of 1927 to settle, during 1928, the remainder of the frozen 'floating' debt with the Banco do Brasil through Stabilisation Office issues. The amount of these liabilities had been officially estimated at 420 thousand contos in 1927,[65] representing not less than 20 per cent of the total budgeted expenditure for 1928.

The other important factor behind the late 1927 upswing was the large income growth in the coffee sector, resulting from the very favourable terms at which this year's bumper crop was financed and sold. As noted above, in the last quarter of 1926, international coffee prices had been hit by the forecasts of the bumper crop and were falling markedly throughout the first half of 1927. This tendency was, however, immediately reversed when the news that the Coffee Institute had obtained enough cash to finance the 1927 crop reached the consuming centres in September. Santos prices, which after exchange stabilisation varied in line with New York, rose from 150 milréis per bag in September 1927 to 200 milréis per bag in June 1928, and were stabilised at this figure by the Institute's intervention.[66]

To translate those prices into the amounts actually received by the farmers one should bear in mind not only the peculiarities of the *defesa* system – that is, the difference between the amounts the farmer pocketed as cash advances after the delivery of his product to the warehouses and the amount he received after his coffee was sold – but also the peculiarities of the coffee production cost function which, as shown below, made average costs extremely sensitive to output variations.

As to the first, the price received by the farmer for the actual sale of his coffee was, obviously, the price ruling at the Santos terminal on the day of the sale, which behaved as mentioned above. However the price received for the coffee deposited at the defence warehouses, i.e., the valuation the *comissários* placed on the farmers' coffee for the purpose of granting them cash advances, was very much determined by the financial system's evaluation of what prices were likely to be by the time the coffee was released for sale. If there were no reasons to expect that prices would fall, competition between *comissários* for handling the largest possible amount of coffee would make it perfectly reasonable for them to grant the customary 60 per cent advances based on a valuation in line with ruling Santos prices.

The state of expectations in relation to future prices by the time the 1927 crop was financed could hardly have been more optimistic: not only had the Institute proved its worth, but the 1928 crop forecast pointed to a rather small crop and prices were actually rising strongly. Under these circumstances the 1927 crop was financed at ever more favourable valuations and, as estimated by Rowe, on a conservative basis, should have averaged 100 milréis per bag for the period during which the crop was being retained.[67]

On the other hand, the behaviour of costs was strongly influenced by the record output of 1927, given the large weight of fixed costs over total costs in coffee production. Including the colonists' wages[68] – which accounted for 45 per cent of total normal costs – but not including interest charges, Rowe estimated fixed costs as constituting over 75 per cent of total costs in a normal crop year[69] and, in spite of the considerable yield variations among plantations of different age, this share of fixed costs varied narrowly between different farms as the yield variations were compensated by several factors such as the higher wages paid in the new districts.[70] With such cost structure, the output increase of over 70 per cent between the normal 1926 and the bumper 1927 crops would mean a decrease in average total costs of over 30 per cent.

Rowe's estimates help one to gain a firmer grasp of the effect this scissor movement of prices and costs had on the behaviour of the farmers' profit margins in 1927. He reckoned that a bag of coffee produced in the average yield zone and delivered to the *reguladores* would cost approximately 53 milréis, or 57.6 milréis if the coffee defence transportation tax was added.[71] This figure represented what farmers would require to cover all their production expenses until the coffee was released and sold. However, given the very favourable prices and expectations then prevailing, this coffee was financed at at least 100 milréis per bag. Morevover, when the coffee from the 1927 crop began to be sold in March 1928, and Santos prices stabilised at 200 milréis per bag, the cost of intermediate yield zone coffee delivered to the port – after allowing for the *comissário's* comission, export duties and interest changes on the cash advanced – added up to only 83 milréis per bag;[72] the sale price was, therefore, maintained at 140 per cent above total farmers' costs. As Rowe put it, if 'the surplus over cost be put at only 80 per cent per bag, so as to be absolutely on the safe side, the farmer stood to get a return of over 35 per cent on his capital. Even the planter in the Old Zone might anticipate a return of at least 25 per cent, while those in the New Zone would see their whole capital back with one more similar season'.[73]

Given the low costs prevailing in 1927, the Institute's price policy in 1927–8 has been deeply criticised as being utterly irresponsible.[74] This point is rather debatable. Firstly it should not be forgotten that there were strong underlying factors behind the price rise, such as the sustained increase in international demand, the growing confidence in the financial strength of the Institute and the prospect of a small crop for 1928, which were quite independent of the Institute's action.

Moreover it is important to recall that the Coffee Institute was now a *political* institution, run by São Paulo politicians and it would be against all rules of commonsense political behaviour to arouse the planters' opposition by trying to force its hand against the mood of the market. In fact the decision to stabilise prices from the second quarter of 1928, at a level which was still 21 per cent below the level at which the period of federal defence had left them, and at a time when the prospects of a small crop warned that costs would rise, might have been by no means an easy one.

The very favourable behaviour of profit margins in the coffee sector at the time of a large crop caused an abnormally large increase in the share of profits, which was bound to affect not only the rate of investment in the coffee industry itself but would spill over to the urban sectors, boosting domestic activity and import levels. On the effects upon the coffee industry more will be said later in connection with the analysis of the 1929–30 downswing. Suffice it to say here that the rise in profits, plus the additional funds the farmers could get on long-term mortgages through the Institute's bank from the end of 1927, did lead to a large increase in planting,[75] especially in the newer zones, and most probably to an increase in property concentration as it has been calcualted that '15 to 20 per cent of the trees in São Paulo changed hands during 1928 and 1929.'[76]

What it is more important to point out here, however, is the overall expansionary impact of the large income growth in the dynamic sector of the economy against the background of increasingly easy money described at the beginning of this section. According to Villela and Suzigan's estimates, real GNP, which had grown by a mere 2.5 per cent in 1926 rose at the amazing rates of 8.6 per cent in 1927 and 16.3 per cent in 1928.[77] As far as the behaviour of the industrial sector is concerned, the high levels of investment prevailing prior to the long recession of 1925–6, as well as the lagged response of the investment proxy variable relative to current production levels, suggest that there existed large margins of idle capacity in industry in 1927, and this was probably a contributing factor to the brisk recovery which took place from the end of 1927[78] and also, given exchange rate stability, for the almost absolute price stability during the boom.[79]

The impressive momentum gathered by the Brazilian boom from late 1927 should not, however, disguise the fact that economic recovery rested on flimsy foundations, i.e., that it was rather dependent on the continuity of the very favourable world economic conditions prevailing since 1926. That the gold standard-cum-foreign debt programme was inherently unstable had already been shown by the pre-war experience. However, as will be presently argued, in the late twenties, the operation of the gold standard had a greater destabilising potential because of its influence upon the financial feasibility of the permanent coffee defence scheme on the lines built by the Institute, given the latter's extreme reliance upon the smooth behaviour of the international economy and on the conduct of domestic monetary policy.

It should be recalled that there was a radical change in the operational features of coffee finance after the fully fledged system of crop retention up-country was built. It was shown above that, with the introduction of the regulating warehouses system, although the planter would normally forward to his *comissário* the warrants issued by the *reguladores* against the deposit of his coffee as soon as he received them, he had to wait much longer for his agent to notify him that his coffee had arrived and was ready for sale. Thus, instead of being able to sell the whole of their crop before the end of the year, the first in–first out system adopted in the management of the stocks at the warehouses would mean that – barring an unlikely difference in the time taken by different planters to deliver their crop to the warehouses – the farmers now received the total proceeds from the sale of their crops distributed over a much longer period.[80]

If that meant that they now needed a larger volume of finance, it was also true that they now had a security to offer in the shape of the warrants of their coffee stocks deposited up-country so that now, after accepting those titles, their *comissários* could place them as a collateral for bank loans, the proceeds of which were used to make the longer advances now needed by the planters in order to cover their current expenditures until their coffee was released for sale. Thus, the fundamental constraint placed on the ability of the private sector financing the coffee trade under the new system of sales regulation was the willingness and, ultimately, the ability of the banking system to go on making advances against coffee warrants without knowing exactly how long it would take before they could be liquidated.

It was the likelihood that this constraint would be normally binding and that, therefore, additional resources would be necessary to fill the gap, when the private system had stretched as far as it could go on a commercially sound basis, that made it necessary to construct the Institute's whole financial support apparatus. Indeed, the chief function of the Banco do Estado de São Paulo, as the Institute's bank, was to act as a lender of last resort to the commercial banks operating in the market for loans secured by coffee warrants. The Institute could influence the overall volume of credit needed to finance the scheme in a direct way through changes in its coffee release policy or in the valuation set for the coffee accepted by its bank as a collateral for loans. However, the use of these weapons was restricted between narrow limits in the more likely case that the Institute wanted to diminish the overall demand for funds, since large outflows from the *reguladores* would have a depressing effect on the price of the commodity which was the basis of the entire credit structure of which the Institute was the ultimate guarantor, while a lowering of the amount advanced per bag was limited by the planters' capacity to endure it. In fact, in discussing the financial feasibility of the new *defesa* system, what it is important to note is that the size of the gap the Institute had ultimately to finance in a given period was directly dependent on three factors quite beyond the Institute's control. The first was, of course, the size of the crop, a larger crop meaning, *ceteris paribus*, a greater strain on the Institute's resources, since it would raise the level of stocks to be held up-country. The second was the state of world demand which, given the policy of automatic regulation of port entries, would affect the financial needs of the defence system in the same way as crop variations. The third was the state of domestic credit conditions which, differently from the first two shocks already mentioned, would affect the Institute's financial requirements, not through an increase in the overall requirements of coffee finance, but through its effect on the private banking system's ability to fulfill its part in it.

What most contemporaries seemed to have overlooked and is most important to realize is that the last two of the above mentioned factors, viz., the state of world demand and domestic credit conditions, were bound to be correlated in a perverse fashion, as far as the Institute's objectives were concerned, while Brazil was on the gold standard. For, as in the case of export economies sudden balance of payments disequilibria were often exogenously determined by a worsening of international economic conditions, a severe tightening of domestic credit was likely to accompany a sudden deterioration in the balance of trade due to a slackening of demand for the staple export.[81] In the case of Brazil this would mean that, when the overall requirements of coffee finance were rising because of slack international demand, the willingness of the private banking sector to lend on coffee would be diminishing, thus increasing the financial burden of the coffee price control authorities.

The scenario would be made much grimmer if the assumed worsening of the international economic outlook was caused by or, at any rate, was simultaneous with a deterioration of the very favourable conditions then prevailing in the principal international financial markets. The reader should keep in mind that the recovery of Brazil's balance of payments position after 1926 can be almost entirely explained by the large surpluses in capital account appearing from that year. In these circumstances, a decrease in the leading financial centres' propensity to lend would severely affect her external position and the contraction in the monetary base which the operation of the gold standard would inevitably bring about would raise the private banking sector's liquidity preference, thus causing a sharp rise in the Institute's financial requirements at a time in which, *ex hypothesi*, its ability to borrow abroad would be severely impaired.

If such a situation developed in an extreme form at the time of a bumper crop, it would hit the coffee price support system in its Achilles heel and the federal authorities would eventually be confronted with the dilemma of either letting the gold standard go or pushing the coffee industry towards the abyss.

6.4   THE ONSET OF THE 1929 BRAZILIAN RECESSION

The above explanation of the potential weakness to which the Brazilian economy was exposed in the late twenties, through its heavy reliance on a stable functioning of the world economy and, especially, of the world's capital markets, will be abundantly verified by the analysis of the events from the end of 1928. However, the actual end of the 1927–8 upswing came in Brazil when international economic conditions – though already strained by the effects the New York stock-market boom was beginning to have in the pace of international long-term lending – were still generally expansionary, and it had important domestic determinants. Although the underlying cause of the downturn was a sudden and continuous deterioration in Brazil's external position from the middle of 1928, the onset of a specifically Brazilian recession was triggered and reinforced by a deliberate restrictive credit policy followed by the Banco do Brasil from September 1928 and, by the beginning of 1929, Brazil would already be into a deepening recession.[82]

The deterioration of Brazil's international payments position by the middle of 1928 was caused by the operation of two independent factors. Firstly there was the shrinkage of the trade surplus, shown in Table 6.1, which was bound to happen, due to the growth of imports which accompanied the boom, against the sluggish behaviour of exports.

Table 6.1   Brazil: 1927–8, half-yearly trade balance (in £ millions)

Period	Exports	Imports	Trade Balance
1927 (second half)	50.2	39.9	10.3
1928 (first half)	48.4	43.1	5.3
1928 (second half)	48.8	47.6	1.2

Source: Brazil: Ministério da Fazenda, *Commércio Exterior do Brasil*, op. cit., several issues.

However the greatest adverse change was due to the sudden fall of Brazil's public borrowing abroad which had totally exogenous causes, namely, the sharp fall in American long-term lending in the middle of 1928, as depicted in Table 6.2. Although the causes of this phenomenon are still open to debate, majority opinion holds that it was mainly due to specifically American developments, such as the diversion of investors' and financial intermediaries' funds into stocks and the call market for brokers' loans as the stock market boom developed in New York, and the restrictive monetary policy followed by the Federal Reserve System from the spring of 1928.[83] Moreover, since conditions in London were not unaffected by these American

Table 6.2   New capital issues for foreign account in New York and London: 1926–8 (nominal values in £ millions)

Period	New York	London
1926	231.3	87.8
1927	313.3	112.4
1928 (first half)	191.3	75.0
1928 (second half)	78.9	73.0

Source: Bank of England Statistical Summary for Central Banks, July 1930. [I wish to thank Professor Donald Moggridge for making these statistics available to me from the Keynes Papers.]

developments,[84] the post-1925 rise in British long-term foreign issues also lost its momentum towards the end of 1928.

Although the available yearly figures on Brazilian foreign long-term borrowing only show a marked decline in 1929,[85] of the twenty foreign long-term loans issued by Brazilian public authorities – including the Coffee Institute – in London and New York during 1927 and 1928, totalling in nominal terms £26.6 million in 1927 and £25.3 million in 1928, not a single loan was floated between July 1928 and May 1929, except for an insignificantly small loan to the state of Bahia floated in August and entirely used for the immediate redemption of its outstanding foreign debt, and the issue of the third series of £1.25 million for mortgages by the Coffee Institute, as agreed with Lazards in 1927.[86] As the United States Consul-General reported in early 1929, during the previous two years 'representatives of New York financial houses had, figuratively, "camped on the door-step" of state and municipal governments, "nibbling" for their business. At one time there were more than half a dozen such representatives here. The situation has now changed.'[87]

It should be recalled that the domestic banking system had been expanding its operations rapidly for some months past. Commercial bank loans, including Banco do Brasil commercial credit operations, had risen by 31.6 per cent in 1927 and the tendency continued into 1928, commercial loans rising by 12 per cent in the first half of the year.[88] However, the end of the buoyant balance of payments position caused a marked decrease in the rate of growth of Stabilisation Office note issues from the middle of the second quarter of 1928. This sharp reversal in the behaviour of the monetary base, coming when the expansion of investment was gathering strength, put a severe strain on the private sector. This strain was amplified, as many contemporary observers realised, by the fact that the high expectations and the very active lending policy of the banks, favoured by the extreme lenience of current Brazilian bankruptcy laws, had led several – including some large – firms to take very risky financial positions as the boom progressed.[89] As a result, when the liquidity crunch began to be felt, the Banco do Brasil was increasingly called upon to rescue some of the troubled firms, either through rediscount or direct lending operations.

The Bank's first reaction was to support the private sector.[90] However concern over the wisdom of sustaining the boom in the prevailing conditions grew, together with the share of titles of doubtful quality in the Bank's commercial portfolio, and opposition to its policy mounted in mid-1928. The critics had all the paradigms of sound gold standard management on their side: the weakening external position, on top of the domestic boom, did not commend the support that the Bank was lending to 'reckless borrowing.' Moreover, as Brazil's gold reserve increased after the opening of the Stabilisation Office, reaching a comfortable 35 per cent of the total outstanding note issue by mid-1928, it stirrred up the feeling that the Banco do Brasil should be ready to take up again its central banking functions at any moment, as was the President's expressed intention. Indeed, the Bank had been increasing its cash holdings throughout 1927, raising its cash reserve ratio – including the banking system's sight deposits with it – from 0.22 at the end of 1926 to 0.42 in August 1928,[91] with a view to resuming those functions, and the critics of the Bank's new protective attitude towards the private sector saw it as likely to endanger its liquidity and to divert the Bank from its priority objective, which was considered the final step in the government's financial reconstruction plan.[92] These criticisms were bound to impress the government, for the President was not likely to force a course that could harm the confidence in his stabilisation programme.

The struggle over the conduct of the Bank's policy was eventually decided in 25 August, with the replacement of Mostardeiro Filho by Leão Teixeira at the presidency of the Bank[93] and, in September, the Bank defined its new directives, taking a series of steps severely to restrict its lending operations to the private sector and to shorten the average maturity of its commercial portfolio. The Board's decisions included putting a ceiling of 5000 contos for credits granted to any individual firm, freezing the limit allowed for its branches' lending operations, limiting loans longer than six months as well as credits for fixed investments or new ventures, and requiring much stricter guarantees for normal credit operations.[94]

This drastic change in the Bank's commercial credit policy had immediate repercussions on the banking system's lending policy and a contraction in other bank's deposits followed, with a short lag. The money supply, whose growth had already fallen heavily with the shrinkage of gold inflows at the Stabilisation Office towards the middle of 1928, stagnated in the fourth quater of the year and started to fall in 1929, as deposits fell and the Banco do Brasil went on relentlessly increasing its cash reserves.[95]

This deflationary whirlpool dragged down activity levels almost immediately and, as early as 10 November, even the conservative *Jornal do Commércio*, commenting on the panic which had almost developed in the Rio money market the day before, following the confirmation of rumours about the increasing number of bankruptcies, was pleading with the new president of the Bank 'to understand that with the responsibilities of the direction of the money market, His excellency should not exaggerate in a direction opposed to that in which his predecessor has, perhaps, exaggerated.'[96] The government, however, kept its new course, in spite of the knowledge that a severe recession, reinforced by its ouwn policy, was under way.[97]

The course of the 1929 recession can be traced through a few indicators. As Table 6.3 shows, business failures soared in the first

Table 6.3   Liabilities of failures in Rio de Janeiro: 1927–9
(in thousand contos)

Period	Liabilities
1927	412
1928	539
1929 (first half)	679
1929 (second half)	721

Source: *BOLSA Monthly Review*, January 1930, p. 70 and *RC-JC*, 1979, p. 52, quoted in Neuhaus, P. (1974). *'A Monetary History of Brazil, 1900–1945'*. Chicago, unpublished PhD dissertation.

half of the year. Real GNP stagnated in 1929 at the previous year's level, and industrial output actually fell by 3.3. per cent.[98] Imports, which had risen 19 per cent in real terms in 1928, started to fall in the first quarter of 1929 in spite of the lagged response of equipment orders.[99] The dizzying but short-lived prosperity had ended and was not to return for many a day.

6.5   THE COLLAPSE OF SÃO PAULO'S COFFEE DEFENCE PROGRAMME

The period from September 1928 to October 1929 would witness a progressive deterioration in São Paulo coffee defence authorities' ability to maintain the policies defined in late 1927. The first blow was delivered by nature: contrary to expert opinion, which held that large crops were followed by some years of low or average yields, due to the exhaustion of the trees, the September 1928 blossoming had been exceptional, and the general opinion was that, barring droughts or frosts, the 1929 crop would be very large, comparable to the 1927 record.

The causes of the sharp increase in average yields, which explains the increase in production in 1927 and 1929, are to be found in a combination of the extremely good weather conditions prevailing during the growth of these crops, together with the changing age distribution of Brazilian coffee trees resulting from new planting up to the mid-twenties. In fact although by 1927 the old – low productivity – zone still accounted for some 60 per cent of São Paulo's coffee trees,[100] the postwar period had seen the first substantial surge of new planting since the 1890s. This increase in planting since the war had been made possible by structural causes such as the external economies created with the opening up of new districts in the west of São Paulo, along the extensions of the Araraquara, Sorocabana and, especially, the Noroeste railways[101] and the recovery of high levels of foreign immigration in the twenties. However, even though these were important inducements, the actual levels of investment and their fluctuations shown in Table A.7 cannot be explained without reference to current profits and credit conditions. The strong stimulus to farmers' current profits given by the operation of the *defesa* system in times of easy money and larger crops and its effect on investment is illustrated by the rise in planting both in 1922–4 and 1927.

This effect has not been emphasised in the literature, which tends to stress the influence of high price expectations maintained by the confidence in the working of the permanent defence system since its beginning in 1922. It is, of course, undeniable that this psychological component did exist, but it is impossible to isolate the effect of confidence in the price support programme from other factors affecting price expectations, such as the very low level of world stocks prevailing up to 1927, raised by the abnormally low yields of the period.[102] Moreover price expectations alone cannot account for the cyclical falls occurring during the period of small crops and tight money between 1924 and 1926, unless it is proven that confidence in the defence system fell in the Institute's early years, in spite of the very high international prices prevailing.

Nevertheless this argument, in its more radical form, is construed so as to show that confidence in the maintenance of artificially controlled high prices led to overinvestment, which was responsible for the collapse of coffee price support in October 1929.[103] There can be little doubt that, as far as supply stocks are concerned, the growth of planting until the coffee year of 1928–9 was in great part responsible for the immense problems *of the early thirties*, although supply considerations alone do not, of course, explain world market disequilibria after 1929. As will be presently shown, to maintain simply that the October 1929 crash was due to 'overproduction' induced by the operation of the coffee defence price policy, i.e., to the occurrence of the 1929 bumper crop, is deeply simplistic and overlooks crucial changes in credit conditions occurring this year, both in Brazil and in her lenders' capital markets, as well as decisive policy decisions taken by the federal government, which drastically affected the financial feasibility of the price support scheme.

It is true that the news of a possible bumper crop came as a shock in late 1928, since world stock levels were very high from 1927 because of the growth in the share held at the coffee defence warehouses, given the 'automatic' sales policy of the Coffee Institute. Nevertheless in spite of anticipations of difficult days ahead the Institute maintained all its outward signs of indefectible confidence against bear attacks and Santos prices were not affected.[104]

However as the months went by it became evident that, irrespective of the crop forecast, the position of the coffee industry was not nearly as good as it had been in 1928. With the sharp increase in Brazilian stocks in 1927, the retention period had steadily lengthened and now planters had to make ends meet with the cash they received as advances for a much longer period – estimated at 16 months in March 1929[105] – and interest payments, of course, rose. Moreover, the 1928 crop had been a small one, totalling 6.8 million bags against the 17.3 million for 1927 for São Paulo, which meant that unit costs had more than doubled relatively to the previous year. The cost of São Paulo coffee placed at the warehouses was estimated at around 118 milréis per bag for the intermediate zone and 153 milréis per bag for the old – low productivity – zone[106] while, since the Institute kept Santos prices stable, farmers were still receiving their advances at the rate of 100 milréis per bag. So when the harvesting of the large crop began, the majority of farmers were pinched for ready money[107] for, although the bulk of productive capacity was concentrated in the medium-sized to large *fazendas* with over twenty thousand trees, the small estates below this size accounted for three-quarters of the total number of coffee farms, as Table 6.4 illustrates.

Clearly the situation was initially manageable because the planters were still receiving the proceeds of the 1927, low cost, crop, but undoubtedly the whole of the coffee industry was now in a much less comfortable position. As time went by, most planters began to find it

Table 6.4 São Paulo: 1927,
Size distribution of coffee farms

Size class (trees)		Number of estates	Total number of trees in size class (millions)
over	200 000	805	302.6
100 000 to	200 000	1 615	242.2
50 000 to	100 000	2 390	179.2
20 000 to	50 000	5 659	198.0
10 000 to	20 000	7 489	112.3
5 000 to	10 000	8 189	61.4
below	5 000	13 751	24.4

Source: Rowe, J.W.F. (1932). *Brazilian Coffee*, London and Cambridge Economic Service, Special Memorandum No. 35, Studies in the Artificial Control of Raw Materials No. 3, London. Table X, p. 89.

increasingly difficult to endure the long period of retention and their support for the Institute's sales policy was slowly undermined, until they began to press for a speed up of the outflow from the *reguladores*.[108]

The restrictive credit policy adopted by the Banco do Brasil from September 1928 would amplify the deflationary impact of the cash flow squeeze in the coffee sector. Indeed, the Bank's change of policy was particularly untimely as far as the São Paulo banks were concerned, for they had seen assets represented by the coffee bills issued by the defence warehouses become increasingly illiquid.

By the end of 1928, however, the federal government also began to nurture favourable opinions as to the beneficial effects of larger stock releases. Its reasons were quite different from those of the planters and stemmed from worries about its ability to maintain the exchange stabilisation programme without heavy gold losses, for the balance of payments response expected from the new restrictive credit policy did not materialise quickly. In December 1928, Washington Luis, through the Governor of São Paulo, instructed the Coffee Institute to lower prices so as to increase exports.[109] The president of the Institute strongly objected to the wisdom of the measure,[110] but started immediately to sell from stocks for future delivery and future prices began to fall.[111]

As expected by the Coffee Institute, this action had an adverse effect on the value of exports, which actually fell in the first quarter of 1929 and, in March, the Banco do Brasil had to intervene strongly in the foreign exchange market to avoid an outflow of gold.[112] Towards the end of the month the Bank saw its foreign exchange reserves dwindle dangerously and the Institute, which had every interest in avoiding a further monetary contraction which a loss of gold would involve, was then instrumental in rescuing it by arranging, through their London bankers, for a £5 million, one-year loan to the Bank in early April,[113] with which the latter could reassert its control over the foreign exchange market.[114]

As the picking of the crop came close, the Coffee Institute set its sails to weather the storm. The first step was, of course, to open negotiations with Lazards to try and obtain additional finance to carry the larger stocks. The second, and an extremely clever move, was to issue new instructions regulating coffee deliveries to the warehouses in order to spread them evenly throughout the coffee year.[115] The new regulations were presented as a technical measure aimed at avoiding the scramble for pre-emption of space in railway cars at the beginning of the shipping of the crop to the *reguladores* and also at preventing the sacking of improperly dried beans which, as was widely acknowledged, was happening and strongly affected the quality of the product.[116] Their basic aim, however, was to minimise the finance needed at the peak load, and illustrates the Institute's intentions of shifting more of the financial burden of carrying the extra large crop onto the planters' shoulders. The third measure was simply to bluff and understate both the size of stocks and of the coming crop, in an attempt to maintain domestic and, especially, foreign confidence in the scheme. In May, the president of the Institute, in a widely publicised speech to representatives of the coffee trade, put defence stocks at the end of the 1928–9 crop year at 8 million bags[117] and the Institute's official crop estimates published in June placed São Paulo production at 13.7 million bags.[118] *Ex post* figures would be 10.3 and 19.5, respectively.[119]

The May speech by Rolim Telles, the president of the Coffee Institute, also provided an opportunity for the first public expression of their silent disagreement with the federal government's views of the relationship between coffee and exchange rate policies for, although Washington Luis continued to reaffirm his support and confidence in the coffee defence programme as indispensable for the success of his stabilisation policy,[120] the government had not yet cancelled the December 1928 instructions to lower coffee prices. In a veiled reply 'to those who think that lower prices would stimulate a larger volume of sales,' Telles concluded that to 'let our prices decline in order to sell more coffee would be equivalent to concluding that buyers were ignorant of economic laws . . . for it would be a silly thing to accumulate stocks of an article whose producers, afraid of over-production were forcing prices down.'[121]

The clash between the Institute and the federal government over this central issue was, however, postponed by an unexpected turn of events later in the month, when widespread calls came from business circles to ease the Bank's credit policy, in view of the depression and the alarming increase in the number of failures. The pressure brought to bear on Washington Luis led to the resignation of Leão Teixeira from the presidency of the Banco do Brasil on 3 June, and his interim replacement of Silva Gordo, then head of the Bank's exchange department and former president of the Coffee Institute's bank.[122]

In the second half of July, the new president of the Banco do Brasil, worried over the fall in coffee prices[123] which he considered to be the cause of pressures on the exchange market, convinced Washington Luis that 'any brisk change in coffee policy would provoke the retreat . . . of consumers and, with the scarcity of trade bills, the likely failure of His Excellency's policy – exchange stabilisation'[124] and the Institute was accordingly instructed to abandon the December 1928 directives.[125]

However by mid-1929, when the coffee control authorities' outlook brightened on the domestic front, tension was growing in London with the weakening of sterling, due to the French loan conversions and the capital outflows induced by the last stages of the New York stock market boom, seriously affecting Lazards' willingness to go on lending to the Institute.[126] Attempting to try and get accommodation in New York was of no use. Contrary to the *Paulistas'* expectations that President Hoover had changed his views on coffee valorisation after his visit to Brazil in 1928, the Department of State turned down a request by American bankers to fund the £5 million customary one-year advances from Lazards to the Institute on the grounds that 'the President had not changed his point of view on the matter and felt that the fact that this was not new money had very little to do with the whole situation.'[127]

Although negotiations in London dragged on, by 23 July the President of the Institute, feeling that 'the financial crisis which menaced the world . . . caused by the scarcity of gold, which was entirely absorbed by the American market, thanks to fabulous interest rates due to the speculation in stocks at the New York stock exchange, which then reached its climax . . . prevented securing foreign credits,'[128] arranged for a stand-by credit of 100 000 contos with the

Banco do Brasil, to be used for rediscount of coffee bills 'if necessary', through an oral agreement with the Bank's new president.[129] This credit was utterly insufficient to meet the financial requirements of the 1929 crop under the usual operational characteristics of coffee defence. Even at the gross underestimates put forward by the Institute for São Paulo's output, if the production of Brazil's foreign competitors and world absorption stayed at the previous crop year level and the relation of other States to São Paulo output was put at 50 per cent, the increase in stocks from 1 July 1929 to July 1 1930 would be about 7.2 billion bags.[130] This would represent a demand for additional finance of the order of 430 000 contos – or 36 000 contos per month under the recently introduced system of coffee delivery to the warehouses – at the 60 milréis per bag guaranteed by the Institute's bank. It is true that the *defesa* managers could expect that the private banking system would help carry the stocks. The latter's likely behaviour, however, could even increase the Institute's financial burden beyond the figures quoted above since, as the private banks were already heavily loaded with coffee bills from the existing stocks, they could, under the present conditions and expectations, refrain from going on lending on coffee after the liquidation of their current commitments.

It is rather unlikely, however, that the Institute's experts, being men with a lifelong experience in the coffee trade, made such a mistake in their estimates of the financial requirements of the new crop. The basic rationale of the Institute's rediscount agreement with the Banco do Brasil was the fear of a sudden break in prices. The Institute managers knew, like everyone conversant with the world coffee market, that coffee demand was strongly price-inelastic in normal demand conditions and that the present bear expectations due to the large crop and the credit tightening prevailing in the major importing centres – which affected the roasters' willingness to carry large stocks – would make it much more so. Moreover they saw that even if a fall in prices should induce importers to share the burden of carrying world stocks with Brazil, it would also seriously impair the Institute's ability to control world prices in the future. In fact, the very idea of postwar permanent coffee defence was based on holding the bulk of world stocks at the price control authorities' warehouses, and to let a substantial part of the stocks go overseas would be to deprive the Institute of its strongest weapon.[131]

All these considerations point to the conclusion that, when the Institute saw its ability to maintain its usual operational framework deteriorate, together with the conditions in world financial markets, it tried at once to guarantee its power at least to control prices at the Santos terminal. For that purpose, as its president showed to the Governor of São Paulo, with the limitation of port stocks at 1.8 million bags, at the ruling prices 'with the minimum capital of 100 000 contos it would be easy for the Defence to avoid the fall in coffee prices at any time.'[132] In fact, the rediscount arrangement with the Banco do Brasil was a last line of defence for market intervention, to bide time either until better conditions for negotiating foreign financial accommodation returned[133] or, if the worst came to the worst, to try and negotiate some further help from the federal government.

Clearly the outcome of any negotiation with the federal authorities was wide open. On the more pessimistic hypothesis of the government flatly refusing any help, the Institute would have to trim its expenditure to the exclusive needs of market intervention, shifting the entire burden of carrying the stock to the coffee sector. This was clearly a situation which could not be sustained for long, even at the low costs of the 1929 crop and with severe reductions in farm labourers' wages.

However in mid-1929 the extent and duration of the world economic crisis ahead was not anticipated. If it proved to be severe or drawn out, and thereby prevent an early improvement in world capital markets, the crisis situation, described as notionally possible in the analysis of the new coffee defence scheme made above, would occur. In this case the Institute managers would be justified in expecting that the federal government would eventually devalue and ease domestic credit conditions, thus placing the coffee control authorities in a much more comfortable position, from which they could even allow an orderly and phased increase in stock releases.

6.6 THE CRISIS OF 1930

At this critical juncture the fate of the coffee defence programme was affected by the breakdown of the São Paulo-Minas Gerais alliance which had guaranteed the political balance for the alternance of heads of government from these two states for the past two presidential terms.

Since Washington Luis's inauguration, Minas Gerais politicians felt that their standing agreement with São Paulo was in jeopardy. Antonio Carlos, now Governor of Minas Gerais and, in normal conditions, the natural government candidate for the 1930 elections, had led the attempted parliamentary opposition to the Monetary Reform Bill in 1926. There were rumours that the President's choice of the so-called 'official' candidate would fall to Julio Prestes, the deputy who introduced the Bill and now Governor of São Paulo.[134] Nevertheless, even as early as July 1927, such influential politicians as ex-President Epitácio Pessoa predicted that the stalemate thus created between the two largest states of the Union would lead to the putting forward of a third name, probably that of Getúlio Vargas, of Rio Grande do Sul, then Minister of Finance and responsible for the implementation of the government's currency reform.[135] In fact, when by mid-1929 the rumours of Washington Luis's support for Prestes turned into 'almost certainty,'[136] Minas Gerais politicians succeeded in signing a secret agreement with Rio Grande do Sul to the effect that if the President refused to support Antonio Carlos, both states would put forward Vargas's candidacy.[137]

Vargas had left the Ministry of Finance in late 1927 to take up the governorship of his state but, as the documents from his private archives clearly show,[138] he was still loyal and on good terms with the President and in no way opposed the federal government's financial policy. In July, when Vargas learnt for certain that his name would be proposed, he wrote to Washington Luis informing him of the Minas Gerais pressure for his candidacy, warning that a refusal to consider it could provoke a political crisis of serious consequences. The President, although taken aback by the unexpected news,[139] reacted quickly and, in the nine days between receiving and answering Vargas's polite ultimatum, succeeded in getting support for Prestes's candidacy in all but one of the remaining states.[140] As the Minas Gerais-Rio Grande do Sul agreement ruled, the President's implicit refusal to consider Vargas's name bound them to launch his candidacy and, in August, the fight began, shattering the political peace reigning since 1926.

The first consequence of an open electoral confrontation between the government and two major states was definitely to place the defence of the gold standard as the utmost priority in economic policy for, although the opposition did not go against it, the President justified the break with Minas Gerais by the wish to guarantee the continuity of the federal government's financial reconstruction plan and Prestes's electoral platform on economic policy centered exclusively on carrying out the transformation of the Banco do Brasil into a central bank with full convertibility of the total note issue.[141] In face of the extremely vulnerable external position of the third quarter of 1929 the government's determination not to allow its exchange stabilisation programme to founder before the March 1930 elections meant that financial help from the federal government for the Institute was unlikely in the foreseeable future and, moreover, that the government was likely to resort to its former restrictive credit policy in the absence of an early improvement in the balance of payments.

The political crisis would also widen the front on which the Institute had to fight its battle, since the opposition immediately seized on the issue of the wisdom of maintaining São Paulo's present retention and price policies. In the annual meeting of the coffee producing states on 19 September, the usual optimistic exposition by the Institute's president met a strong rebuttal from the Minas Gerais representative who criticised the present coffee release policy as too rigid, proposing that 'the [signatory] states, in special cases, could raise the amounts released.'[142] Parliamentary opposition voiced the same criticisms, aimed at the Institute's rearguard of discontented farmers in São Paulo, the largest electoral stronghold of the government candidate.[143]

The realities of the new political and economic situation would eventually bring the President back to disagreement with the Institute's views. Ample financial help for coffee was now out of the question because of its effects on the exchanges, but even any form of support which would enable the Institute to support prices was politically dangerous. The retention period had risen to twenty months in September 1929, and the government wavered again over the question of whether price support was bringing any benefit to the balance of payments position, since it was not yet convinced of the perverse effect of larger stock releases.[144]

The government's change of mind marked the end of the brief interlude of the *Paulista* Silva Gordo at the presidency of the Banco do Brasil. On 11 September Guilherme da Silveira, a Rio industrialist and banker, was nominated to bring the leading institution in the money market back to its previous restrictive course. Telles, the President of the Coffee Institute, forecasting the change in the Bank's credit policy and worried by the federal government's wobbling on the question of coffee prices during the first half of the year, tried to confirm the stand-by credit agreed with Silva Gordo in July. However, in his own words, the 'federal government, again with a different financial orientation, refused to grant the agreed rediscount facility and, furthermore, understood that the immediate lowering of coffee prices would remedy the situation.'[145]

The president of the Institute came to Rio and tried personally to convince Washington Luis of the necessity to support prices, but the latter had made up his mind: 'Coffee does not concern me anymore;', he explained, as recollected by Telles, 'has not England given up the defence of rubber? To maintain the exchange rate I have the balance of the Stabilisation Office which is enough for the necessary remittances up to the end of my mandate and to keep the stabilisation rate.'[146]

In a desperate attempt, Telles went at once to the Banco do Brasil, pressing the same points to Silveira, arguing the past administration's compromise with the Institute and pointing out that a monetary contraction now could place the coffee industry in an intolerable situation, but only to hear that 'coffee was the disgrace of the country . . . the fall in coffee prices would be beneficial to Brazil, since more coffee would be sold and thus foreign exchange would be forthcoming.'[147]

As the news of the government position leaked, the expectations of a price break led to a run by coffee bill holders on the Institute bank. In September 1929, the bank's rediscount operations were suspended, so as to spare the remainder of its liquid reserves for market intervention while the question of the Banco do Brasil's refusal was discussed between the federal government and the Governor of São Paulo.[148] The President, however, would not give in and, on 11 October, Prestes signed Telles's resignation as the State Secretary of Finance, which meant the end of the Institute's resistance to the federal government's directives. In the words of Rowe's dramatic reconstruction of this day at the Santos Coffee Exchange:

> At the morning session . . . the broker who usually conducted the Institute's operation sat quietly in his place and made no bid to buy. But, while very astonished, the market appears to have thought that he was engaged upon some new bluff, and no attempt was made to call it by offers to sell at reduced prices. At the afternoon session, however, he again remained silent, and the market suddenly realised that the end had come.[149]

Prices immediately plummeted, falling by the maximum statutory limit for several days, until, on 29 October, the Santos and Rio

Coffee Exchanges closed, while representatives of the trade posed the problem again at the federal government's doorstep. By the end of the year, when the fall was finally arrested, prices stood at a third below their previous level.[150]

The collapse of coffee prices in October 1929 caused by the federal government's *volte face* on the coffee problem would seriously hit both the coffee industry and, contrary to the President's expectations, the balance of payments position. Towards the end of the year the contraction of income would accelerate in most consumer countries and affect the demand for coffee for many months hence. Moreover, as predicted by the Institute, after the demoralisation of the Brazilian price support scheme, buyers did not start actively bidding again until very late, particularly so in the extremely unfavourable business climate which followed the Wall Street crash. All these adverse circumstances would make coffee one of the outstanding casualties of the widespread fall in food and raw material prices in the early stages of the world depression.[151] Coming on top of the already extremely depressed domestic economic conditions then prevailing, the cumulative coffee and external balance problems would launch a crisis of unprecedented magnitude in 1930.

The immediate effect of the collapse of coffee prices was to cause the whole domestic system of coffee finance to grind to a halt. This had already happened to some extent when the Institute Bank stopped rediscounting coffee bills before the crash, but the real freeze-up only came when the collapse of prices affected the liquidity of the ultimate debtor in the system – the planter. The planters had received advances at the rate of 100 milréis per bag for the coffee being sold in the last months of 1929, i.e., the first arrivals of the 1928–9 crop. If two years' interest, export taxes and commission are added, the expenses incurred in selling their coffee can be placed at over 140 milréis per bag.[152] To finance the planters during the retention period, the *comissários* had borrowed to the limit from the banks who were also carrying large positions of coffee bills. Thus, when prices collapsed to below 120 milréis per bag, the planters simply could not settle their debts.[153]

When all transactions stopped, with the closure of the Coffee Exchanges, opinions varied widely about the ways in which to restore the normal working of the coffee industry. The interests directly engaged in the coffee trade, ranging from planters to São Paulo banks, wanted, of course, plain cash as a way out of the paralysis provoked by the crisis. Following the suspension of trade, a delegation of planters and *comissários* went to Rio to press Washington Luis to either declare a general moratorium – a solution probably preferred by the planters – or to issue Stabilisation Office notes against the £10 million free gold reserve formerly belonging to the Treasury and now held by the Banco do Brasil to help the coffee industry, as was being proposed by financial interests in São Paulo.[154] The President, however, firmly refused to accept either of these proposals. The moratorium, it was argued, was unnecessary since it was already *de facto* in force in the existing situation, while easing money was out of the question, given the federal government's determination to support its stabilisation programme.[155]

London's Brazilian creditors – with the obvious exception of Lazards, the Institute's foreign bankers and a newcomer in dealings with Brazil – had for a long time been critical of the financial soundness of the coffee price support scheme.[156] Schroeders, the traditional bankers of the São Paulo government, had not banked for the Coffee Institute, bound by their previous stance against artificial coffee price control as a member of the consortium led by Rothschilds, which since the time of the Montagu mission had issued federal government loans. Now, with Lazards having backed down, the sudden collapse, although calling for immediate support to avoid a serious balance of payments crisis which could prevent São Paulo and the federal government honouring their debts, immensely increased the traditional bankers' bargaining power to impose the liquidation of the defence scheme as a condition for bailing São Paulo out of its troubles.

The opposition supporting Vargas, which had made the need for changes in the Institute's price and retention policy an electoral issue and supported the planters' early demands for a speedier liquidation of stocks, had to maintain coherence and, since it did not oppose the government's stabilisation programme, its position on economic policy issues became indistinguishable from the government's and foreign creditors'. Although trying to expose the fact that by defending the exchange rate, the government was sacrificing the coffee industry, the opposition, through its leading spokesman on economic affairs, opposed further financial help to coffee by the Banco do Brasil.[157]

However as the Jornal do Commércio correctly interpreted the mood of the coffee industry after the meeting with Washington Luis, 'the interested parties . . . were not willing to discuss abstract themes. They wished the Union's help. The claim for this support was the more justified as the crisis was the result of the policies of the governments of the Union and São Paulo.'[158] Clearly, after the crash there was no politically conceivable course of action open in the short run to the federal government other than to let the Banco do Brasil dishoard a fraction of the large cash reserves it had accumulated in the past years to clear the debris its own action had precipitated, while joining forces with São Paulo in an attempt to get some help from their foreign bankers to put the state's financial system back on its feet without undue pressures on the balance of payments.

On 30 October, the president of the Banco do Brasil went to São Paulo to work out a financial arrangement to place the banks in a more liquid position. Throughout the five days' negotiations, Silveira pressed the condition that the Institute should reduce coffee prices for balance of payment reasons.[159] Finally it was decided that the Bank was to start rediscounting warehouse deposit certificates at the rate of 40 milréis per bag.[160] The new valuation was a third below the previous minimum guaranteed by the Institute but, when trade reopened later in November, the Institute succeeded in holding prices stable around 120 milréis per bag and the intervention by the Banco do Brasil was undoubtedly instrumental in helping avoiding a crisis of unforeseeable proportions. In that way 130 000 contos were lent up to the end of the year[161] and almost 160 000 up to March 1930.[162]

At the same time, São Paulo, backed by the federal government, started negotiations in London with Schroeders, Rothschilds and Barings for a permanent solution to their problems. Although it proved impossible to raise any substantial amount at short notice, owing to the uncertain situation in world financial markets in early November 1929, and to the unpredictability of the outcome of the coming presidential elections in Brazil, by the middle of November a £2 million short-term loan was granted to São Paulo, together with the pledge of a larger future operation to fund the Institute's short-term liabilities, against Brazilian assurance of the early liquidation of the coffee stocks presently held at the farms and *reguladores*, i.e., the abandonment of permanent coffee defence.[163] The conditions accepted by the Brazilians during these negotiations were also instrumental in allowing New York participation in the present and future operation, since the Department of State gave, of course, its *nihil obstat* after receiving guarantees from the American house involved that it had 'entered into the transaction only after receiving governmental assurance that the coffee valorisation plan, heretofore in force, will be substantially modified in a sense favourable to American consumers.'[164]

The course of coffee policy had been set and the loan negotiations were no more than the final act of the drama begun in December 1928. The President was now to hold obstinately to his only objective of preserving the stabilisation plan. However, as the evolution of the balance of payments would demonstrate, this was only possible on the unlikely hypothesis of amassing ample foreign credits.

The disastrous effects of the sudden coffee price fall upon the value of exports from the last quarter of 1929 would forcefully prove the point which the former Institute managers had been trying to impress on the federal government for months before the crash. The monthly value of Brazilian exports fell from an average of £8.7 million in the third quarter of 1929 to £8.3 million in October, £7.3 million in November and £6.9 million in December and, on a yearly basis, from £94.8 million in 1929 to £65.7 million in 1930, in spite of a 7 per cent increase in the quantity of coffee exported.[165]

From October 1929, Brazil's balance of payments difficulties became acute because, in spite of the falling import level since the onset of the 1929 recession, the slump in exports was accompanied by a large increase in short-term capital outflows stemming from internal and external causes.[166] On 7 December, the Banco do Brasil withdrew its support to the foreign exchange market so as to spare its foreign exchange reserves for remittances on government account.[167] Even after the Ministry of Finance had taken the unusual step of issuing temporary exchange control regulations in January 1930,[168] and in spite of heavy overdrafts by the Banco do Brasil on its foreign correspondents,[169] the Bank was only able to regain control of the market by allowing gold to flow out of the Stabilisation Office.[170]

The loss of gold continued on an increasing scale until March 1930, and the deflationary pressures stemming from the contraction in the monetary base, amplified by the natural precautionary behaviour of the private banking sector during the crisis, offset many of the beneficial effects of the slow process of debt liquidation in São Paulo which had begun after the Bank's intervention, the additional help from the foreign loan, and the Institute's successful re-stabilisation of coffee prices.[171]

The bulk of the burden of adjustment in the coffee sector fell on producers and *comissários*. Failures of commission houses became frequent and large numbers of farmers in the old zone abandoned their crops.[172] The general squeeze in farmers' current revenues caused a marked deterioration of labour conditions in the rural areas. Day labourers lost their jobs, while the colonists accepted money wage cuts of 35 to 40 per cent in exchange for permission to grow food crops among the coffee trees.[173] In March the unofficial election returns gave Prestes, the government's candidate, the presidential mandate.[174] By the end of April arrangements for the large coffee loan agreed in November were concluded and a nominal £20 million long-term loan was issued by São Paulo in London, New York and several other European markets. It was announced that the loan – characteristically entitled the Coffee Realisation Loan – was to allow the sale 'gradually and in an orderly manner of the present stock, and place future crops in the market currently . . . so as to prevent accumulation of stocks in the future,'[175] and was issued together with a series of regulations as to the future marketing of Santos coffee to be effective from 1 July, and a new tax of 3 shillings per bag was charged to the planters for its service.

In view of future events it is otiose to analyse the economic consequences of the 1930 coffee loan. What it is important to note is that, as mentioned above, the motive for this loan was to provide for the funding of the Institute's short-term obligations[176] – amounting to £7 million, in addition to the £5 million one-year loan issued by the Banco do Brasil in 1929 – and, as underwriters only subscribed less than £17 million of the amount offered for sale[177] its immediate balance of payments effect was a drop in the ocean as far as the needs of the federal government exchange rate policy were concerned.

However the similarities between the economic crises and policy responses generated by the collapse of the gold standard in 1930 to those of 1914 cannot fail to strike the modern observer. In spite of the already unbearable and growing deflationary pressures caused by the overvalued exchange rate, the government still stuck to its far-fetched objective of full convertibility[178] and opened negotiations for a foreign loan to suport the gold standard.

On 20 March a representative of Rothschilds arrived in Rio for negotiations with the federal government,[179] but nothing came of this visit. Probably in view of better prospects in New York, the President-elect left for the United States on 23 May. However, his attempts proved unsuccessful and, as a last resort, he decided to sail to London, but found that the bankers maintained their position 'as reluctant to offer any assistance unless Brazil invited some outside expert to investigate and reorganise financial methods on the lines of the Montagu mission.'[180] Washington Luis, however, refused to do so, for fear of the political consequences of such an act in the very tense political situation in the aftermath of the presidential elections.[181]

With the failure of the loan negotiations, the federal government had unsuccessfully fired its last shot to save what was left of the 1926 financial reconstruction programme. Almost immediately afterwards – though not abolishing the gold standard legislation – the government withdrew the exchange control regulations and instructed the Banco do Brasil to step down market intervention in order to keep its still large holdings of Office notes to settle the necessary remittances on government account.[182] The milréis was left to find its own level and the gold outflows – which had been stopped from the end of April, during the loan negotiations – resumed.[183]

Industrial output fell by 4.7 per cent and imports of capital goods by the industrial sector by 46 per cent in 1930.[184] The real effects of the depression were made worse by the fiscal crisis at both federal and state levels of government, caused by the huge contraction both in the volume of imports (which affected federal tariff revenue) and the value of exports, which hit state revenues coming mainly from *ad valorem* export duties;[185] all public works started during the boom were discontinued and large and small states went into arrears with their debt payments.[186] In August, as the British Ambassador observed, the situation was so tense that 'no man can be held to be a responsible and serious observer who does not dwell on national bankruptcy, commercial ruin and even revolution,'[187] and described Washington Luis as a 'broken and disappointed man, who has lost all his former self-confidence, and who cannot be brought to take any action whatever.'[188]

In September this evidently unbearable situation finally moved the President to urge Prestes to comply with the London bankers' conditions and issue an invitation for a financial mission. The President-elect, however, considered that he would prefer to await his formal inauguration, and Rothschilds were accordingly informed that an invitation might be sent only by 15 November.[189]

Prestes, however, would never reach the Presidency. On 3 October, anti-government armed risings, led by Vargas's supporters and young military officers, broke out in the three states which had supported his candidacy. The revolutionary troops swept the country, meeting little opposition, converging on Rio and São Paulo and, when the threat of a bloody civil war grew, a group of high-ranking army officiers from the Rio headquarters deserted the government, swinging the military balance against it.[190] Besieged with his cabinet in the undefended presidential palace, the President was taken, on 24 October, by the timely intervention of the Cardinal Archbishop of Rio to the Fort of Copacabana, from where he would leave for sixteen years' exile in Europe and the United States. The Vargas era was about to begin.

7 Conclusions

The evidence presented in the preceding chapters has an important bearing upon existing interpretative generalisations about the political motivations of economic policy making during the First Republic, briefly reviewed in the Preface to this book. Even though the works by Pelaez and others had the merit of stressing the resilience of orthodox doctrines within influential circles – a rather uncontroversial fact at the time and not only in Brazil – the evidence presented in the present study certainly does not support their strong claim about the permanent orthodox bias of *actual* economic policies. After its heyday at the time of Finance Ministers Murtinho and Bulhões, which can be conceived as the culmination of a reaction launched by orthodox opinion after the monetary explosion and exchange rate collapse of the early days of the Republic, orthodoxy was always on the defensive, only temporarily regaining enough influence to carry policy proposals through in the mid-twenties, when great external, fiscal and monetary disequilibria recurred. The explanations put forward in the preceding pages for the motives of the adoption of the gold standard in 1906 and 1926 as well as the policies actually followed during, for instance, Epitácio Pessoa and early Bernardes governments can hardly be said to have an orthodox inspiration – notwithstanding public men's frequent utterances in favour of 'sound finance' – and were, in fact, carried out against the views held by the most representative sectors of orthodox opinion.

Criticism of the traditional view needs greater elaboration. In no way is it intended here to deny that the political representatives of the coffee and related trading and financial interests from São Paulo held a hegemonic position in the Brazilian state. They assumed this position during the nineties, based on the unique economic and political resources they held to take the leadership in the process of reconstruction of a workable political system as explained in Chapter 1. The preservation of their position was guaranteed by the enormous significance that São Paulo coffee production maintained for the performance of the economy, by the power-centralising political system their very leaders designed at the turn of the century and, last but not least, by their capacity to integrate the interests of the growing industrial bourgeoisie of their state in their own channels of political representation, given the absence of important objective economic contradictions with the industrialists' more limited corporative claims and the latter's extreme dependency on a good performance by the coffee industry.

It must be noted, however, that the power of São Paulo was not absolute and it did not always have the control of the extremely effective federal political machinery its historical leaders built at the turn of the century. Instances such as the 1910 presidential elections, when São Paulo supported the opposition candidate – who included federal commitment to coffee valorisation in his electoral platform – and lost, could be multiplied to illustrate this point. However to probe further in this direction would take us far beyond the scope of this study. For the purpose of the present argument it is only necessary to postulate the simple notion that if the hegemonic position held by any class cannot but be founded on the importance it holds in some fundamental instance of economic activity, it cannot be overlooked that the exercise of political hegemony is not a one-way affair: it presupposes, as noted by Gramsci, 'that a certain balance of compromises be formed, that, in other words, the leading group makes some sacrifices of an economic-corporative kind.'[1] Nevertheless, traditional literature, which derives all its *a priori* appeal from the uncontroversial (but not always properly understood) fact of *Paulista* hegemony, has shown a remarkable lack of interest in considering how this simple truth holds in pre-1930 republican economic policy making.

It is to this question that the following critical remarks are addressed. What will be argued below is that the traditional notion that, as a straightforward corollary to the political hegemony of the coffee interests, federal economic policies consistently favoured the sectoral interests of this group, is incorrect. Based on the facts presented in the review of economic policies carried out in the preceding chapters, a strong case will be made against the two stylised facts which form the empirical basis of support of the traditional view, viz., that the federal government was always ready to bow to pressures for price support schemes coming from the coffee trade, and that it systematically favoured low exchange rates.

Let us start by considering the view that the federal government always gave its support to coffee valorisation and that this was motivated by the intention to protect the sectoral interests of the industry. It should be recalled from the outset that the federal government (a) effectively denied support in crucial instances such as 1906 and 1929, (b) did not promote the constitution of a permanent federal institution responsible for coffee valorisation, as requested by São Paulo in the first half of the twenties, and eventually handed over its informal responsibility for price support back to the government of that state, and (c) only intervened sporadically in 1908, 1917, 1921 and, through the Banco do Brasil, in 1923. The reasons for this changing attitude have been discussed in some detail in this work. On the one hand it was shown that, on several occasions, pressures for federal support were effectively countervailed by the influence of other politically strong groups: the opinion of the government's London bankers on the risks of valorisation was decisive in blocking it in 1906; the fierce opposition from the Minas Gerais bench at the Chamber to President Pessoa's permanent valorisation plan – stemming from their fears of its monetary consequences – was instrumental in shelving it in 1921; the united opposition of these very same groups against federal involvement in coffee schemes, plus United States government's strong opposition to commodity control schemes in the mid-twenties were responsible for President Bernardes' decision definitely to abandon it in 1924; and, as argued in Chapter 6, the tense domestic political situation and the opinion of Brazil's international creditors did influence President Washington Luis's adamant attitude against granting federal financial help to the São Paulo Coffee Institute in 1929.

On the other hand the instances in which federal support was effectively granted to the coffee industry were at times when there were evident signs that severe balance of payments and induced domestic disequilibria would ensue if coffee prices were left subject to the influence of market forces, and this cannot be interpreted as clear evidence that the support given was primarily motivated by the intention to give preferential treatment to this particular trade; rather as a clearly necessary and timely stabilisation policy. It must not be overlooked that in a specialised export economy, where macroeconomic instability usually stems from external shocks, the stabilisation of the price of the staple export is the most efficient anti-cyclical policy in the short run.[2] This was particularly true in the case of Brazil, since coffee prices had a great potential instability, being subject to exogenous disturbances coming both from fluctuations in world demand as well as from large supply shocks, and the country's quasi-monopolistic position in world markets greatly simplified the implementation of such policies. Public interference did, in fact, exert a beneficial stabilising influence, avoiding major external disequilibria with damaging consequences to overall economic performance.[3] Therefore even the cases in which the federal government intervened in coffee markets cannot be used as *prima facie* evidence of its wish to protect the sectoral interests of the coffee industry since, on those occasions, the national interests and those of the latter coincide.

The discussion of the alleged bias of exchange rate policy in favour of the leading export sector needs a longer digression. It will be recalled that during the period under analysis Brazil experienced two types of exchange rate system: floating rates under managed fiduciary currency and fixed rates under the gold standard. Under the latter – as during 1906–14 or 1927–30 – the policy adopted in the presence of external disequilibria was to try and maintain the then overvalued exchange parity, even at the cost of large monetary contractions, while the authorities attempted without success to obtain some form of foreign financial assistance to redress external balance. In those cases, of course, it does not seem valid to speak of devaluation-prone policies, since the contrary is true.

Of the periods in which Brazil remained under floating rates there are the peace-time years of 1889–1906 and 1919–26 which present the greatest interest from the point of view of the present discussion for, during the war, exchange rates were kept roughly stable, mainly for fiscal and price stabilisation reasons, at the level they found after the early and rapid adjustment from pre-war parity.

It is interesting to note that these two long peace-time periods show a striking similarity as far as the evolution of the external position and macroeconomic policies are concerned. The early years of both are marked by a reversion of previously very favourable external conditions and large exchange rate depreciation the government was in no position to countervail. The exchange rate collapses tended to provoke severe and cumulative budget and monetary disequilibria as well as inflationary pressures for reasons connected with structural and institutional features of the Brazilian economy abundantly discussed in the preceding chapters. Moreover, as external equilibrium was re-established on a fragile basis through the working of automatic adjustment mechanisms induced by price and income changes following the external shocks and exchange rate depreciation and the government encountered difficulties in borrowing abroad, those sudden external disequilibria were also followed by periods of very low levels of official international reserves and the federal authorities were not able to prevent recurrent pressures on the external value of the milréis. It was the anxiety over this lack of effective control over the exchange rate, growing inflationary pressures and the disarray of public finances which, on these two occasions, eventually made the need to break the vicious circle of exchange rate and price instability, fiscal disequilibrium and monetary expansion for inflationary deficit financing the main objective of economic policy.

Thus, as shown in Chapters 1 and 4, the great exchange rate collapses of 1890–2 and 1920–2 were, after a period of great domestic instability and threat of further external disequilibria, followed by negotiations with international bankers aimed at achieving this objective, and from them resulted in either case the extremely restrictive monetary and fiscal policies of the Campos Salles and Bernardes administrations. Those deflationary interludes – which, unlike the exchange rate collapses which ultimately motivated them, were the result of conscious policy options – had, moreover, the explicit aim of achieving a substantial exchange rate *appreciation* and so cannot possibly be reconciled with the presuppositions of the traditional view.

These two occasions on which the federal government switched to very restrictive monetary and fiscal policies were followed, however, by sharp improvements in the value of exports and, especially, in Brazil's ability to borrow abroad as a result of general upswings in world investment. Exogenous increases in foreign exchange receipts at times when the level of imports was still depressed resulted in the rapid exchange rate appreciations of 1905 and 1925–6, drastically altering the nature of the problem the restrictive policies had been designed to solve. The outcome was, on both occasions, and as in many other primary producing countries, the eventual adoption of the gold standard which, by promising to prevent further uncontrolled and disruptive appreciation after domestic costs, prices and incomes had adapted to the lower exchange rate levels, as well as, under the favourable conditions then prevailing, to shift away from dear money, could not fail to have the enthusiastic support of *all* domestic producers. Furthermore, as the creation of gold-stabilisation devices had an important effect on the country's capacity to borrow abroad, enabling public authorities at all levels to take advantage of the favourable conditions then obtaining in international capital markets to finance public works programmes, common-sense political behaviour by the leading regional oligarchies resulted in further, and by no means negligible, support to the adoption of the gold standard.

The above discussion shows that the view, so ingrained in the literature, that the depreciating trend of the milréis throughout the First Republic was an intentional consequence of policy decisions needs qualification. Although the secular fall of the exchange rate obviously favoured export activities – and hence the coffee industry – this falling trend is totally explained by the exchange rate collapses of the early nineties and early twenties which resulted from severe external shocks whose effects the federal executive was not able to offset, even though it tried to reverse it to the point of eventually resorting to very restrictive policies on both occasions. Moreover to affirm unqualifiedly, as is often done, that the creation of the Conversion and Stabilisation Offices was motivated by the intention to protect the sectoral interests of the coffee trade seems also a gross over-simplification.

As stressed above the criticisms put forward in the preceding paragraphs are not incompatible with the view that the São Paulo political oligarchy held a hegemonic position within the state before 1930. What must be clear is that, as shown in this work, the potential instability of Brazil's external position, her extreme and growing dependency on imported fuel and many industrial intermediary goods, and some institutional features of her monetary and fiscal systems did result – in a period in which her transactions with the rest of the world were free from controls and the behaviour of the world economy far from being smooth – in frequent exogenous fluctuations in the country's external position with destabilising domestic implications. The political consequences of these periodical crises were exacerbated by their distributive effects and not unfrequently presented a serious menace to the political cohesion of the state. On these occasions the debate on economic policy tended to gravitate towards broader issues relating to the design of instruments to provide a greater degree of monetary, budget, exchange rate and price stability. These were occasions on which, because the need to maintain or restore financial stability and to keep open or re-enact access to foreign financial centres became crucial for political stability, monetary and fiscal orthodoxy thrived and the political oligarchies of São Paulo – which, incidentally, by no means represented the average coffee planter – by the very fact that they held a hegemonic position within the state, were bound to take a less corporative view on the issues at stake and compromise. The only intention of the critical remarks made above is to question, on the basis of fact, oversimplified but widely accepted generalisations concerning economic policy making during the period covered by the present study and to point to the need for further research by political historians towards a deeper understanding of the rationale of economic demands and relative political strength of the relevant classes or regional groups than the one presently available.

A second set of general conclusions stemming from the present study relates to the operation of external adjustment mechanisms in peripheral countries in the relatively free international economic environment prevailing before the Great Depression.

The Brazilian experience under the gold standard highlights some negative features of its operation in debtor nations with high export price instability, and tends to confirm the view that available theoretical models used to explain self-equilibrating balance of payments adjustment mechanisms under the standard, by their stylised nature 'shed more light on the myth of the gold standard than on the historical reality.'[4] Brazilian balance of payments dynamics under the gold standard, as discussed in Chapters 2 and 6, was found to follow the pattern suggested by Ford's pioneering study on Argentina, being to a large extent dominated by the behaviour of the capital account. The adoption of the gold standard happened at times when Brazil's participation in an international lending boom coincided with export price recovery leading to balance of payments surpluses and upward pressures on the exchanges. Given the passive role of the monetary authority after the switch to gold, being unable to sterilise the gold inflows because of the narrowness of domestic capital markets, the surplus balance of payments position leads to credit expansion, fuelling the upswing launched by increased net exports and domestic investment financed by foreign borrowing.

As long as the underlying causes of the upswing persist, current account adjustment proceeds basically through income induced increase in imports.[5] Thus, the overall payments equilibrium upon which monetary stability depends becomes ever more dependent on the maintenance of foreign investors' propensity to lend and on the maintenance of favourable prices for the staple export and, given the swiftness with which these can change, increasingly vulnerable. If foreign lending or export prices collapse and fail to recover after the process of import growth has gathered momentum and substantially eroded the trade surplus, the ensuing sharp monetary contraction can be extremely painful, as witnessed by the 1913–4 and 1929–30 experiences.

On the other hand the analysis of the adjustment process under floating rates showed that the fall in imports caused by a sharp milréis depreciation and credit stringency created by the bearish behaviour of domestic banks were fundamental elements of the adjustment process following external shocks in the short run, but that coffee price support – when enacted, as in the early twenties – also played an important part in it. Although external adjustment took place at the cost of inducing high rates of inflation and severe budget imbalances, real output losses were small.

Finally it should be added that the evidence presented here points to the need to give a prominent place to the role of external constraints in explaining the discontinuity in Brazilian economic policy making from the thirties towards greater government intervention and control, as opposed to the traditional analyses based almost solely on considerations of domestic political conflict following the collapse of the First Republic. With the benefit of hindsight one can infer that during the pre-1930 regime governments failed to devise means to promote the necessary structural changes needed for greater macroeconomic stability, such as greater export diversification and import substitution, a change towards a budget structure less vulnerable to external shocks, and so on. Nevertheless, by operating in a world economic order which, although not free from severe dislocations, did preserve or rapidly restore its basic institutional characteristics, governments in the First Republic were able to achieve some degree of macroeconomic stability without disrupting, except in the marketing of coffee, the free play of market forces, even if at the cost of growing public foreign indebtedness.

The dramatic external disequilibrium experienced by Brazil in the early thirties, following the total breakdown of the world monetary system imposed, however, the introduction of trade and exchange controls, bilateral trade agreements and, last but not least, a drastic re-scheduling and, eventually a unilateral moratorium on the service of the public foreign debt. These measures were unthinkable in peace-time before 1930 – and, in effect, only began to be reluctantly implemented almost a year after the rise of Vargas when further negotiations for British financial assistance proved futile – for, given the country's external vulnerability and its domestic implications, there was an ever present need to keep open the access to international capital markets. The latter's absolute collapse, the beggar-my-neighbour policies followed by some leading industrial countries and the problems posed by coffee overproduction up to 1933, by completely changing this outlook, ironically created the possibility of overcoming Brazil's long-standing problem of maintaining domestic stability in the face of external shocks, without any of the structural or institutional changes which would be needed in the scenario of pre-1930 international conditions and economic policy wisdom.

It is important to note, moreover, that, given the inherited structure of the economy, these policies were introduced for purely macroeconomic stabilisation reasons and, although trade and exchange controls proved in the long-run to be the most powerful single instrument for the re-allocation of real resources towards the transformation of the supply structure of the Brazilian economy, their introduction was not part of any industrialising political project. If these arguments are accepted, one should conclude that, contrary to much of the received historiography, it is in the deep changes undergone by the rules of the game governing international economic relations since the Great Depression, and not in a supposed recomposition of the political basis of the state following the 1930 Revolution, that the political rationale and feasibility of post-1930 economic policies and structural changes must be sought.

Appendix: Statistical Tables

Table A.1 Brazil: 1900–30, real output indices (1939 = 100)

Year	Haddad's Estimates			Villela and Suzigan's Estimates			Fishlow's Estimates		
	Agriculture	Industry	Total	Agriculture	Industry	GNP	Agriculture	Industry	GDP
1900	27.2	11.0	18.1	–	–	–	–	–	–
1901	32.9	11.3	20.7	–	–	–	–	–	–
1902	31.5	11.7	20.6	–	–	–	–	–	–
1903	32.1	12.0	21.0	–	–	–	–	–	–
1904	32.1	12.6	21.3	–	–	–	–	–	–
1905	32.3	12.9	22.0	–	–	–	–	–	–
1906	33.3	13.6	24.8	–	–	–	–	–	–
1907	39.4	14.8	25.0	–	–	–	–	–	–
1908	36.5	14.8	24.2	–	–	–	–	–	–
1909	36.6	18.0	26.7	–	–	–	–	–	–
1910	38.2	18.8	27.4	–	–	–	–	–	–
1911	36.7	20.5	29.0	–	–	–	–	–	–
1912	39.4	22.7	31.0	–	–	–	–	–	–
1913	41.1	22.9	31.0	–	–	–	–	–	–
1914	41.5	20.9	31.5	–	–	–	–	–	–
1915	43.2	23.6	31.6	–	–	–	–	–	–

1916	42.0	26.3	31.9	—	—	—	—	—	—
1917	47.0	28.6	34.9	—	—	—	—	—	—
1918	43.5	28.3	34.2	—	—	—	—	—	—
1919	44.8	32.5	36.9	—	—	—	—	—	48
1920	53.3	34.2	41.5	57.8	34.7	47.4	59	41	48
1921	55.5	33.6	42.3	60.5	34.3	48.9	61	40	48
1922	55.8	39.9	45.6	60.3	39.7	50.4	63	48	53
1923	58.0	45.2	49.5	61.4	47.4	53.3	64	48	54
1924	58.6	44.7	50.2	63.5	39.6	52.8	64	48	55
1925	56.7	45.2	50.2	61.5	39.9	51.7	62	49	55
1926	58.5	46.3	52.8	63.7	39.5	53.1	62	50	56
1927	64.8	51.3	58.5	69.2	42.7	57.7	68	55	61
1928	76.7	54.9	65.2	82.1	46.1	67.1	76	58	67
1929	76.9	53.7	65.9	82.1	44.5	66.9	77	56	67
1930	77.8	50.1	64.5	82.9	42.4	66.4	79	52	66

Sources: Haddad, C.L.S., *op. cit.*, pp. 10–11 and Haddad, C.L.S., Crescimento Econômico do Brasil, 1900–76, in Neuhaus, P. (ed.) *Economia Brasileira: uma visão histórica*, Campus, Rio de Janeiro, 1980, p. 24; Villela, A.V. and W. Suzigan, *op. cit.*, Table XII, p. 431 and Table XVI, p. 436; Fishlow, A., *op. cit.*, p. 357.

Table A.2 Brazil: 1901–30, selected domestic activity and capital formation indicators (1939 = 100)

Year	Fuels	Quantity Index of Imports of		Capital Goods to Industry	Apparent Consumption of	
		Raw Materials	Capital Goods		Cement	Steel
1901	21.4	39.2	68.7	56.8	5.1	10.3
1902	22.9	47.2	33.9	31.7	8.0	18.2
1903	22.6	50.7	38.6	38.0	8.7	18.1
1904	24.2	52.2	42.3	41.3	12.8	19.7
1905	26.3	59.7	64.7	62.3	17.7	21.8
1906	29.7	64.9	62.5	66.1	24.6	27.2
1907	32.4	73.8	94.1	93.0	24.5	32.8
1908	33.3	61.8	99.2	96.4	27.0	37.7
1909	34.5	64.3	117.5	102.9	27.5	32.2
1910	41.3	84.7	136.6	118.7	36.1	44.6
1911	44.4	90.7	185.6	153.6	36.7	50.7
1912	64.5	102.5	271.5	205.3	50.1	64.1
1913	60.1	104.4	223.0	152.6	63.5	74.6

Year						
1914	43.1	52.0	87.7	63.4	24.7	37.7
1915	37.9	46.5	33.3	25.2	19.8	24.5
1916	36.6	54.7	43.0	32.2	23.2	24.3
1917	28.5	39.8	46.6	32.0	13.4	22.1
1918	20.8	44.9	42.9	36.9	7.1	13.1
1919	39.9	61.0	93.1	64.6	27.1	37.5
1920	41.0	72.8	148.5	108.1	23.6	58.0
1921	38.5	52.6	115.9	125.8	21.4	25.0
1922	43.2	72.0	97.4	91.5	43.6	34.9
1923	51.6	80.4	127.8	119.4	30.5	43.8
1924	62.1	100.6	182.8	151.0	43.3	75.4
1925	77.6	110.8	267.0	209.2	45.9	73.3
1926	76.2	109.7	226.1	154.7	55.9	73.7
1927	92.7	113.7	191.3	124.3	67.8	84.8
1928	98.3	130.9	234.7	133.2	74.3	101.3
1929	108.4	122.2	275.0	184.7	86.2	113.8
1930	92.9	86.4	106.3	99.7	64.4	53.8

Source: Villela, A.V. and W. Suzigan, *op. cit.*, Table VII, p. 437 and Table XXI, p. 442.

Table A.3   Brazil: 1889–1930 price indices

Year	Cost of Living in Rio (1919 = 100)	Implicit GDP Deflator (1939 = 100)
1889	15.6	–
1890	16.8	–
1891	21.5	–
1892	30.8	–
1893	32.9	–
1894	31.9	–
1895	30.2	–
1896	38.6	–
1897	45.8	–
1898	48.3	–
1899	47.4	–
1900	41.1	–
1901	33.8	–
1902	31.2	–
1903	31.8	–
1904	33.7	–
1905	30.2	–
1906	36.8	–
1907	34.9	–
1908	35.7	40.0
1909	33.9	39.3
1910	31.5	41.0
1911	35.1	41.9
1912	37.9	45.0
1913	37.2	40.0
1914	35.1	34.7
1915	50.0	39.3
1916	52.7	47.5
1917	63.9	51.7
1918	95.9	56.0
1919	100.0	60.9
1920	109.8	72.5
1921	92.6	61.4
1922	89.2	67.0
1923	120.5	87.2
1924	148.4	96.8
1925	160.2	114.6
1926	144.7	93.9
1927	147.8	91.8
1928	148.1	108.4
1929	156.2	98.4
1930	127.7	86.5

Sources: Cost of Living in Rio from Villela, A.V. and W. Suzigan, *op. cit.*, Table VII, p. 424. Implicit GDP Deflator from Haddad, C.L.S., *op. cit.*, Table 76, p. 191.

Table A.4   Brazil: 1901–30, foreign trade indices (1928 = 100)

Year	Quantity Indices		Price Indices		Terms of Trade	Capacity to Import
	Imports	Exports	Imports	Exports		
1901	29.8	73.4	40.8	29.5	72.3	53.1
1902	31.0	70.9	41.2	26.1	63.3	44.9
1903	31.7	69.2	41.6	27.0	64.9	44.9
1904	32.2	60.6	43.1	32.2	74.7	45.3
1905	37.8	65.5	32.6	36.4	81.0	53.1
1906	39.6	77.5	34.2	26.0	76.0	58.9
1907	45.4	82.7	38.5	26.2	68.1	56.3
1908	40.3	73.5	38.1	24.2	63.5	46.7
1909	43.1	79.8	37.2	32.1	86.3	68.9
1910	53.8	63.8	35.9	37.1	103.3	65.9
1911	59.2	66.3	36.3	38.2	105.2	69.7
1912	70.3	72.2	36.6	39.1	106.8	77.1
1913	69.2	76.6	39.4	32.5	82.5	63.2
1914	37.7	68.1	40.4	27.9	69.1	47.1

continued on p. 178

Table A.4   continued

Year	Quantity Indices		Price Indices		Terms of Trade	Capacity to Import
	Imports	Exports	Imports	Exports		
1915	28.8	90.7	54.8	28.0	52.7	47.8
1916	31.4	80.1	69.9	35.8	51.2	41.0
1917	25.0	85.2	90.9	35.3	38.8	33.1
1918	25.2	71.0	106.1	40.3	38.0	27.0
1919	36.7	95.6	98.3	57.4	58.4	55.8
1920	48.0	86.6	117.8	51.0	43.3	37.5
1921	33.2	86.7	137.9	49.7	36.0	31.2
1922	40.8	93.1	109.5	63.1	57.6	53.6
1923	54.9	102.1	111.7	81.4	72.9	74.4
1924	73.3	92.3	103.0	105.5	102.4	94.5
1925	86.8	90.8	105.3	111.5	105.9	96.2
1926	84.3	90.0	86.8	89.3	102.9	92.6
1927	84.0	99.9	105.5	91.9	87.1	87.0
1928	100.0	100.0	100.0	100.0	100.0	100.0
1929	101.3	105.2	94.2	92.4	98.1	103.2
1930	62.9	111.5	100.9	65.7	65.1	72.6

Source: Villela, A.V. and W.Suzigan, *op. cit.*, Table XX, p. 441.

Table A.5 Brazil: 1889–1930, commodity composition of exports (in percentages over total value of exports)

Year	Coffee	Traditional Primary Exports Rubber	Traditional Primary Exports Other[a]	Total	Other Exports
1889	66.5	9.8	17.7	94.0	6.0
1890	67.7	9.7	16.7	94.1	5.9
1891	64.7	9.9	20.4	95.0	5.0
1892	71.4	9.8	14.2	95.4	4.6
1893	67.8	10.6	17.5	95.9	4.1
1894	68.5	11.7	15.6	95.8	4.2
1895	68.7	15.5	12.2	96.4	3.6
1896	69.4	13.3	12.8	95.5	4.5
1897	63.8	16.3	16.1	96.2	3.7
1898	55.3	21.3	18.3	94.9	5.1
1899	56.6	24.0	14.2	94.8	5.2
1900	56.9	19.6	19.1	95.6	4.4
1901	59.0	21.2	16.1	96.3	3.7
1902	55.8	20.0	19.2	95.0	5.0
1903	51.7	26.4	16.2	94.3	5.7
1904	50.6	28.4	15.8	94.8	5.2
1905	48.0	32.3	14.6	94.9	5.1
1906	52.0	26.5	16.8	95.3	4.7
1907	52.7	25.3	16.9	94.9	5.1
1908	52.2	26.7	15.8	94.7	5.3

continued on p. 180

Table A.5 continued

Year	Coffee	Traditional Primary Exports Rubber	Traditional Primary Exports Other[a]	Total	Other Exports
1909	52.5	29.7	13.6	95.8	4.2
1910	42.3	39.1	14.2	95.6	4.4
1911	60.4	22.5	12.7	95.6	4.4
1912	62.4	21.6	11.9	95.9	4.1
1913	62.3	15.9	17.3	95.5	4.5
1914	57.7	15.1	20.9	93.7	6.3
1915	59.7	13.0	20.4	93.1	6.9
1916	51.9	13.3	21.9	87.1	12.9
1917	36.6	11.9	24.5	73.0	27.0
1918	31.1	6.6	28.0	65.7	34.3
1919	56.3	4.9	21.1	82.3	17.7
1920	49.1	3.3	25.9	78.3	21.7
1921	59.6	2.1	21.1	82.8	17.2
1922	64.5	2.1	21.2	87.8	12.2
1923	64.4	2.5	19.1	86.0	14.0
1924	75.8	2.1	12.1	90.0	10.0
1925	72.0	4.9	14.6	91.5	8.5
1926	73.8	3.6	13.9	91.3	8.7
1927	70.7	3.2	16.9	90.8	9.2
1928	71.5	1.5	16.8	89.8	10.2
1929	71.0	1.6	15.7	88.3	11.7
1930	62.6	1.2	17.6	81.4	18.6

(a) Includes sugar, raw cotton, cocoa, tobacco, maté, leather and furs.
Source: Brazil. Anuário Estatístico do Brasil, 1939–40, cit., Table III.7, pp.1377–78.

Table A.6 World coffee production, stocks and prices: 1889–1930

Year	Production (in million bags)				World Stocks on June 30th (in million bags)			Prices	
	São Paulo	Brazil	Mild Countries	World Total	'Visible' Stocks	Brazil Interior	World Total	Brazil (milréis per 10 kg)	New York (cents per pound)
1889	1.87	4.40	4.01	8.42	2.43	—	2.43	6.65	16.00
1890	2.91	5.52	3.76	9.28	1.90	—	1.90	8.15	19.00
1891	3.65	7.69	4.24	11.94	2.99	—	2.99	10.10	20.00
1892	3.21	6.53	4.74	11.27	3.16	—	3.16	12.20	14.00
1893	1.72	5.04	4.36	9.40	2.16	—	2.16	15.80	16.40
1894	3.98	7.23	4.53	11.76	3.06	—	3.06	14.70	14.70
1895	3.09	6.00	4.39	10.39	2.49	—	2.49	14.20	16.60
1896	5.10	9.31	4.60	13.91	3.98	—	3.98	10.70	11.10
1897	6.16	11.21	4.84	16.05	5.44	—	5.44	8.55	7.50
1898	5.58	9.32	4.40	13.72	6.18	—	6.18	7.30	6.50
1899	5.70	9.42	4.38	13.80	5.73	—	5.73	7.80	6.70
1900	7.97	11.28	3.78	15.07	6.83	—	6.83	5.85	6.40
1901	10.16	16.14	3.64	19.79	11.30	—	11.30	4.65	6.40
1902	8.35	12.94	3.72	16.66	11.87	—	11.87	4.20	6.60
1903	6.39	11.10	4.89	15.99	12.28	—	12.28	4.90	7.00

continued on p. 182

Table A.6 World coffee production, stocks and prices: 1889–1930

Year	Production (in million bags)				World Stocks on June 30th (in million bags)			Prices	
	São Paulo	Brazil	Mild Countries	World Total	'Visible' Stocks	Brazil Interior	World Total	Brazil (milréis per 10 kg)	New York (cents per pound)
1904	7.43	10.52	3.92	14.44	11.22	—	11.22	5.15	8.10
1905	6.98	10.84	3.95	14.79	9.70	—	9.70	4.25	8.60
1906	15.39	20.19	3.60	23.78	16.38	—	16.38	not quoted	7.90
1907	7.20	11.00	3.86	14.86	14.13	—	14.13	3.45	7.60
1908	9.53	12.91	4.00	16.91	12.82	—	12.82	3.40	8.34
1909	12.12	15.32	3.80	19.12	13.73	—	13.73	3.80	8.80
1910	8.46	10.85	3.68	14.52	11.08	—	11.08	5.85	10.40
1911	10.58	13.04	4.34	17.37	11.00	—	11.00	7.55	14.18
1912	9.47	12.13	4.91	17.05	10.29	—	10.29	6.90	16.00
1913	11.07	14.47	5.80	20.26	11.32	—	11.32	5.00	13.17
1914	9.21	13.47	4.39	17.86	7.52	—	7.52	4.30	11.46
1915	11.71	15.96	4.81	20.77	7.08	—	7.08	4.85	9.57
1916	9.94	12.74	3.95	16.69	7.76	—	7.76	5.50	10.55
1917	12.21	15.84	3.01	18.85	11.77	—	11.77	4.15	10.16
1918	7.25	9.71	4.50	14.21	10.02	—	10.02	10.75	12.71
1919	4.15	7.50	7.68	15.18	6.70	—	6.70	14.00	24.78
1920	10.25	14.50	5.79	20.28	8.52	—	8.52	8.00	10.09
1921	8.20	12.86	6.93	19.79	8.59	—	8.59	14.75	10.38
1922	7.05	10.10	5.70	15.89	5.33	—	5.33	20.20	14.30

1923	10.37	14.89	6.87	21.76	5.03	—	5.03	23.50	14.84
1924	9.19	14.59	6.76	21.35	5.00	4.60	9.60	37.00	21.31
1925	10.09	15.46	7.05	22.51	4.46	1.90	6.36	26.00	24.55
1926	9.88	15.85	7.07	22.92	4.42	2.80	7.22	22.80	22.30
1927	17.98	27.12	8.00	35.12	5.30	3.30	8.60	27.00	18.68
1928	8.81	13.62	8.66	22.28	5.33	13.10	18.43	30.50	23.20
1929	19.49	28.23	8.27	36.50	5.57	10.30	15.87	22.50	22.00
1930	10.10	16.55	8.63	25.18	6.38	23.70	30.08	16.25	13.00

Source: Production : Figures for São Paulo and Brazil up to 1909 represent port arrivals at Santos and all Brazilian ports; for the period 1910–1930 the data show actual figures. Figures for the Mild Countries represent exports from other coffee producing countries. Data from Brazil. Departamento Nacional do Café, *Anuário Estatístico*, 1938, *cit.*, p. 14 and table facing p. 264.

World Stocks: Visible Stocks include port stocks in Europe, the United States and Brazil plus coffee afloat from Brazil to the United States and Europe. Brazil Interior stocks represent quantities stored in the Coffee Institute's regulating warehouses. Data from Brazil, Departamento Nacional do Café, *op. cit.*, table facing p. 264 and Rowe, J.W.F., *op. cit.*, Table II, p. 85.

Prices: Brazilian prices are average Santos spot prices for all grades up to 1907 and Santos 7 grade from 1908 onwards during the crop year starting on July 1st of the year shown. New York prices represent average spot prices for all grades in the New York terminal during the crop year starting on July 1st for data up to 1907, and average spot price for the Santos 4 grade in New York during the calendar year from 1908 to 1930. Figures from Brazil, Departamento Nacional de Café, *op. cit.*, p. 173 and table facing p. 264, and Rowe, J.W.F., *op. cit.*, Table IV, p. 86.

Table A.7 São Paulo: 1909–1930, number of trees, new planting and average yield of coffee trees

Crop Year	Number of Trees in Bearing (millions)	New Planting (millions)	Average Yield (kg per thousand trees)
1909–10	696.7	1.5	1043.8
1910–11	696.7	13.0	728.5
1911–12	696.7	20.0	911.1
1912–13	720.9	34.8	788.2
1913–14	722.4	43.0	919.4
1914–15	735.4	-5.9	751.4
1915–16	755.4	-4.4	930.1
1916–17	791.2	19.7	753.8
1917–18	834.2	28.3	878.2
1918–19	828.3	27.3	525.2
1919–20	823.9	49.9	302.2
1920–21	843.6	2.2	729.0
1921–22	871.9	14.8	564.3
1922–23	899.2	81.4	470.4
1923–24	949.1	75.7	655.5
1924–25	951.3	29.3	579.6
1925–26	966.1	35.5	626.6
1926–27	1047.5	77.1	565.9
1927–28	1123.2	173.8	960.5
1928–29	1152.5	36.1	458.6
1929–30	1188.0	-90.5	984.3

Note: New planting in year t equals the difference between the number of trees in bearing in years t+4 and t+3. This is based on the fact that it takes from three to four years for a coffee tree bearing its first commercial crop.

Sources: Mc Creery, W.G. and M.L. Bynum, op. cit., p. 59; Brazil. Departamento Nacional do Café, Anuário Estatístico, cit., p. 40, and Table A.6.

Table A.8 Monthly world coffee prices[1]: 1906–1930 (in US$ cents per pound)

	1906	1907	1908	1909	1910	1911	1912	1913	1914	1915	1916	1917	1918
January	8.62	7.06	8.27	8.02	91.6	13.86	15.43	15.73	12.05	9.98	9.31	10.89	10.61
February	8.37	7.12	8.44	8.36	9.19	13.34	15.45	14.95	12.06	9.89	9.84	10.58	10.53
March	8.31	7.25	8.54	8.76	9.31	13.22	15.70	13.98	11.63	9.86	10.19	9.95	10.91
April	8.09	7.03	8.59	9.06	8.97	12.91	16.20	13.44	11.66	10.22	10.44	10.44	11.15
May	7.28	7.65	8.61	9.09	9.31	12.89	15.92	13.31	11.69	9.98	10.74	10.64	10.88
June	8.22	7.69	8.78	9.31	9.34	13.19	16.11	12.19	12.29	9.53	10.70	10.50	10.88
July	8.31	7.39	8.71	9.06	9.61	13.77	16.08	11.79	11.94	9.50	10.67	10.15	11.43
August	8.44	8.00	8.31	8.76	10.09	13.91	15.61	12.00	12.61	9.39	10.89	10.17	11.47
September	8.31	8.03	8.12	8.69	14.41	14.53	16.22	12.17	11.50	8.84	11.53	9.95	12.70
October	7.75	8.05	8.16	8.81	11.84	16.21	16.73	13.44	10.11	9.03	11.03	9.66	14.40
November	7.44	7.72	8.03	8.79	12.74	16.47	16.47	12.89	10.00	9.35	10.75	9.47	15.25
December	7.19	7.85	7.56	8.91	13.86	16.92	16.04	12.13	10.03	9.31	10.48	9.47	22.25

continued on p. 186

Table A.8 continued

	1919	1920	1921	1922	1923	1924	1925	1926	1927	1928	1929	1930
January	21.69	25.75	9.53	12.26	15.53	16.00	28.25	24.03	19.58	22.10	24.00	14.70
February	21.41	24.75	9.91	12.52	15.94	18.34	27.56	24.08	18.44	22.50	24.60	14.40
March	21.25	24.30	9.48	13.38	15.56	20.18	26.35	23.20	18.13	23.00	24.80	14.20
April	21.43	24.13	9.50	14.64	14.94	19.40	24.47	22.16	17.94	22.60	24.50	14.10
May	23.13	24.19	9.18	14.56	14.70	19.13	22.66	22.38	17.15	23.60	23.80	13.80
June	26.44	23.53	9.47	14.50	14.59	19.02	24.78	22.78	16.91	23.80	23.30	13.20
July	28.60	19.91	9.42	14.54	13.58	20.61	23.75	22.81	16.88	23.80	22.50	13.10
August	29.56	15.83	10.38	14.51	13.88	21.63	23.34	22.50	16.98	23.80	22.20	11.50
September	26.43	13.84	11.50	15.06	14.31	22.81	23.97	22.13	17.75	23.70	22.40	12.10
October	25.63	12.00	11.88	15.10	14.75	24.91	23.09	20.63	20.66	23.50	19.80	13.20
November	26.50	10.98	12.13	15.25	15.13	27.03	23.56	20.75	22.13	23.10	17.70	11.60
December	25.33	9.94	12.19	15.25	15.22	26.68	22.75	20.13	21.66	23.20	15.20	10.50

[1] Monthly averages of New York spot prices. Up to April 1907 prices refer to the Rio-7 grade; afterwards to the Santos-4 grade.

Sources: RC-JC, 1907, p. 109 and Rowe, J.W.F., *op. cit.*, Table IV, p. 86.

Table A.9 Brazil: 1889–1930, yearly exchange rates (90-day sight exchange rate on London, in pence per milréis)

Year	Exchange Rate	Year	Exchange Rate
1889	26.4	1910	16.2
1890	22.6	1911	16.1
1891	14.4	1912	16.1
1892	12.0	1913	16.1
1893	11.3	1914	14.8
1894	10.1	1915	12.6
1895	9.9	1916	12.1
1896	9.0	1917	12.8
1897	7.7	1918	13.0
1898	7.2	1919	14.5
1899	7.4	1920	14.6
1900	9.5	1921	8.4
1901	11.4	1922	7.2
1902	12.0	1923	5.4
1903	12.0	1924	6.0
1904	12.2	1925	6.1
1905	15.9	1926	7.2
1906	16.2	1927	5.9
1907	15.2	1928	5.9
1908	15.2	1929	6.0
1909	15.2	1930	4.9

Source: Brazil. IBGE, Anuário Estatístico do Brasil, 1939–40, cit., p. 1354.

Table A.10 Brazil: 1905–1930, monthly exchange rates (90-day sight exchange rate on London, in pence per milréis)

	1905	1906	1907	1908	1909	1910	1911	1912	1913	1914	1915	1916	1917
January	13.78	17.16	15.41	15.16	15.16	15.14	16.12	16.11	16.26	16.06	13.87	11.56	12.00
February	13.76	16.98	15.41	15.16	15.16	15.08	16.01	16.11	16.22	16.05	12.75	11.67	11.89
March	14.58	16.19	15.16	15.16	15.06	15.06	16.01	16.14	16.14	15.89	13.01	11.73	11.84
April	16.06	15.37	15.16	15.16	15.14	15.45	16.05	16.19	16.08	15.83	12.20	11.64	12.05
May	16.42	15.70	15.19	15.16	15.09	15.84	16.16	16.11	16.09	15.86	12.28	12.05	13.31
June	16.19	16.59	15.19	15.16	15.09	16.34	16.09	16.14	16.05	16.05	12.42	12.30	13.66
July	16.64	16.86	15.20	15.16	15.09	16.65	16.09	16.16	16.06	15.81	12.83	12.59	13.36
August	17.53	16.86	15.26	15.16	15.09	17.06	16.11	16.14	16.08	13.53	12.31	12.56	13.05
September	17.24	16.37	15.19	15.16	15.11	17.81	16.18	16.14	16.08	11.95	12.09	12.36	12.86
October	15.92	15.44	15.19	15.16	15.19	17.37	16.20	16.20	16.08	12.56	12.25	12.19	13.05
November	16.44	15.47	15.19	15.16	15.26	17.22	16.20	16.28	16.08	13.59	12.25	12.00	13.12
December	16.72	15.39	15.20	15.16	15.25	16.16	16.20	16.23	16.08	14.05	12.09	11.97	13.69

	1918	1919	1920	1921	1922	1923	1924	1925	1926	1927	1928	1929	1930
January	13.75	13.08	17.73	9.72	7.50	5.94	6.17	5.92	7.42	5.86	5.95	5.95	5.62
February	13.42	13.16	18.22	9.75	7.58	5.94	6.73	5.69	7.34	5.91	5.96	5.95	5.64
March	13.34	13.25	17.51	9.39	7.76	5.75	6.45	5.62	7.20	5.91	5.96	5.93	5.79
April	13.11	13.58	16.37	8.51	7.69	5.56	6.28	5.44	7.03	5.87	5.96	5.94	5.87
May	13.05	14.42	16.37	8.33	7.64	5.44	6.09	5.23	7.36	5.89	5.96	5.94	5.88
June	12.98	14.52	15.00	7.81	7.62	5.47	6.01	5.50	7.73	5.89	5.96	5.94	5.71
July	12.22	14.51	14.14	7.17	7.51	5.48	6.01	5.70	7.75	5.87	5.94	5.94	5.40
August	12.28	14.42	13.67	7.95	7.37	5.19	5.45	5.70	7.67	5.89	5.95	5.94	5.05
September	12.14	14.50	12.51	8.23	6.94	5.20	5.33	6.08	7.58	5.91	5.95	5.94	5.14
October	12.51	14.72	12.14	8.12	6.31	5.08	5.47	6.76	7.01	5.94	5.96	5.94	5.29
November	13.51	16.48	11.58	7.86	6.56	4.84	6.06	7.42	6.42	5.92	5.96	5.87	5.23
December	13.70	17.64	10.45	7.67	6.28	5.22	6.01	7.31	5.94	5.94	5.94	5.66	5.46

Source: Brazil. Camara Syndical dos Corretores de Fundos Públicos da Capital Federal, *Relatório*, Imprensa Nacional, Rio de

Table A.11 Brazil: 1889–1930, main identifiable balance of payments items (in $ millions)

Year	Exports	Imports	Trade Balance[a]	Interest on Public Debt[b]	Balance of Current Account Items	New Long-Term[c] Public Loans	Amortization of Public Debt	Balance of Capital Account Items	Total Balance
1889	28552	24002	4550	1000	3550	19837	8027	11810	15360
1890	26382	24019	2363	1319	1044	—	208	–208	836
1891	27136	25565	1571	1309	262	—	318	–318	–56
1892	30854	26302	4552	1294	3258	—	399	–399	2859
1893	32007	26215	5792	1464	4328	2857	403	3307	7635
1894	30491	27145	3346	1448	1898	—	558	–558	1340
1895	32586	29212	3374	1423	1951	4305	564	4868	6819
1896	28333	27880	453	1942	–1489	—	615	–615	–2104
1897	25883	22990	2893	1907	986	—	1743	–1743	–757
1898	25019	23536	1483	1078	405	—	1574	–1574	–1169
1899	25545	22563	2982	375	2607	—	1196	–1196	1411
1900	33163	21409	11754	453	11301	—	706	–706	10595
1901	40662	21377	19285	1312	17973	1001	216	785	18758
1902	36437	23279	13158	2357	10801	—	227	–227	10574
1903	36883	24208	12675	2860	9815	7860	419	7441	17256
1904	39430	25915	13515	3000	10515	1735	464	1271	11786
1905	44643	29830	14813	3204	11609	5855	656	5199	16808
1906	53059	33204	19855	4189	15666	9161	657	8504	24170
1907	54177	40528	13649	4742	8907	5366	2060	3306	12213
1908	44155	35491	8664	8284	380	6263	3396	2867	3247

continued on p. 190

Table A.11   continued

Year	Exports	Imports	Trade Balance[a]	Interest on Public Debt[b]	Balance of Current Account Items	New Long-Term[c] Public Loans	Amortization of Public Debt	Balance of Capital Account Items	Total Balance
1909	63724	37139	26585	6904	19681	3802	2214	1588	21269
1910	63092	47872	15220	6473	8747	15505	3624	11881	20628
1911	66839	52822	14017	6959	7058	8697	5975	2722	9780
1912	74649	63425	11224	6944	4280	3669	4857	-1158	3122
1913	65451	67166	-1715	7596	-9311	19133	6913	12212	2901
1914	46803	35473	11060	7505	3555	4200	1498	2252	5807
1915	53951	30088	23863	4977	18886	—	2616	-2616	16270
1916	56462	40369	16093	5417	10676	270	1435	-1165	9511
1917	63031	44510	18521	6540	11981	—	3078	-3078	8903
1918	61168	52817	8351	8264	87	—	5212	-5212	-5125
1919	131133	80275	50858	8555	42303	2730	3657	-927	41376
1920	111496	119652	-8156	10799	-18955	—	2826	-2826	-21781
1921	58262	59060	-798	9540	-10338	23471	1670	21801	11463
1922	82655	58785	23870	10928	12942	9751	2300	7271	20213
1923	73635	50952	21681	9763	11918	—	2078	-2078	9840
1924	95671	72249	23422	9395	14027	—	1939	-1939	12088
1925	102875	84443	18432	8349	10083	3000	1782	1218	8865
1926	94254	79876	14378	8846	5532	25788	1773	24015	29547
1927	88689	79634	9055	10415	-1360	23972	2889	21083	19723

1928	97426	90669	6757	12400	−5643	23506	4509	18997	13354
1929	94831	86653	8178	13239	−5061	2500	5560	−3060	−8121
1930	65746	53619	12127	13509	−1382	17849	6131	11718	10336

Notes:

(a) The trade balance actually approximates the value of the balance of merchandise trade plus outpayments for insurance and freights since in Brazilian trade statistics exports were valued FOB while imports were valued CIF, and the share of total foreign trade carried by Brazilian merchant ships was quite small.

(b) Includes annual commissions and fees paid to the issuing banks.

(c) Nominal value of all Federal, State, Municipal and coffee long-term foreign loans issued during the year net of the usual discount and commissions charged by the underwriting banks. It excludes all funding loans issued for payments of current interest and amortization on past loans, the 1901 issue of Rescission Bonds for purchase of foreign owned interest-guaranteed railways, and the 1908 and 1922 coffee loans for purchase of foreign held short-term coffee bills financing the stocks bought in 1907 and 1921, respectively.

Sources: Brazil. IBGE, *Anuário Estatístico do Brasil, 1939–40*, pp. 1358–59, and Bouças, V.F., *op. cit.*, passim. The values in pounds sterling of constant gold parity taken from these sources were converted to current "paper", pound value, for the period 1918–1925, using the exchange rates given in Brazil. IBGE, *Anuário Estatístico do Brasil, 1939–40*, p. 1359 and in Table A.9, above.

Table A.12 Brazil: 1890–1930, yearly revenue and expenditure of the federal government
(in thousand contos)

Year	Budgeted Revenue	Budgeted Expenditure	Surplus (+) or Deficit (–)	Effective Revenue	Effective Expenditure	Surplus (+) or Deficit (–)	Index of Real Effective Deficit at 1939 Prices (1908=100)
1890	150.8	151.2	0.4	195.2	220.6	–25.4	n.a
1891	150.8	151.2	0.4	228.9	220.6	8.3	n.a
1892	208.0	205.9	2.1	227.6	279.3	51.7	n.a
1893	233.3	211.6	21.7	159.8	300.6	–40.8	n.a
1894	233.5	250.6	17.1	165.0	372.7	–107.7	n.a
1895	270.2	295.7	–25.5	307.7	344.7	–37.0	n.a
1896	354.6	296.0	58.6	346.2	368.9	–22.7	n.a
1897	339.3	313.2	26.1	303.4	379.3	–75.9	n.a
1898	342.6	324.6	18.0	324.0	668.1	–344.1	n.a
1899	351.1	346.0	5.1	320.8	295.4	25.4	n.a
1900	508.8	393.3	111.5	307.9	433.5	–126.6	n.a
1901	453.4	351.1	102.3	304.5	334.5	–30.0	n.a
1902	360.8	318.4	42.4	343.8	297.7	46.1	n.a
1903	341.3	338.7	2.6	415.4	363.2	52.2	n.a
1904	359.4	362.2	–2.8	442.8	463.5	–20.7	n.a
1905	371.0	381.5	–10.5	401.0	374.9	26.1	n.a
1906	382.6	369.2	13.4	431.7	423.4	8.3	n.a
1907	457.6	409.1	48.1	536.1	522.2	13.9	n.a
1908	435.9	447.6	–11.9	441.2	511.0	–69.8	100
1909	463.0	422.3	40.7	449.9	518.3	–68.4	100

Year							
1910	501.0	446.1	54.9	524.8	623.5	−98.7	138
1911	490.2	503.8	−13.6	563.5	681.9	−118.4	162
1912	517.6	547.4	−29.8	615.4	789.2	−173.8	221
1913	579.9	628.3	−48.4	654.4	762.9	−108.5	155
1914	587.2	596.9	−9.7	423.2	766.7	−343.4	567
1915	523.8	509.7	14.1	404.3	688.5	−284.2	414
1916	589.1	592.7	−3.6	477.9	686.5	−208.6	252
1917	630.0	630.0	—	537.4	801.4	−264.0	293
1918	716.1	642.0	74.1	618.8	867.1	−248.3	254
1919	740.7	674.2	66.5	525.7	931.6	−305.9	288
1920	738.4	735.4	3.0	922.2	1226.2	−304.5	241
1921	873.9	861.0	12.9	891.0	1189.3	−298.3	278
1922	1028.5	(*)	(*)	972.2	1428.3	−456.1	390
1923	1144.8	1124.1	20.7	1269.1	1569.1	−311.0	204
1924	1438.7	1355.1	83.6	1588.4	1629.8	−41.4	24
1925	1389.8	1428.5	−38.7	1741.8	1760.2	−18.4	9
1926	1588.4	1430.9	157.5	1647.9	1867.9	−219.9	134
1927	1799.2	1787.4	11.8	2039.5	2025.9	13.5	−8
1928	2088.9	2088.8	0.1	2216.1	2350.1	−133.6	7
1929	2212.5	2118.6	93.9	2201.2	2422.4	−221.1	129
1930	2283.3	2257.4	25.9	1677.9	2510.5	−832.6	552

(*) The expenditure budget for 1922 was not sanctioned by the President of the Republic.
Sources: DOU, several issues, and Brazil. IBGE, *Anuário Estatístico do Brasil, 1939/40*, *cit.*, p. 1410. The conversion of the part of budgeted revenue and expenditure expressed in "gold" milréis was made at the average exchange rate of the year the budgets were drafted. Last column was calculated using the GDP deflator shown in Table A.3, above.

Table A.13 Brazil: 1890–1930, federal government revenue structure (in thousand contos)

| Year | Tax Revenue | | | | | | Revenue from Public Services | Sundry Items | Total Federal Revenue |
| | Indirect Taxes | | | | Direct Taxes | Total | | | |
	Import Duties	Consumption Tax	Stamp Duty	Other					
1890	101.0	—	9.1	33.5	18.5	161.1	17.8	15.3	195.2
1891	106.8	—	10.4	25.1	23.1	165.4	23.2	31.3	228.9
1892	111.3	0.3	8.4	55.3	9.8	185.1	28.5	14.0	227.6
1893	132.6	0.8	7.0	67.2	7.1	214.8	33.3	11.7	259.8
1894	136.1	0.8	7.5	69.7	4.6	218.7	36.1	10.2	265.0
1895	159.8	0.8	8.9	80.2	2.7	252.4	39.4	15.9	307.7
1896	263.6	1.6	8.5	32.9	3.0	282.6	47.1	16.5	346.2
1897	226.2	2.0	9.4	8.0	2.7	248.3	43.1	12.0	303.4
1898	220.4	13.1	9.0	11.4	3.1	257.0	47.9	19.1	324.0
1899	200.3	25.5	10.2	12.5	5.8	254.0	47.2	19.6	320.8
1900	164.9	36.7	14.5	26.8	5.4	248.3	46.6	13.0	307.9
1901	174.4	31.5	15.2	13.7	5.3	240.1	48.5	16.3	304.9
1902	200.0	34.0	14.0	12.5	4.6	265.8	46.8	31.2	343.8
1903	204.1	35.4	12.6	11.6	4.6	268.3	49.8	97.3	415.4
1904	213.3	35.4	13.1	13.0	4.9	279.7	52.7	110.4	442.8
1905	241.3	35.2	13.9	19.2	5.0	314.6	46.6	39.8	401.0
1906	266.9	43.5	13.7	18.9	5.4	348.4	49.1	34.2	431.7
1907	307.3	48.0	15.2	24.4	6.0	400.9	51.7	83.5	536.1
1908	253.4	44.6	15.6	11.0	5.7	330.5	48.8	62.0	441.3
1909	249.2	45.7	15.7	11.7	2.6	324.9	52.2	72.8	449.9

1910	308.1	54.6	18.6	11.1	3.0	395.4	49.6	79.8	524.8
1911	339.1	59.8	23.1	20.9	3.8	446.7	54.8	62.0	563.5
1912	371.8	62.6	24.8	23.9	4.5	487.6	61.6	66.2	615.4
1913	367.7	65.1	25.5	21.0	4.6	483.9	73.5	97.0	654.4
1914	209.1	52.2	20.1	17.8	3.7	302.9	66.5	53.8	423.2
1915	165.0	67.9	24.7	21.2	16.4	295.2	68.9	40.2	404.3
1916	198.9	83.8	28.2	20.3	18.7	349.9	77.7	50.3	477.9
1917	169.4	117.7	31.1	23.4	23.7	365.3	96.3	75.8	537.4
1918	183.2	119.7	34.1	22.9	12.7	372.6	182.1	64.1	618.8
1919	226.9	131.9	42.4	29.2	9.4	439.8	127.1	58.8	625.7
1920	373.7	175.6	59.6	31.7	10.6	651.2	134.5	136.5	922.2
1921	345.6	154.1	64.4	34.4	18.8	617.3	145.4	128.3	891.0
1922	333.7	165.2	68.2	41.5	26.3	634.9	159.1	178.2	972.2
1923	505.5	258.2	88.3	58.2	41.6	951.8	191.4	114.9	1258.1
1924	607.1	299.1	102.1	133.7	24.2	1166.2	203.4	218.8	1588.4
1925	772.9	312.4	108.7	148.1	34.2	1376.3	222.3	143.2	1741.8
1926	622.3	363.9	116.2	147.7	35.6	1285.7	214.1	148.1	1647.9
1927	871.0	402.9	124.9	148.3	61.3	1608.4	236.3	194.8	2039.5
1928	978.6	440.3	130.7	152.0	70.3	1771.9	286.4	158.2	2216.5
1929	967.3	426.7	136.9	156.7	77.6	1765.1	294.0	142.1	2201.2
1930	652.7	352.2	110.2	153.4	65.5	1334.8	258.4	85.5	1677.9

Sources: Brazil. IBGE, *Anuário Estatístico do Brasil*, 1939–40, *cit.*, pp. 1410–1411, Villela, A.V. and W. Suzigan, *op. cit.*, Table IV, pp. 418–419 and Table V, pp. 420–421, and Brazil, Ministério da Fazenda, *Balanço Geral da União*, 1927, *cit.*, pp. 251–303.

Table A.14 Brazil: 1890–1930, federal government expenditure structure
(in thousand contos)

	Consumption	Debt Service	Gross Fixed Capital Formation	Subsidies and Transfers	Other	Total
1890	134.1	54.5	23.8	8.2	–	220.6
1891	142.5	50.7	17.2	10.2	–	220.6
1892	192.4	51.7	25.1	10.1	–	279.3
1893	208.0	59.2	23.1	10.2	–	300.6
1894	293.3	48.4	19.3	11.6	–	372.7
1895	250.9	60.3	21.4	12.1	–	344.7
1896	272.9	59.4	22.9	13.7	–	368.9
1897	288.6	64.9	12.1	13.7	–	379.3
1898	274.6	355.4	24.7	13.4	–	668.1
1899	182.0	63.8	17.4	14.5	17.7	295.4
1900	228.4	179.9	10.8	14.4	–	433.5
1901	218.4	92.0	8.7	15.4	–	334.5
1902	186.4	84.8	10.7	15.8	–	197.7
1903	201.6	91.9	32.7	15.2	21.8	363.2
1904	196.1	108.0	76.9	17.1	65.3	463.5
1905	206.6	97.1	53.2	18.0	–	374.9
1906	242.6	105.4	57.6	17.8	–	423.4
1907	291.4	108.1	103.4	19.3	–	522.2
1908	295.3	105.8	79.2	18.9	11.7	511.0
1909	304.8	127.5	67.4	18.6	–	518.3
1910	319.8	168.9	113.5	21.3	–	623.5
1911	379.8	139.1	138.4	24.6	–	681.9
1912	408.8	144.4	189.4	34.8	11.8	789.2
1913	392.9	164.8	166.3	38.9	–	762.9
1914	414.0	138.0	164.8	49.9	–	766.7
1915	322.2	170.0	148.7	47.6	–	688.5
1916	232.7	261.5	149.0	43.3	–	686.5
1917	242.8	299.7	189.9	69.1	–	801.4
1918	288.7	256.7	252.3	69.4	–	867.1
1919	369.8	248.7	238.5	74.6	–	931.6
1920	511.5	327.5	295.6	92.1	–	1226.7
1921	567.3	243.8	305.6	72.5	–	1189.3
1922	681.3	303.9	367.1	76.0	–	1428.3
1923	960.3	464.4	58.0	72.3	14.1	1569.1
1924	986.0	477.5	91.3	75.0	–	1629.8
1925	1087.8	468.2	125.0	79.2	–	1760.2
1926	1187.8	446.3	155.0	78.6	–	1867.7
1927	1247.9	627.9	74.9	81.1	–	2025.9

Table A.14   continued

	Consumption	Debt Service	Gross Fixed Capital Formation	Subsidies and Transfers	Other	Total
1928	1337.2	775.5	124.5	112.8	–	2350.1
1929	1453.4	731.5	116.3	121.2	–	2422.4
1930	1860.3	419.2	113.0	118.0	–	2510.5

Note: Figures from 1915 to 1922 represent budgeted expenditures. The effective figures for these years are not available.
Sources: Table A.12, above, and Villela, A.V. and W. Suzigan, op. cit., Table 11, pp. 414–415.

Table A.15   Brazil: 1890–1930, outstanding issue of long-term federal bonds (in thousand contos)

1890	539	1911	620
1891	537	1912	678
1892	542	1913	726
1893	537	1914	759
1894	535	1915	782
1895	534	1916	864
1896	636	1917	938
1897	637	1918	1012
1898	637	1919	1042
1899	637	1920	1113
1900	511	1921	1344
1901	571	1922	1447
1902	570	1923	1778
1903	564	1924	2032
1904	581	1925	2138
1905	569	1926	2096
1906	558	1927	2162
1907	553	1928	2162
1908	547	1929	2450
1909	559	1930	2534
1910	592		

Source: Brazil. Ministério da Fazenda. Resenha Estatística da Caixa de Amortização, 1960/61, quoted in Ferreira, E.F., Administração da Dívida Pública e a Política Monetária no Brasil, IBMEC, Rio de Janeiro, 1974, p. 12.

Table A.16 Brazil: 1889–1930, the money stock and its components (in thousand contos)

End of period	Outstanding Note issue	Cash Held by the Banco do Brasil	Cash Held by Other Banks			Cash Held by the Public	Sight Deposits			Money Stock (M_1)	Rate of Growth of Money Stock (%)
			Till Money	Deposits at the Banco do Brasil	Total		Banco do Brasil	Other Banks	Total		
1889	218.9	9.7	60.4	18.0	78.4	148.8	25.8	95.8	121.6	270.4	–
1890	335.0	12.3	107.6	34.6	142.4	214.8	55.4	268.5	323.9	538.7	99.2
1891	501.3	28.3	138.2	23.9	162.1	334.8	91.2	385.4	476.6	811.4	50.6
1892	552.7	21.7	117.0	7.7	124.7	414.0	80.9	225.2	306.1	720.1	–11.2
1893	617.4	19.1	122.6	8.5	131.1	475.7	70.0	187.7	257.7	733.4	1.8
1894	694.9	34.3	173.3	10.9	184.2	487.3	77.2	220.8	298.0	785.3	7.1
1895	687.7	39.7	157.8	10.1	167.9	490.2	82.6	228.9	311.5	801.7	2.1
1896	714.5	31.3	192.7	9.8	202.5	490.5	86.1	243.9	330.0	820.4	2.3
1897	757.2	24.2	211.2	3.9	215.1	521.8	84.9	278.5	363.3	885.1	7.9
1898	773.9	25.9	189.5	3.5	193.0	558.5	80.8	273.8	354.6	913.1	3.2
1899	732.4	21.9	166.5	2.1	168.6	544.1	79.1	246.6	325.7	869.8	–4.7
1900	701.9	21.3	149.4	4.3	153.7	531.2	33.2	169.3	202.5	733.7	–15.6
1901	682.6	28.6	139.9	1.7	141.6	514.1	16.2	147.5	163.7	677.8	–7.6
1902	676.2	41.5	118.4	0.3	188.7	516.3	20.2	149.5	169.8	686.1	1.2
1903	675.0	44.7	107.2	–	107.2	523.1	27.8	133.0	160.7	683.8	–0.3
1904	673.3	61.0	93.7	–	93.7	518.6	59.9	146.6	206.5	725.0	6.0
1905	669.5	58.3	103.8	–	103.8	507.3	60.8	158.2	218.9	726.3	0.2
1906-I	668.3	43.7	99.5	·	99.5	525.1	46.1	154.4	200.5	726.7	–0.1
1906-II	674.6	32.7	93.1	–	93.1	548.7	33.8	151.7	185.6	734.3	1.1
1906-III	689.4	26.5	90.7	–	90.7	572.2	29.4	157.1	186.6	758.8	3.3
1906-IV	705.0	25.0	89.9	–	89.9	590.1	27.4	160.3	187.6	777.7	2.5
1907-I	721.1	22.1	91.2	–	91.2	607.8	31.7	166.9	198.6	806.4	3.6
1907-II	736.6	23.0	94.0	–	94.0	619.5	41.9	175.9	217.8	837.4	3.8
1907-III	744.0	32.5	99.9	–	99.9	611.6	61.8	182.3	244.2	855.7	2.2
1907-IV	742.1	47.2	104.0	–	104.0	590.9	80.7	184.3	265.0	855.9	0.0

1908-I	738.6	57.3	105.8	—	105.8	575.5	98.4	186.7	285.1	860.6	0.6
1908-II	734.0	62.6	106.4	—	106.4	565.0	106.1	185.0	291.1	856.1	-0.5
1908-III	729.0	62.8	107.7	—	107.7	558.5	116.3	185.2	301.5	860.0	0.4
1908-IV	726.1	59.6	106.0	—	106.0	560.5	118.7	184.6	303.2	863.8	0.4
1909-I	725.8	48.7	103.9	—	103.9	573.3	114.1	183.6	297.7	871.0	0.8
1909-II	751.0	40.2	110.3	—	110.3	600.5	108.6	188.2	296.8	897.2	3.0
1909-III	776.1	35.3	116.1	—	116.1	624.7	110.1	198.7	308.8	933.5	4.0
1909-IV	821.2	40.7	127.2	—	127.2	653.3	102.6	204.8	307.2	960.5	2.9
1910-I	864.9	47.4	138.2	—	138.2	679.4	99.7	221.8	321.5	1000.8	4.2
1910-II	903.4	52.0	146.4	—	146.4	705.0	104.7	239.8	344.4	1049.4	4.8
1910-III	911.4	48.5	147.1	—	147.1	715.7	108.5	248.9	357.5	1073.2	2.3
1910-IV	924.4	52.7	154.8	—	154.8	717.0	114.6	260.9	375.5	1092.4	1.8
1911-I	926.0	53.4	159.4	1.2	160.6	713.2	127.1	286.8	413.9	1127.1	3.2
1911-II	935.6	47.4	164.9	1.8	166.7	723.4	133.8	306.3	440.1	1163.5	3.2
1911-III	947.2	46.1	171.8	1.8	173.6	729.3	138.1	326.6	464.7	1194.1	2.6
1911-IV	963.0	48.1	177.2	1.8	179.0	737.7	140.5	349.9	490.5	1228.1	2.8
1912-I	976.4	46.7	176.0	2.0	178.0	753.7	137.3	365.8	503.1	1256.8	2.3
1912-II	988.5	41.2	171.4	0.6	172.0	775.9	136.1	361.0	497.1	1272.9	1.3
1912-III	993.1	37.3	167.8	—	167.8	788.1	135.2	354.3	489.5	1277.6	0.4
1912-IV	992.3	34.9	165.1	—	165.1	792.3	134.5	345.9	480.5	1272.8	-0.3
1913-I	981.6	35.8	164.7	—	164.7	781.0	137.0	338.7	475.8	1256.8	-1.2
1913-II	964.4	37.1	166.8	—	166.8	760.5	141.5	332.6	474.1	1234.6	-1.8
1913-III	941.9	37.8	171.4	—	171.4	732.6	138.0	325.7	463.7	1196.4	-3.1
1913-IV	922.7	38.3	179.2	—	179.2	705.2	133.6	311.8	445.4	1150.6	-3.8
1914-I	915.4	38.5	188.7	—	188.7	688.2	131.5	289.3	420.7	1108.9	-3.6
1914-II	927.4	36.5	211.8	—	211.8	679.1	126.1	278.1	404.2	1083.3	-2.3
1914-III	947.5	35.3	239.6	—	239.6	672.6	125.1	276.7	401.8	1074.4	-0.8
1914-IV	969.6	32.6	260.2	—	260.2	676.8	113.6	280.8	394.4	1071.2	-0.3
1915-I	993.8	31.0	279.8	—	279.8	683.0	103.8	294.8	398.6	1081.6	1.0

continued on p. 200

Table A.16   continued

End of period	Outstanding Note issue	Cash Held by the Banco do Brasil	Cash Held by Other Banks			Cash Held by the Public	Sight Deposits			Money Stock (M₁)	Rate of Growth of Money Stock (%)
			Till Money	Deposits at the Banco do Brasil	Total		Banco do Brasil	Other Banks	Total		
1915-II	1020.6	29.8	299.8	–	299.8	691.0	91.8	325.8	417.6	1108.6	2.5
1915-III	1047.0	30.6	305.4	–	305.4	711.0	85.0	345.6	430.6	1141.6	3.0
1915-IV	1077.0	30.0	312.8	–	312.8	734.2	72.4	360.2	432.6	1166.8	2.2
1916-I	1111.2	32.6	321.2	–	321.2	757.4	74.8	376.2	451.0	1208.4	3.6
1916-II	1146.8	34.8	320.8	–	320.8	791.2	80.2	405.0	485.2	1276.4	5.6
1916-III	1169.4	36.0	316.8	–	316.8	816.6	84.4	427.0	511.4	1328.0	4.0
1916-IV	1198.2	35.0	313.6	–	313.6	849.6	85.6	460.6	546.2	1395.8	5.1
1917-I	1233.4	34.0	311.8	–	311.8	887.6	91.0	497.2	588.2	1475.8	5.7
1917-II	1274.8	32.4	316.4	–	316.4	926.0	92.0	541.4	633.4	1559.4	5.7
1917-III	1323.9	29.8	337.0	–	337.0	957.0	93.4	587.0	680.4	1637.4	7.3
1917-IV	1392.8	28.2	371.4	–	371.4	993.2	80.6	676.0	756.6	1749.8	6.9
1918-I	1463.0	28.0	397.2	–	397.2	1037.8	72.4	741.4	813.8	1851.6	5.8
1918-II	1534.2	28.2	422.0	–	422.0	1084.0	63.6	825.4	889.0	1973.0	6.5
1918-III	1594.6	37.6	450.0	–	450.0	1107.0	78.4	889.4	967.8	2074.8	5.1
1918-IV	1643.0	49.0	463.4	–	463.4	1130.6	90.2	956.4	1046.6	2177.2	4.9
1919-I	1679.6	58.0	457.0	–	457.0	1164.6	112.4	973.0	1085.4	2250.0	3.3
1919-II	1708.2	64.6	474.4	–	474.4	1169.2	132.8	1009.0	1141.8	2311.0	2.7
1919-III	1727.4	80.2	482.8	–	482.8	1164.4	151.2	1006.4	1157.6	2322.0	0.5
1919-IV	1749.0	81.6	504.8	–	504.8	1162.6	158.6	1025.2	1183.8	2346.4	1.0
1920-I	1773.0	83.6	542.8	–	542.8	1146.6	164.4	1029.0	1193.4	2340.0	-0.2

1920-II	1799.2	90.2	603.0	–	603.0	1105.8	187.2	1045.4	1232.6	2338.4	-0.7
1920-III	1827.0	102.6	668.0	–	668.0	1056.4	212.0	1069.0	1281.0	2337.4	-0.4
1920-IV	1862.0	103.4	724.4	–	724.4	1034.2	286.6	1127.8	1414.4	2448.6	4.7
1921-I	1904.2	113.6	738.4	–	738.4	1052.2	343.2	1062.2	1405.2	2457.4	0.3
1921-II	1953.6	121.0	752.0	39.8	752.0	1080.6	428.4	1146.4	1574.8	2655.4	8.0
1921-III	2012.0	120.0	721.0	67.0	760.8	1171.0	488.4	1233.8	1722.2	2893.2	8.9
1921-IV	2076.0	123.0	682.8	97.6	749.8	1270.2	564.8	1319.2	1884.0	3154.2	9.0
1922-I	2141.6	124.8	624.0	139.6	721.6	1392.8	569.6	1362.0	1931.6	3324.4	5.3
1922-II	2209.0	126.0	601.4	182.0	741.0	1481.6	610.2	1570.2	2180.4	3662.0	10.1
1922-III	2259.4	127.0	564.4	186.2	746.4	1568.0	653.0	1638.2	2291.2	3859.2	5.4
1922-IV	2291.2	129.8	570.8	190.0	757.0	1590.6	675.8	1694.2	2370.0	3960.6	2.6
1923-I	2340.2	121.6	537.6	190.0	727.6	1681.0	676.0	1735.0	2411.0	4092.0	3.3
1923-II	2412.4	127.4	551.0	190.0	741.0	1734.0	703.8	1825.2	2529.0	4263.0	4.2
1923-III	2467.8	123.2	548.0	177.8	725.8	1796.8	697.0	1860.4	2557.4	4354.0	2.1
1923-IV	2534.8	122.8	530.2	170.2	700.4	1881.8	676.8	1877.4	2554.2	4436.0	1.2
1924-I	2665.0	123.8	509.8	151.2	661.0	2031.4	681.0	1905.6	2586.6	4618.0	4.1
1924-II	2768.4	127.8	528.6	137.2	665.8	2112.0	690.8	1949.8	2640.6	4752.6	2.9
1924-III	2816.6	124.4	523.0	149.0	672.0	2169.2	684.4	2008.6	2693.0	4862.2	2.3
1924-IV	2845.4	122.0	520.4	149.2	669.6	2203.0	679.4	2059.2	2738.6	4941.6	1.6
1925-I	2861.4	119.6	537.8	142.8	680.6	2204.0	879.0	2116.2	2795.2	4999.2	1.2
1925-II	2812.8	128.4	539.8	158.4	698.2	2144.6	663.4	2082.8	2746.2	4890.8	-2.1
1925-III	2753.2	140.0	514.6	185.2	699.8	2098.6	641.2	2062.0	2703.2	4803.2	-1.8
1925-IV	2704.8	165.2	527.6	172.6	700.2	2012.0	688.2	1993.4	2681.6	4693.6	-2.2
1926-I	2672.0	174.8	556.4	173.8	730.2	1940.8	708.8	1922.2	2631.0	4571.8	-2.6
1926-II	2638.2	185.4	538.4	184.4	722.8	1914.4	695.8	1864.6	2560.4	4474.8	-2.1
1926-III	2610.6	187.6	542.6	186.6	729.2	1880.4	721.0	1924.2	2645.2	4525.6	1.1

continued on p. 202

Table A.16   continued

End of period	Outstanding Note issue	Cash Held by the Banco do Brasil	Cash Held by Other Banks			Cash Held by the Public	Sight Deposits			Money Stock (M₁)	Rate of Growth of Money Stock (%)
			Till Money	Deposits at the Banco do Brasil	Total		Banco do Brasil	Other Banks	Total		
1926-IV	2591.8	208.4	553.6	184.4	738.0	1829.8	745.2	1973.8	2719.0	4548.8	1.6
1927-I	2595.4	187.6	528.2	190.6	718.8	1879.6	716.6	1992.8	2709.4	4589.0	0.9
1927-II	2677.0	210.2	502.2	198.0	700.2	1964.6	707.0	2091.6	2798.6	4763.2	3.8
1927-III	2801.0	274.2	501.0	212.0	713.0	2025.8	760.6	2181.2	2941.8	4967.6	4.3
1927-IV	2951.8	356.6	504.0	238.8	742.8	2091.2	783.4	2318.6	3102.0	5193.2	4.5
1928-I	3105.2	401.0	499.4	259.6	759.0	2204.8	819.8	2401.2	3221.0	5425.8	4.5
1928-II	3250.4	472.4	513.2	291.2	804.4	2265.0	825.2	2563.0	3388.2	5654.0	4.2
1928-III	3327.6	553.0	495.0	321.4	816.4	2279.6	854.6	2651.6	3506.2	5785.8	2.3
1928-IV	3369.6	615.0	498.2	322.8	821.0	2256.4	840.8	2701.6	3542.4	5798.8	0.2
1929-I	3385.6	639.2	501.8	303.2	805.0	2244.6	827.8	2676.8	3504.6	5749.2	-0.8
1929-II	3395.4	677.6	521.6	293.6	815.2	2196.2	820.2	2680.2	3500.4	5696.6	-0.9
1929-III	3357.8	705.2	520.4	278.0	798.4	2132.2	820.8	2614.6	3435.4	5567.6	-2.2
1929-IV	3254.8	671.4	532.4	259.8	792.2	2051.0	758.4	2538.0	3296.4	5347.4	-3.9
1930-I	3110.2	577.8	545.2	256.0	801.2	1987.2	697.2	2481.4	3178.6	5165.8	-3.3
1930-II	2998.6	500.6	545.6	296.4	802.0	1952.4	647.2	2407.8	3055.0	5007.4	-3.1
1930-III	2888.0	435.6	526.0	255.0	781.0	1926.4	688.4	2298.6	2987.0	4913.4	-1.8
1930-IV	2817.6	381.2	524.6	255.4	780.0	1911.8	757.2	2270.2	3027.4	4939.2	0.5

Sources: Pelaez, C.M. and W. Suzigan, op. cit., Tables A.1, A.2 and A.3, pp. 395 ff. The series presented in this table were smoothed by a moving average process from 1906–I. For that reason, the figures for the Outstanding Note Issue shown above for 1906–1930 differ from the totals presented in Table A.17, as the latter represent actual end of period figures.

Table A.17 Brazil: 1889–1930, breakdown of outstanding note issue by issuing authority (in thousand contos)

End of Period	Treasury	Private Banks of Issue	Conversion Office	Banco do Brasil Rediscount Department	Banco do Brasil Issue Department	Stabilisation Office	Total
1889	207.6	11.3	—	—	—	—	218.9
1890	207.1	127.9	—	—	—	—	335.0
1891	155.2	346.1	—	—	—	—	501.3
1892	206.6	346.1	—	—	—	—	552.7
1893	271.4	346.0	—	—	—	—	617.4
1894	349.5	345.4	—	—	—	—	694.9
1895	346.9	340.8	—	—	—	—	687.7
1896	373.8	340.7(*)	—	—	—	—	714.5
1897	757.2	—	—	—	—	—	757.2
1898	773.9	—	—	—	—	—	773.9
1899	732.4	—	—	—	—	—	732.4
1900	701.9	—	—	—	—	—	701.9
1901	682.6	—	—	—	—	—	682.6
1902	676.2	—	—	—	—	—	676.2
1903	675.0	—	—	—	—	—	675.0
1904	673.3	—	—	—	—	—	673.3
1905	669.5	—	—	—	—	—	669.5
1906-I	669.3	—	—	—	—	—	669.3
1906-II	669.0	—	—	—	—	—	669.0
-III	667.0	—	—	—	—	—	667.0
1906-IV	664.8	—	37.3	—	—	—	702.1
1907-I	664.7	—	83.8	—	—	—	748.5
1907-II	662.2	—	92.2	—	—	—	754.4
1907-III	660.0	—	93.4	—	—	—	758.4

continued on p. 204

Table A.17 continued

End of Period	Treasury	Private Banks of Issue	Conversion Office	Banco do Brasil Rediscount Department	Banco do Brasil Issue Department	Stabilisation Office	Total
1907-IV	643.5	—	99.9	—	—	—	743.4
1908-I	640.8	—	97.8	—	—	—	738.6
1908-II	636.7	—	94.7	—	—	—	731.4
1908-III	635.5	—	92.2	—	—	—	727.8
1908-IV	534.7	—	89.4	—	—	—	724.1
1901-I	634.0	—	85.8	—	—	—	719.8
1909-II	632.4	—	92.9	—	—	—	725.3
1909-III	632.2	—	102.5	—	—	—	734.7
1909-IV	628.4	—	225.2	—	—	—	853.6
1910-I	626.6	—	223.2	—	—	—	849.8
1910-II	624.8	—	320.0	—	—	—	944.8
1910-III	623.8	—	223.2	—	—	—	847.0
1910-IV	621.0	—	304.0	—	—	—	925.0
1911-I	619.0	—	275.6	—	—	—	894.6
1911-II	617.0	—	298.5	—	—	—	915.5
1911-III	614.0	—	337.9	—	—	—	951.9
1911-IV	612.5	—	378.5	—	—	—	991.8
1912-I	611.1	—	371.3	—	—	—	982.8
1912-II	609.7	—	363.6	—	—	—	973.3
1912-III	638.3	—	379.3	—	—	—	987.6
1912-IV	607.0	—	406.0	—	—	—	1013.0
1913-I	605.4	—	408.1	—	—	—	1013.5
1913-II	603.8	—	374.3	—	—	—	987.1
1913-III	602.2	—	316.9	—	—	—	919.1
1913-IV	601.5	—	295.3	—	—	—	896.8

1914-I	601.2	—	244.0	—	—	845.2	—
1914-II	600.4	—	206.4	—	—	806.8	—
1914-III	759.2	—	174.9	—	—	934.1	—
1914-IV	822.5	—	157.8	—	—	980.3	—
1915-I	838.3	—	134.7	—	—	973.0	—
1915-II	839.3	—	103.9	—	—	943.2	—
1915-III	889.6	—	95.7	—	—	985.3	—
1915-IV	982.1	—	94.6	—	—	1076.7	—
1916-I	1015.6	—	94.6	—	—	1110.2	—
1916-II	1040.6	—	94.6	—	—	1135.2	—
1916-III	1060.6	—	94.6	—	—	1155.2	—
1916-IV	1122.5	—	94.6	—	—	1217.1	—
1917-I	1137.5	—	94.6	—	—	1232.1	—
1917-II	1177.5	—	94.6	—	—	1272.1	—
1917-III	1265.3	—	94.6	—	—	1359.9	—
1917-IV	1389.4	—	94.6	—	—	1484.0	—
1918-I	1455.7	—	76.2	—	—	1550.3	—
1918-II	1534.2	—	57.8	—	—	1592.0	—
1918-III	1549.2	—	39.4	—	—	1588.6	—
1918-IV	1679.2	—	20.9	—	—	1700.1	—
1919-I	1709.1	—	20.5	—	—	1729.6	—
1919-II	1729.1	—	20.1	—	—	1749.2	—
1919-III	1729.1	—	19.7	—	—	1748.8	—
1919-IV	1729.1	—	19.3	—	—	1748.4	—
1920-I	1729.0	—	19.3	—	—	1748.3	—
1920-II	1729.0	—	19.3	—	—	1748.3	—
1920-III	1729.0	—	19.3	—	—	1748.3	—
1920-IV	1828.9	—	19.3	—	—	1848.2	—
1921-I	1880.2	—	19.3	40.9	—	1940.4	—

continued on p. 206

Table A.17 continued

End of Period	Treasury	Private Banks of Issue	Conversion Office	Banco do Brasil Rediscount Department	Banco do Brasil Issue Department	Stabilisation Office	Total
1921-II	1879.8	—	19.3	82.6	—	—	1981.7
1921-III	1878.3	—	19.3	140.8	—	—	2038.4
1921-IV	1874.1	—	19.3	151.0	—	—	2044.4
1922-I	1870.0	—	19.3	32.7	—	—	1922.0
1922-II	1865.9	—	19.3	115.1	—	—	2000.3
1922-III	1861.8	—	19.3	160.1	—	—	2041.2
1922-IV	1857.4	—	19.3	336.4	—	—	2213.1
1923-I	1855.7	—	—	312.4	—	—	2168.1
1923-II	1854.0	—	—	399.3	—	—	2253.3
1923-III	1852.3	—	—	399.3	—	—	2251.6
1923-IV	1850.7	—	—	399.3	207.0	—	2457.0
1924-I	1847.5	—	—	399.3(**)	416.0	—	2662.8
1924-II	2243.6	—	—	—	377.1	—	2620.7
1924-III	2240.4	—	—	—	414.2	—	2654.6
1924-IV	2237.1	—	—	—	709.9	—	2947.0
1925-I	2215.2	—	—	—	726.9	—	2942.1
1925-II	2193.2	—	—	—	673.0	—	2866.2
1925-III	2154.1	—	—	—	592.0	—	2746.1
1925-IV	2115.0	—	—	—	592.0	—	2707.0
1926-I	2074.5	—	—	—	592.0	—	2666.5

1926-II	2034.0	—	592.0	—	2626.0
1926-III	2000.0	—	592.0	—	2592.0
1926-IV	1977.3	—	592.0	—	2659.3
1927-I	1977.3	—	592.0	—	2569.3
1927-II	1977.3	—	592.0	9.9	2579.2
1927-III	1977.3	—	592.0	86.7	2656.0
1927-IV	1977.3	—	592.0	435.6	3004.9
1928-I	1977.3	—	592.0	619.7	3189.0
1928-II	1951.7	—	592.0	761.5	3305.2
1928-III	1951.7	—	592.0	791.0	3334.7
1928-IV	1951.7	—	592.0	835.3	3379.0
1929-I	1951.7	—	592.0	850.8	3394.5
1929-II	1951.7	—	592.0	852.3	3396.0
1929-III	1951.6	—	592.0	856.6	3400.2
1929-IV	1951.6	—	592.0	850.7	3394.3
1930-I	1951.4	—	592.0	651.1	3194.5
1930-II	1951.4	—	592.0	340.6	2884.0
1930-III	1951.3	—	592.0	134.1	2677.4
1930-IV	1930.4	—	170.0	128.8	2689.2

(*) In 1897 Treasury notes were substituted for the outstanding private banks' note issue.

(**) In May 1924 the Treasury notes issued by the Banco do Brasil's Rediscount Department became Treasury liability.

Note: Treasury issues between 1921-IV and 1924-IV, and Conversion Office issues from 1917-IV to 1919-IV were linearly interpolated between actual end of year figures.

Sources: Ministério da Fazenda, Balancetes da Caixa de Amortização, in *DOU*, several issues, Brazil, Camara Syndical dos Corretores de Fundos Públicos da Capital Federal, *Relatório*, Imprensa Nacional, Rio de Janeiro, 1902; *RC-JC*, several issues; Banco do Brasil, Balancete da Carteira de Redescontos, in *DOU*, several issues.

Abbreviations

The following abbreviations are used in the endnotes of this book.

BBBM	Arquivo do Banco do Brasil, *Atas das Reuniões de Diretoria*, Brasília.
BBR	Banco do Brasil, *Relatório do Banco do Brasil*, Typ. do Jornal do Commércio, Rio de Janeiro, yearly.
DOU	Brazil, Imprensa Nacional, *Diário Oficial da União*, Rio de Janeiro, daily.
FO 368	Public Record Office, *Foreign Office Files, Brazil, General Correspondence: Commercial*, London.
F0 371	Public Record Office, *Foreign Office Files, Brazil, General Correspondence: Political*, London.
FRUS	United States. Department of State, *Foreign Relations of the United States*, U.S.G.P.O., Washington, yearly.
MFR	Brazil. Ministério da Fazenda, *Relatório Apresentado ao Presidente da República dos Estados Unidos do Brasil pelo Ministro de Estado dos Negócios da Fazenda*, Imprensa Nacional, Rio de Janeiro, yearly.
RA	Archives of N.M. Rothschild and Sons, London.
RC-JC	Jornal do Commércio, *Retrospecto Commercial*, Typ. do Jornal do Commércio, Rio de Janeiro, yearly.
SAJ	*The South American Journal and Brazil and River Plate Mail*, London, weekly.
T 160	Public Record Office, *Treasury Files: Finance*, London.
UK-DCR	United Kingdom. Foreign Office and the Board of Trade, *Diplomatic and Consular Reports (Annual Series): Brazil*, HMSO, London, yearly; title changes.
USNA RG-59	The National Archives of the United States, *Record Group 59: Records of the Department of State Relating to Internal Affairs of Brazil*, Washington.

Notes and
References

Preface

1. See especially C.M. Pelaez, 'As consequências econômicas da ortodoxia monetária, cambial e fiscal no Brasil entre 1889–1945', in *Revista Brasileira de Economia*, (Jul/Sep, 1971). With minor qualifications this view is also put forward in A.V. Villela, and W. Suzigan, *Política do Governo e Crescimento da Economia Brasileria* (IPEA/INPES, Rio de Janeiro, 1973).
2. See, for instance, B. Fausto, *Pequenos Ensaios de História da República (1889–1945)* Cadernos CEBRAP nº 10, 2ª edição (Brasiliense, São Paulo, n.d.) and B. Fausto, *A Revolučao de 1930: historiografia e história* (Brasiliense, São Paulo, 1970).
3. As Fausto puts it, 'the essential fact is that the agrarian-exporting nucleus in spite of attritions, achieved its basic objectives . . . A rapid mention to the valorization plans serves to illustrate how they always triumphed in adverse circumstances thanks, chiefly, to the solid regional basis of São Paulo,' and that 'the maintenance of the exchange rate at low levels [was intended to] proportionate a larger income in national currency to the coffee sector.' B. Fausto, *Pequenos Ensaios de História da República*, pp. 10–11.
4. Such as, for instance, the great gap between the structures of domestic supply and demand, which made the domestic price level extremely dependent on exchange rate variations, or the large share of import taxes in federal revenue and of foreign debt service in expenditure which made the government budget position also very much dependent on the external value of the milréis.

1 The Shaping of the First Republic: an Introduction.

1. See S. Buarque de Holanda, 'Do Império à República', in S. Buarque de Holanda, (ed.), *História Geral da Civilização Brasileira, Tomo II*, volume 5 (Difel, São Paulo, 1972).
2. The classic contemporary references on the economic problems and policies of the period are J.P. Wileman, *Brazilian Exchange* (Galli Brothers, Buenos Aires, 1896) and J.P. Calógeras, *Política Monetária do Brasil* (Cia. Ed. Nacional, São Paulo, 1960) (first edn 1910). See also J.F. Normano, *Brazil, a study of economic types* (Univ. of North Carolina Press, Chapel Hill, 1935). The recent works by C.M. Pelaez, 'As concequências econômicas' and A.V. Villela and W. Suzigan, *Política do Governo e Crescimento* quoted above, also deal with the

211

period. The present appraisal of economic policy-making during the first republican decade is, however, still far from satisfactory, owing basically to the dearth of reliable statistical information.

3. See Table A.16. On the reforms see G.H.B. Franco, 'Reforma Monetária e Instabilidade Durante a Transição Republicana' (unpublished M.Sc. Dissertation, Departamento de Economia, Pontifícia Universidade Católica do Rio de Janeiro, 1982).

4. The halt of foreign capital inflows was not just a consequence of political uncertainties associated with the fall of the Empire but reflected the overall contraction in British foreign lending following the Baring crisis. The Argentine origin of the crisis destroyed the European investor's confidence in South American securities and between 1886–90 and 1891–5 British long-term investments in the continent fell by 82 per cent and, as a proportion of total British foreign lending, from 27.7 to 10.2 per cent. See M. Simon, 'The pattern of new British portfolio foreign investment, 1866–1914', in Adler J.H. (ed.), *Capital movements and economic development* (St. Martin's Press, New York, 1970).

5. For data on coffee mentioned in this section refer to Table A.6.

6. If one bears in mind that there is a period of 3 to 4 years between the planting of a coffee tree and its bearing a commercial crop, the production statistics of Table A.6 clearly show the growth of planting after about 1891. A contemporary observer noted that 'between 1888 and 1898 the number of trees had tripled.' A. Lalière, *Le café dans l'état de Saint Paul, Brésil* (Augustin Challamel, Paris, 1909) p. 36.

7. It should be kept in mind that Brazil derived at that time around two-thirds of her export earnings from coffee. Brazil's dominant position in the world's coffee market can be gauged from Table A.6.

8. Amongst Brazilian economic policy-makers the opinion that there was a negative correlation between the money supply – as crudely measured by the total outstanding note issue – and the exchange rate was almost unanimously held. But as a result of the prevailing universal ignorance about the mechanics of floating exchange rate systems they did not possess a coherent explanation for this relation and even its fundamental causal link in the Brazilian case, namely the effect of credit expansion on imports, was entirely overlooked.

9. See Table A.6.

10. The sterling value of official remittances abroad rose 3.5 times from 1896 to 1897 and in both years they were larger than the trade surplus. For data on the rate of exchange see Table A.9.

11. Prudente de Moraes to Campos Salles, 18.2.1898. Quoted in F. de Assis Barbosa, 'A Presidência Campos Salles', *Luso-Brazilian Review*, vol. V (June 1968) p.4. Indeed the Finance Minister had been for some time sounding Rothschild's opinion on the viability of suspending for some time the foreign debt payments. To that the bankers replied that they would discuss these proposals if the government pledged to build in London a reserve large enough to allow it not to operate in the Rio exchange market for a long period. J.P. Calógeras, *Política Monetária do Brasil*, p. 321.

12. So, if we call:
    t_i — the specific tariff rate on product i
    g — the percentage to be paid "in gold"
    r — the current exchange rate in pence per milréis
    r^* — the formal sterling parity of the milréis, established in 1842 at 27d, the actual specific tariff in milréis, T_i, to be paid by importers would be $T_i = t_i (1\text{-}g) + t_i g \frac{r^*}{r} = t_i (1+ag)$, where a is the market premium on sterling.
13. See J.P. Calógeras, *Política Monetária do Brasil* p. 324. The ruling exchange rate was then a litle over 7d.
14. Ibid. pp. 332–3.
15. This was not part of the July 1899 legislation but as the bankers were later to remind their representative in Rio it resulted from a 'tacit understanding with the Brazilian Government.' N.M. Rothschild & Sons to Lynch (telegram), 15.2.24, in *RA* 111/220 File no. 3. These reserves are usually referred to in the literature as the Paper Money Guarantee Fund.
16. The large note withdrawals occurred up to the end of 1901 as the Treasury drew upon the London loan. From 1898 to 1901 the note issue fell by 12.8 per cent to a level lower than the one it had stood at on December 1894. See Table A.16.
17. See J.P. Calógeras, *Política Monetaria do Brasil* Chapter XX. There is a modern account of the crisis but one which admittedly draws heavily upon Calógeras in P. Neuhaus, 'A Monetary History of Brasil, 1900–1945' (Ph.D. Dissertation, Chicago, 1974) pp. 6–11.
18. D. Joslin, *A Century of Banking in Latin America* (Oxford University Press, 1963) p. 145.
19. J.P. Calógeras, *Política Monetária do Brasil* p. 346. The Banco da República was one of the few and certainly the most important domestic bank operating in the foreign exchange market, the largest share of which was held by the foreign banks since they concentrated their business on the finance of foreign trade and held the majority of foreign companies' accounts. On this see A.S.J. Baster, *The International Banks* (P.S. King and Son, London, 1935) pp. 154 ff.
20. This interpretation of the onset of the crisis is given in D. Joslin, *A Century of Banking*, pp. 144–5. Calógeras misunderstood some of its details. Cf. J.P. Calógeras, *Política Monetária do Brasil*, p. 346.
21. The Brazilian trade balance had a tendency to show a larger surplus in the second half of the calendar year under the influence of coffee exports, for although the picking of the crop starts late in April the necessity of processing the beans at the plantations prevented it from reaching the ports before July. As imports do not follow an identifiable seasonal pattern, being influenced by several short-term factors, the balance had a tendency to move into lower surpluses or small deficits towards the second quarter of the year.
22. See Table A.16. The small reductions in the note issue from 1902 to 1904 seem to have been made mainly on technical grounds.
23. C.J.C. de Almeida, *Banco da República do Brasil: Relatório apresentado ao Exmo. Sr. Ministro da Fazenda pelo Director da Carteira de*

Câmbio, 1902–1906 (Typ. do Jornal do Commércio (Rio de Janeiro, 1906) p. 4.

24. A concise presentation of the debates on the coffee question during the decade preceding the 1906 valorisation scheme is found in T.H. Holoway, *The Brazilian Coffee Valorization of 1906* (Logmark Edition, Madison, 1975) pp.32–43. See also A. de E. Taunay, *Pequena história do café no Brasil* (INC, Rio de Janeiro, 1945) Chapter XX.

25. Given the depressed international price level, the exchange rate rise was the cause of the large fall in milréis export prices between 1898 and 1902. See Tables A.9 and A.6

26. J.P. Calógeras, *Política Monetária do Brasil*, p. 366.

27. See Tables A.12, A.16 and A.17.

28. See V. Viana, *O Banco do Brasil* (Typ. do Jornal do Commércio, Rio de Janeiro, 1926) p. 765.

29. For details of the legislation see J.P. Calógeras, *Política Monetária do Brasil*, pp. 403–07 and V. Viana, *O Banco do Brasil*, Part Nine, Chapters II and III.

30. See, for instance, *MFR*, 1905, p. xxvii.

2. The Pre-war Gold Standard

1. See C.J.C. Almeida, *Banco da República do Brasil*, p. 18.

2. T.H.Holloway, *Brazilian Coffee Valorization*, pp. 44–45. The bill had been submitted to Congress in 1903 but met strong opposition. J.P. Calógeras, *Política Monetária do Brasil*, p. 416.

3. The extent of flowering of the trees in September is the usual indicator on which early forecasts of the size of the next year's crop are based.

4. The average Havre price in 1905 had been 47 francs per bag.

5. This proposal also resulted from more immediate fears that the transfer of the £15 million, in the short time required to effect the surplus coffee purchases, would lead to further appreciation of the milréis.

6. Successive presidential addresses to Congress stressed that large foreign borrowing by the state and local authorities was not a practice to be indulged in because of its destabilising effects on the rate of exchange and the international political consequences of default.

7. *SAJ*, 6.10.1906.

8. As ex-Finance Minister Murtinho publicly stated: 'Those who preach immediate convertibility [below par] accept that the State should act dishonestly. When the rate of exchange reaches its par, not through artificial means nor through the action of accidental circumstances, but through the realities of public wealth, we can then declare convertibility.' *RC-JC*, 1905, p. 174.

9. *MFR*, 1906, pp. iv–xiv.

10. *SAJ*, 5.5.1906.

11. This rate was only slightly below the market rate and was considered to be the equilibrium rate by the Banco do Brasil. Cf. C.J.C. de Almeida, *Banco da República do Brasil*, p. 23.

12. This account of the early negotiations is largely based on T.H. Holloway, *Brazilian Coffee Valorization*, pp. 56–64, and in a U.S. Depart-

ment of State memorandum on the valorisation scheme written ca. 1912 to be found in *USNA RG-59*, 832.61333/99, pp. 4–8.

13. According to a contemporary authoritative estimate these expenditures would amount annually to one and half times the state's revenue in 1905. P. Ferreira Ramos, *La question de la valorisation du café au Brésil*, Conference faite au Cercle d'Etudes Coloniales d'Anvers le 29 Janvier 1907 (Anvers, Imp. J.E. Buschmann, 1907) quoted in T.H. Holloway, *Brazilian Coffee Valorization*, p. 66.

14. Besides the obvious support from domestic producers, the reform was loudly praised by the foreign banks. See *SAJ*, 27.4.1907, and *MFR*, 1908, p. xxi.

15. That the alleged motive behind the creation of the Conversion Office was – quite apart from anything specifically related to coffee valorisation – the willingness to prevent disruptive exchange rate appreciations which the Banco do Brasil was unable to control is plainly stated by the Finance Minister in his 1908 report. See *MFR*, 1908, p. xv.

16. Argentina, Mexico and other minor countries had recently linked their currencies to gold in similar circumstances.

17. A.F. Bloomfield, *Monetary policy under the international gold standard, 1880–1914* (Federal Reserve Bank of New York, New York, 1959).

18. C.J.C. de Almeida, *Banco da República do Brasil*, p. 18.

19. Cf. R. Triffin, *The Evolution of the International Monetary System: Historical Reappraisal and Future Perspectives*, Princeton Studies in International Finance no. 12) (Princeton Univ. Press, Princeton, 1964) pp. 6–8.

20. In Brazil, the reduction of the exportable surplus of the major export products due to domestic demand growth was not significant.

21. The characteristics of these cyclical foreign investment booms typical of the pre-war international economy, and their consequences to the capital importing countries under the gold standard were clearly described by Taussig. See V.W. Taussig, *International Trade* (Macmillan, New York, 1927) p. 130. For a fuller, more recent, apraisal see A.G. Ford, *The Gold Standard: 1880–1914. Britain and Argentina* (Clarendon Press, Oxford, 1962) Chap. VII.

22. Imports of gold by the banks and their deposit in the Office by increasing their cash reserves enabled them to extend themselves. It should be noted in passing that the notes issued by the Office did not circulate freely amongst the public to any large extent, and were held as cash reserves by the banking system. See *Brazilian Review*, 31.12.1907.

23. The effects on the money stock are shown in Tables A.16 and A.17.

24. The construction of complete balance of payments statistics for the period covered by this study is not possible since no reliable data on private remittances abroad on income or capital account are available. Nevertheless an effort was made to estimate the balance of other main foreign transactions. These statistics are shown in Table A.11.

25. See F.C.B. Nunes, and J.R. Silva, *Tarifa das Alfândegas*, vols. I–IV (A. Coelho Branco, Rio de Janeiro, 1929–1932).

26. In June, the Brazilian Minister of Public Works told the British

government's representative in Rio that the federal government had decided to advance the £3 million to São Paulo. Haggard to Grey, 24.6.1907, in *FO* 368/91 23416/650. See also *SAJ*, 6.7.1907, p. 19, and Haggard to Grey, 12.9.1907, in FO 368/91 38838/650.

27. He wrote: 'It is true that if the withdrawal of 7 million bags of coffee should influence the market with a beneficial effect on prices, the inverse result would obtain if the state of São Paulo was coerced by lack of resources to release unreservedly the coffee stored. Having in mind the possibility of this latter circumstance and the unfavourable consequences to the national economy which will result from it, it seems correct to concede the help which . . . the São Paulo government asks'. *MFR*, 1908, pp. 87–8.

28. A brief but enlightening account of the crisis in the London money market can be found in J.H. Clapham, *The Bank of England: A History*, Volume II (Cambridge Univ. Press, 1944) pp. 389–394. See also R.S. Sayers, *The Bank of England 1891–1944*, Volume 1 (Cambridge Univ. Press, 1976), Chapter 4.

29. *UK-DCR*, 1909, p. 17.

30. Evidence on Brazilian loans in London from *Monthly Investor's Manual* 1907 and 1908. On the short-term capital outflows see *MFR*, p. xxii.

31. See Table A.17.

32. J.H. Clapham, *Bank of England*, p. 394.

33. The Banque de France was the lender of last resort for banks responsible for providing a large share of funds for the purchases, since around 40 per cent of the stocks were held by French or Belgian importers. See the statement on the coffee position sent by the Governor of São Paulo to the President of the Republic in the second half of this year, reproduced in *SAJ*, 12.12.1908.

34. The limits were 9 million bags for the 1908 crop year (July 1908–June 1909), 9.5 millions for 1909 and 10 millions for 1910 onwards. The limitation was clearly intended to prevent a fall in the value of the coffee stock which secured the loan and to allow its rapid liquidation, since the proceeds of future sales from the stock would be exclusively devoted to this end.

35. The seven members committee was headed by Baron Schroeder whose firm issued two-thirds of the new loan, and was composed of representatives of other creditors and one man from São Paulo. The latter would have veto powers but could be overruled in arbitration by the Governor of the Bank of England.

36. The effects of these exogenous fluctuations on domestic stability, in the two leading South American countries under the gold standard, were clearly perceived by a contemporary Chilean economist: "Ainsi, par exemple, en 1907, à l'époque de la grande crise monétaire des États-Unis de l'Amérique du Nord, le marché de la République Argentine, qui se trouvait dans la situation la plus tranquille et la plus prospère, se vit obligé cependant a subir une certaine contraction monétaire . . . Aussitôt que la crise monétaire fut passé, l'or revint plus abondamment que jamais dans la République Argentine, où il

était attiré par les bonnes récoltes et par l'inversion des capitaux étrangers. Tout cela prouve que la contraction qui se fit sentir et dont il fallait chercher les causes hors du pays, avait peut-être évitée en adoptant un régime de billets de banque bien organisé. . . . A peu près à la même époque et pour le même motif, il se produisait au Brésil un fait analogue a celui que nous avons observé en Argentine". G. Subercaseaux, *Le Papier-Monnaie* (Giard, Paris, 1920) pp. 418–19.

37. Data on daily exchange rates in Rio are available in Brazil, Câmara Syndical da Junta de Corretores de Fundos Públicos, *Relatório* (Imprensa Nacional, Rio de Janeiro, 1910) The gold import point had also been reduced by the very low interest rates prevailing in London in mid-1909. On this see R. Ortigão, *A Moeda Circulante do Brasil*, Typ. do Jornal do Commércio, Rio de Janeiro, 1914) p. 131.

38. *MFR*, 1910, p. xxvi.

39. *MFR*, 1910, p. xxiii.

40. *SAJ*, 1.1.1910 and 15.10.1910.

41. *MFR*, 1910, pp. xxviii–xxix.

42. *MFR*, 1911, p. 76 and Hambloch to Grey, 3.7.1911, in *FO 368/515* 28759/875.

43. The new President – Hermes da Fonseca, an Army officer – had been elected against fierce opposition by São Paulo politicians and still declared himself in favour of a gradual exchange appreciation. See his interview to a Rio newspaper quoted in *SAJ*, 3.12.1910. However, the choice of the Finance Minister fell on a man who had been one of the signatories of the first coffee valorisation proposal of 1906, and clearly represented a compromise with the opposition to the orthodox view on exchange rate policy. On this see R. Ortigão, *A Moeda Circulante no Brasil* (Typ. do Jornal do Commércio, Rio de Janeiro, 1914), p. 136.

44. See Tables A.12 and A.14.

45. *SAJ*, 24.6.1911 and 1.7.1911.

46. Since Ministry of Finance expenditure was relatively incompressible, budget-balancing cuts in other areas would have to slash one third of their current expenditure, even supposing that revenue remained at the same level.

47. In July 1910 the valorisation stocks were still at 97 per cent of their level at the end of 1908. *SAJ*, 27.8.1910.

48. The restriction had been renewed for another five years in 1907.

49. See Tables A.6 and A.8.

50. Evidence that the Department of State was not informed can be found in Knox to Attorney General, 21.5.1912, in *USNA RG-59* 832.61333/91a.

51. See Table A.8. There can be little doubt that the New York sale was the cause of the 1913 price break. The coffee sold represented about 20 per cent of the normal yearly consumption in the United States and the American share of Brazilian coffee exports fell from 46 percent in 1912 to 36 per cent in 1913; the decrease in imports by the United States in 1913 accounted for 80 per cent of the total fall in coffee exports.

52. See his exposition of the financial outlook at a ministerial meeting in April, reported in *SAJ*, 12.4.1913. Serious efforts to reduce expenditure

began to take shape, especially after Salles's replacement by Rivadávia Corrêa at the Finance Ministry in May, but were insufficient to provide any substantial relief.
53. See Table A.17.
54. American Consul-General to Secretary of State, 12.8.1913, in *USNA RG-59*, 832.51/61.
55. H.M. Legation in Rio, Annual Report for 1913, p. 13, in *FO 371*/1915 5814/1814.
56. Ibid. See also *SAJ*, 16.8.1913.
57. As one of Lord Rothschild's sons who led the mission put it to one American diplomat in Rio 'he and the other members of his house have not been able to ascertain exactly how this country stands today financially inasmuch as the Federal Government has not struck a budget balance for five years, and they are very unfavourably impressed with the indications of waste and extravagance in Government expenditures which are entirely unwarranted by the revenues.' American Consul General to Secretary of State, 7.10.1913, in *USNA RG-59* 832.51/62.
58. This was generally done under pressure from their foreign creditors. See, for instance, *SAJ*, 2.4.1910. In 1912, a government bill making these loans conditional on previous federal approval was defeated in the Senate. Between 1900 and 1912 state and local authorities' foreign indebtedness grew from £5.7 million to £49.1 million and, as a share of total public foreign debt, from 12 per cent to 37 per cent in the same period. Data from Brazil, IBGE, *Anuário Estatístico do Brasil*, 1947, pp. 506–7 and Brazil, Ministério da Fazenda (Secretaria Técnica do Conselho de Economia e Finanças), *Finanças do Brasil*, vol. III (Rio de Janeiro, 1932) pp. 76–81.
59. See Table A.16.
60. *SAJ*, 28.3.1914 and 25.4.1914. See also Morgan to Secretary of State, 30.6.1914, in *USNA RG-59* 832.51/69.
61. The terms were considered unrealistic and unnecessarily high-handed even in some sectors of the British financial press. *The South American Journal*, for instance, in an editorial article on the Brazilian loan negotiations, commented that: 'the implications which may be read into the conditions which have been tentatively put forward by the European bankers as a basis for their financial assistance have been somewhat resented by Brazilian politicians. It is not exactly fair to assume that the Republic is "in extremis", or that its conditions are analogous to those of the turbulent States of Eastern Europe, whose fiscal affairs have passed under the tutelage of the "haute finance." Brazil is no doubt quite prepared to accede to terms sufficiently onerous but consistent with her dignity and the real demands of her position'. *SAJ*, 6.6.1914.
62. The British Foreign Office instructed the Rio legation 'to press the Brazilian Government to meet outstanding British claims out of the proposed new loan and to point out that a continued failure to settle is likely seriously to impair Brazilian credit in England,' and the French Minister in Rio informed the Brazilian government that the loan

'would not be admitted to quotation at Paris unless some arrangement for settlement of French claims were previously made.' See Robertson to Grey, 9.12.1914, in *FO 371*/1916, 9101/27845, and 9.7.1914, in *FO 371*/1916, 31188/27845.
63. Morgan to Secretary of State, 14.7.1914, in *USNA RG-59*, 832.51/70

3 The World War

1. Cf. W.H. Lough, *Financial developments in South American countries*, U.S. Department of Commerce, Special Agents Series no. 103 (USGPO, Washington, 1915) pp. 24–5, and Sommers to Secretary of State, 11.9.1914, in *USNA RG-59*, 832.516/1.
2. W.H. Lough, *Financial developments in South America* p. 24.
3. C. Pacheco, *História do Banco do Brasil (História Financeira do Brasil desde 1808 até 1951)*, vol. IV (AGGS, Rio de Janeiro) p. 72.
4. These loans could only be given on two accounts: either to expand the bank's discount operations against commercial or government paper, thus helping to finance the coffee crop and relieve some government creditors who had received bonds as payment during the pre-war slump or, alternatively, to buy Conversion Office notes or gold at par so as to enable the Banco do Brasil to get hold of the gold backed notes held in the private banking system's cash reserves. On this see *SAJ*, 3.10.1914.
5. See Legislative Decree no. 2863, of 24.8.1914.
6. C. Pacheco *História do Banco do Brasil*, p. 72.
7. Roughly one-third of the bank loans went to the Banco do Brasil, one-fourth to the large Banco Commercial e Industrial de São Paulo, while the rest 'was scattered among the various domestic banks, chiefly in the coffee-growing districts.' W.H. Lough, *Financial Developments in South America* p. 24.
8. *SAJ*, 3.10.1914.
9. See Table A.10.
10. See V.F. Bouças, *Finanças do Brasil*, vol. XIX, Dívida Externa, 1824–1945, Ministério da Fazenda, Secretaria do Conselho Técnico de Economia e Finanças (Rio de Janeiro, 1955) p. 254.
11. See *SAJ*, 19.9.1914, and Morgan to Secretary of State, 22.9.1914, in *USNA RG-59* 832.51/78.
12. The loans included in the agreement represented 84.3 per cent of the outstanding foreign debt of the federal government by the end of 1914. Cf. V.F. Bouças, *Finanças do Brasil*, table facing p. 262.
13. Ibid. p. 256.
14. See Table A.11
15. For a recent endorsement of this traditional view compare, for instance, P. Neuhaus, *Monetary History of Brazil*, p. 40.
16. G. Hardach, *The First World War, 1914–1918* (Allen Lane, London, 1977) p. 13–19.
17. See Table A.4. Coffee exports increased from 11.2 million bags in 1914 to 17.1 million bags in 1915. Cf. *RC-JC*, 1915, p. 7.

18. See G. Hardach, *First World War*, pp. 22–27. The blacklisting of the large German-owned São Paulo coffee exporting firms was probably the most effective measure in this connection.
19. Cf. *RC-JC*, 1915, p.7.
20. *MFR*, 1915, pp. 27–28.
21. Cf. Tables A.12, A.13 and A.14.
22. See Mensagem Presidencial de 1915, in *DOU*, 4.5.1915, and *BBBM*, minutes of meeting of 5.11.1914.
23. Mensagem Presidencial de 1915, in *DOU*, 4.5.1915 and *RC-JC*, 1917, p. 20.
24. 'No solid prediction could made [at the end of 1914] of the duration and the result of the war, just started . . . The state of Federal revenue in 1915 was another question without answer . . . In such an uncertain situation the government could not and should not follow the path of [note] emissions.' *MFR*, 1915, pp. 6–7.
25. The new moratorium regulations provided that 25 per cent of each debt should be settled on January 15, 35 percent on February 15 and the remainder on March 15. See W.H. Lough, *Financial Developments in South America* p. 25.
26. *SAJ*, 2.1.1915.
27. See Decrees no. 11471 of 3.2.1915, no. 11478 of 4.3.1915, and no. 11570 of 5.5.1915.
28. See *SAJ*, 27.3.1915. By August 1915 the bills were reported to be 'unsaleable at 75 per cent of their nominal value.' See Peel to Grey, 9.8.1915, in *FO 371/2294*, A 122521/86594/6.
29. See *BBBM*, minutes of meetings held at 5.12.1914 and 10.12.1914. See also *SAJ*, 27.3.1915.
30. See Table A.16. On the behaviour of the private banks see *BBR*, 1915, pp. 19–20.
31. See *RC-JC*, p. 7.
32. On this see J.M. Bello, *A History of Modern Brazil, 1889–1964* (Stanford U.P., 1966) p. 231, and Peel to Grey, 13.7.1915, in *FO 371/2294*, A 104910/104910/6.
33. 'The loss of custom revenues represents, thus, a lasting situation to the Treasury until the end of the war . . . and there one finds the element which now characterizes as a revenue crisis the difficult situation of the public finances . . . The problem to be solved consists then in keeping budget balance until the normal level of revenue from custom duties is reestablished.' *MFR*, 1915, p. 28.
34. See Table A.14.
35. *MFR*, p. 9.
36. Ibid. p. 15.
37. Ibid. p. 16.
38. See Table A.8.
39. In October 1914, a Bill had been presented by a São Paulo senator on these lines but was opposed on the grounds that the August credit relief measures were sufficient to meet the financial needs of the coffee industry. They were also strongly criticised by the London bankers of both the federal and the São Paulo governments. See *SAJ*, 24.10.1914,

13.3.1915 and 1.5.1915. Compare also Morgan to Secretary of State, 16.9.1915, in *USNA RG-59* 832.515/5.
40. See Table A.6
41. Cf. *MFR*, 1915, pp. 13–14.
42. The aggregate reserve ratio of the private banks stood at 92.0 per cent at the end of the first half of 1915, against the 32.5 per cent of the Banco do Brasil. Data sources are the same as Table A.16.
43. P. Neuhaus, *Monetary History of Brazil* p. 47.
44. For a description of and complaints about some statutory limitations on the Bank's rediscount operations, which actually hampered its ability to help the money market, see *BBR*, 1915, pp. 18–19.
45. On this see C. Pacheco, *História do Banco do Brasil* vol. IV, Chapter IV. The number of Banco do Brasil branches jumped from 7 in 1915 to 37 in 1918. Cf. V. Viana, *O Banco do Brasil* pp. 1032–1033.
46. See Legislative Decree no. 2986 of 28.8.1915 and Executive Decrees no. 11693 and no. 11694, of 28.8.1915. The Executive by-laws stipulated the settlement of the Treasury Bills half in cash and half in *apólices* at a discount of 15%.
47. Of the 350 000 contos issued, apart from the 50 000 handed over to the Banco do Brasil, only 11 000 contos were spent in loans to planters through the Bank, while 153 000 contos went to pay federal arrears and 136 000 contos to meet expenditure relating to the 1915 budget. See *RC-JC*, 1917, p. 20.
48. See Tables A.16 and A.17.
49. See Tables A.3, A.12 and A.14.
50. It should be noted, however, that the data presented in Table A.4 may over-estimate the fall in terms of trade since the export price index is based on the normal, peacetime, composition of exports, which, as shown below, changed considerably during the war.
51. See Tables A.4 and A.11.
52. For data on coffee, see Table A.6.
53. Cf. J.H. Williams, 'Latin American Foreign Exchange and International Balances During the War', *The Quarterly Journal of Economics*, vol. XXXIII (May 1919) pp. 449–50.
54. Cf. *MFR*, 1916, p. 22.
55. The classical statement is to be found in R. Simonsen, *A evolução industrial do Brasil* (Empresa Gráfica Revista dos Tribunais, São Paulo, 1939).
56. See, for instance, W. Dean, *A Industrialização de São Paulo (1880–1945)*(Difel, São Paulo, 1971) Chap. IV; A.V. Villela, 'Surto industrial durante a guerra de 1914–1918', *Ensaios Econômicos: homenagem a Octávio Gouvêa de Bulhões* (APEC, Rio de Janeiro, 1972) and A. Fishlow, 'Origins and Consequences of Import Substitution in Brazil', E.L. Di Marco (ed.), *International Economics and Development: Essays in honour of Raul Prebisch* (Academic Press, New York, 1972).
57. On the behaviour of the Brazilian capital goods industry during the war see L.A.C. Corrêa do Lago, F.L. de Almeida, e B.M.F. Lima, *A Indústria Brasileira de Bens de Capital: origens, situação recente, perspectivas* (FGV, Rio de Janeiro, 1979) pp. 36–55.

58. The apparent consumption of cement fell from 465.3 thousand tons in 1913 to 51.7 thousand tons in 1918. Cf. A.V. Villela, and W. Suzigan, *Política do Governo e Crescimento*, Table XVII, p. 423.

59. As the *Jornal do Commércio* put it, 'the Government succeeded in relieving the congestion of the credit institutions' portfolios, thus allowing the reestablishment of commercial activity. The banks, which were saturated with bills and titles, re-enacted their transactions and the increase in business was noticeable throughout the country. Confidence returned.' *RC-JC*, 1917, p. 11.

60. *MFR*, 1916, pp. 20–1.

61. Ibid. p. 21.

62. See Law no. 3213, of 31.12. 1916.

63. See Decree no. 11741, of 5.2.1915 and Decree no. 11510, of 7.3.1915. Compare also Morgan to Secretary of State, 14.9.1916 in *USNA RG-59* 832.51/22.

64. *MFR*, 1916, p. 4.

65. As stated by the Finance Minister in retrospect, the settlement of these debts 'could unfavourably affect the exchanges . . . and the concern with exchange rate stability had dominated the management of public finances.' *MFR*, 1916, p. 4.

66. See Table A.4.

67. See *MFR*, p. 49.

68. J. Atkin, 'Official Regulation of British Overseas Investment, 1914–1931', *Economic History Review* (July 1970) pp. 324–5.

69. On post-1914 American foreign financial policy see C.W. Phelps, *The Foreign Expansion of American Banks: American Branch Banking Abroad* (The Ronald Press, New York, 1927) Chap VIII and IX, and C.P. Parrini, *Heir to Empire: United States Economic Diplomacy, 1916–1923* (Univ. of Pittsburgh Press, 1969) Chapter V.

70. In his official address to the Conference, McAdoo pointed to 'the imperative necessity for close relations between the American States . . . freed as far as possible from the dangers which constantly menace their economic development through European complications.' See *SAJ*, 20.5.1916.

71. See the British Consul-General Memorandum, dated 13.8.1916, enclosed in Peel to Grey, 17.8.1916, in *FO 368*/1496, A 178535/14225/6.

72. Ibid. See also Peel to Grey, 19.10.1916, in *FO 371*/2640, A 229048/125948/6.

73. Polk to Morgan, 21.10.1916, in *USNA RG-59* 832.51/125.

74. Morgan to Secretary of State, 23.10.1916, in *USNA RG-59* 832.51/313.

75. Vice-Consul (São Paulo) to Secretary of State, 13.5.1916, in *USNA RG-59* 832.00/135.

76. See *DOU*, 13.4.1917 and 6.12.1917, and the Board of Trade Memorandum enclosed in *FO 371*/2690, A 193212/183580/6.

77. On this see the Secret Memorandum by the British War Trade Intelligence Department, dated 5.5.1916, in *FO 368*/1495, A 90845/90845/6.

78. Ibid. See also *SAJ*, 1.4.1916.

79. *SAJ*, 25.3.1916.

80. Cf. Peel to Grey, 6.9.1916, in *FO 371*/2640, A 195196/148395/6.

81. *SAJ*, 18.3.1916. See also the Secret Memorandum prepared by the British Admiralty, dated 23.12.1916, enclosed in *FO 371/2640*, A 252290/183580/6.

82. As the Brazilian Finance Minister expressed it to the American Ambassador in this connection 'the Allied powers are again organizing pressure, as yet of an indirect character, to force Brazil's hand'; he went on to say that 'he would rather resort to another issue of paper money than to yield to pressure.' Morgan to Secretary of State, 14.9.1916, in *USNA RG-59* 832.15/22.

83. A fuller account of the issues discussed in this section is to be found in W. Fritsch, 'Brazil and the Great War: 1914–1918', *Rivista di Storia Economica*, Second Series, vol. II (International Issue), 1985.

84. On this see G. Hardach, *First World War*, pp. 41–3.

85. Ibid. p. 43. The losses from the submarine attacks could only be effectively diminished from mid-1917 with the introduction of the convoy system by the Allies. On this see J.A. Salter, *Allied Shipping Control: an experiment in international administration* (Oxford Univ. Press, 1921) pp. 307–9 and 363.

86. Peel to Balfour, 23.3.1917, in *FO 368/1706*, A 87132/43559/6.

87. *SAJ*, 13.1.1917.

88. See Brazilian Minister of Finance to Rothschilds (telegram), 3.3.1917, enclosed in Rothschild to Balfour, 5.3.1917, in *FO 368/1706*, A 48452/43559/6.

89. Rothschild to Balfour, 5.3.1917, in *FO 368/1706*, A 48452/43559/6.

90. See the relevant papers in *FO 368/1706*, A 58984, A 64965, A 77618 and A 87051/43559/6.

91. See Table A.6

92. See Table A.16.

93. Cf. P. Neuhaus, *Monetary History of Brazil*, p. 46.

94. See the Memorandum of the Counsellor for the Department of State, dated 17.5.1917, in *FRUS*, 1917, Supplement 1, The World War, pp. 283–4.

95. Morgan to Secretary of State (telegram), 18.5.1917, in *FRUS*, 1917, Supplement 1, The World War, pp. 284–5.

96. *SAJ*, 26.5.1917.

97. *SAJ*, 12.6.1917.

98. See Table A.8. Cf. also J.W.F. Rowe, 'Brazilian Coffee', London and Cambridge Economic Service, Special Memorandum no. 35, Studies in the Artificial Control of Raw Materials no. 3 (London, 1932) p. 9.

99. A. Delfim Netto, *O Problema do Café no Brasil*, (FGV/SUPLAN, Rio de Janeiro, 1979) p. 91.

100. See Law no. 3316, of 16.8.1917, and *MFR*, 1918, p. VIII.

101. Cf. G. Hardach, *First World War*, p. 102.

102. On this see *MFR*, 1918, p. XVII, *RC-JC*, 1917, pp. 26–7, and Morgan to Secretary of State, 8.1.1918, in *USNA RG-59*, 832.85/70 and enclosures therein.

103. Cf. *RC-JC*, 1918, p. 3.

104. On this see B. Fausto, *Trabalho Urbano e Conflito Social (1890–1920)* (Difel, São Paulo, 1977) especially Chaps VI and VII.

105. *RC-JC*, 1918, p. 3.
106. See B. Fausto, *Trabalho Urbano*, pp. 233ff.
107. *RC-JC*, 1917, p. 6.
108. 'Mr. Antonio Carlos . . . did not take into consideration the proposal to aggravate the tax burden put forward by the Ministry of Finance . . . and tried to cut expenditures . . . .' *RC-JC*, 1917, p. 16.
109. For a justification of this new approach based on the arguments that the tax burden was already excessive and that the government was about to derive a substantial additional revenue from the German ships deal with France, see *MFR*, 1918, pp. vi–vii.
110. Antonio Carlos's conservatism on monetary policy is best illustrated by a report he prepared for the Joint Congress Finance Committee in August 1914, against the Bill providing for the emergency Treasury note issue after the outbreak of the war. The report was labelled 'terrorist' by a contemporary non-orthodox authority. See L.R. Vieira Souto, *O Papel-Moeda e o Câmbio* (Imprimerie de Vaugirard, Paris, 1925) p. 90.
111. See Sharp (Paris) to Secretary of State, 11.1.1918, in *USNA RG-59* 832.85/53 and the report from the Manager of the São Paulo branch of the London and River Plate Bank, dated 22.1.1918, enclosed in *FO 371/3167*, A 65282/64280.
112. A. d'E. Taunay, *Pequena história do café*, p. 325.
113. J.H. Williams, *Foreign Exchange and International Balances*, p. 457.
114. A. d'E. Taunay, *Pequena história do café*, p. 366.
115. At that time, 'There was not a single empty warehouse in Santos. It was not unusual to see old buildings, long since condemned by the sanitary authorities, being hurriedly adapted to receive the shipments arriving from the interior.' Ibid. pp. 355–66.
116. See *SAJ*, 2.3.1918, and Morgan to Secretary of State (telegram), 28.2.1918, in *USNA RG-59* 832.85/73.
117. Morgan to Secretary of State, 2.10.1918, in *USNA RG-59* 832.85/93.
118. See Legislative Decree no. 3361, 26.10.1917. Cf also *MFR*, 1918, pp. XII–XV.
119. Executive Decree no. 13110, of 19.7.1918. Professor Pelaez mistakenly dates this measure as having been taken in July 1917. Cf. C.M. Pelaez, 'As Consequências econômicas', p. 51.
120. A. d'E. Taunay, *Pequena história do café*, p. 365.
121. See Table A.8.
122. See the statement on the effects of the frost made by the Governor of São Paulo on 14.7.1918, cited in Taunay, A. d'E., *Pequena história do café*, p. 365.
123. See Table A.11.
124. See Table A.1.

4 The Impact of the World Postwar Boom and Slump: 1919–22

1. D. Joslin, *A Century of Banking in Latin America* (Oxford University Press, 1963) p. 217.

2. D. Aldcroft, *From Versailles to Wall Street, 1919–1932* (Allen Lane, London, 1977) pp. 64 ff.
3. W.A. Lewis, *Economic Survey, 1919–1939* (Allen and Unwin, London, 1949) p. 18.
4. See, for instance, J.A. Dowie, '1919–1920 is in Need of Attention', *Economic History Review*, (August, 1975).
5. Cf. League of Nations, *Economic Fluctuations in the United States and the United Kingdom, 1918–1922*, (Geneva, 1942) *passim*, D.H. Aldcroft, *Versailles to Wall Street*, pp. 65–7, and W.A. Lewis, *Economic Survey*, p. 19.
6. Cf. League of Nations, *Economic fluctuations, U.S. and U.K.*, pp. 13–19, D.H. Aldcroft, *Versailles to Wall Street*, p. 66 and S. Howson, 'The Origins of Dear Money 1919–1920', *Economic History Review*, XXCII (February 1974) pp. 88 ff.
7. See League of Nations, *Economic Fluctuations, U.S. and U.K.*, pp. 18–19.
8. See Table A.6. This was due almost exclusively to the recent growth of planting in Colombia.
9. Total output rose by 5.9 per cent and industrial output by 14.8 per cent in 1919. See Table A.2.
10. *BBR*, 1919, pp. 14 ff.
11. Between March 1919 and March 1920 there was a 40 per cent appreciation against sterling and 160 per cent against the French franc. Cf. *Federal Reserve Bulletin* (August, 1920) p. 817.
12. *BBR*, 1921, p. 6. During the postwar import boom, the United States – which supplied between 12 to 15 per cent of Brazilian imports before the war – still maintained the leading position attained during the European conflict supplying over 47 per cent of total Brazilian imports in 1919. After 1919, the American share fell rapidly, stabilising between 20 to 30 per cent in the mid-twenties, while Britain's and to a minor extent, Germany's share rose.
13. See Table A.16.
14. See, for instance, *BBR*, 1917, p. 19–24 and *BBR*, 1918, pp. 96 ff.
15. *Jornal do Commércio*, 29.5.1917.
16. P. Neuhaus, *Monetary History of Brazil*, pp. 54 ff.
17. A.C. Ribeiro de Andrade, *Bancos de Emissão no Brasil* (Liv. Leite Ribeiro, Rio de Janeiro, 1923) p. 363. This version is confirmed by Homero Batista himself. In the last Banco do Brasil board meeting he presided he made a farewell address almost exclusively centered on his attempts to transform the Bank into an 'issue and rediscount Bank' and on the lack of support he found in the Executive. See *BBBM*, meeting of 3.1.1919.
18. Cf. *BBR*, 1918, pp. 104 ff.
19. In his *A Reforma Monetária*, he had stated: 'Among fiduciary issues I prefer the banking type; but I do not consider it to be indispensible for its good quality that it should correspond always to an equal metallic backing in the vaults of the issuing Banks as sustained by the bullionists . . . The essential condition of the good fiduciary currency is the limitation of its quantity to the real needs of circulation.' Cf. A.

Cavalcanti, *A Reforma Monetária* (Imprensa Nacional, Rio de Janeiro, 1891) p. 37.
20. Cf. *MFR*, 1919 pp. v and xxiii.
21. J.M. Bello, *Brazil, 1889–1964*, pp. 242 ff.
22. See *BBR*, 1920, p. 8. See also Tables, A.3, A.16 and A.17.
23. *BBR* , 1920, p. 8. See also V. Viana, *O Banco do Brasil*, pp. 805–6.
24. *BBR*, 1920, p. 8.
25. *MFR*, 1920 pp. 289–90.
26. C. Pacheco, *História do Banco do Brasil*, p. 169. The works of the Committee are printed in *MFR*, 1920, pp. 291 ff.
27. D.H. Aldcroft, *Versailles to Wall Street*, pp. 67–8.
28. League of Nations, *Economic Fluctuations, U.S. and U.K.*, pp. 8 and 19–20. See also M. Friedman, and J. Schwartz, *A Monetary History of the United States, 1867–1960* (N.B.E.R. Studies in Business Cycles no. 12, Princeton Univ. Press, 1963) pp. 231–5 and S. Howson, *Domestic Monetary Management in Britain, 1919–1938* (University of Cambridge, Department of Applied Economics Occasional Paper 48, Cambridge Univ. Press, 1975) pp. 23–6.
29. See Table A.4. and A.8.
30. J.W.F. Rowe, 'Brazilian Coffee', p. 22.
31. See A. Delfim Netto, *O Problema do Café*, pp. 100–101.
32. J.W.F. Rowe, 'Brazilian Coffee', p. 22.
33. *BBR*, 1921, p. 6. Another important inducement to the growth of imports may have been the erosion of the protective effect of the Brazilian tariff during the war, when the adjustments then made in the specific milréis rates through increases in the gold tariff quota did not offset the joint effects of world inflation and postwar exchange rate appreciation. The relation between tariff revenue and the value of imports, although probably also reflecting a change in the commodity composition of imports, fell from an average of 39 per cent in 1910–12 to 16 per cent in 1919. Data from Tables A.11 and A.13.
34. Cf. A. d'E. Taunay, *Pequena história do café*, p. 268.
35. W.L. Schurz, *Valorization of Brazilian Coffee*, Supplement to Commerce Reports, Trade Information Bulletin no. 73, October 16, 1922, United States Bureau of Foreign and Domestic Commerce (U.S. G.P.O., Washington, 1922) p. 2.
36. *SAJ*, 25.9.1920 and 9.10.1920. See also *MFR*, 1920, pp. 118–35.
37. Brazil. Câmara dos Deputados, *Documentos Parlamentares: Meio Circulante*, vol. 12 (Typ. do Jornal do Commércio, Rio de Janeiro, 1922) pp. 3–11 and 61–92.
38. As late as December 1920 the Minister of Finance answered a written request for federal support to coffee markets from the Rio Commercial Association stating that although the government 'sees with dccp feelings the fall in prices of several Brazilian products, it would be senseless to throw itself into the task of supporting them in world markets through commercial operations.' Letter of H. Batista to the President of the Rio Commercial Association, 7.12.1920, in *MFR*, 1920, pp. 183–95.
39. Morgan to Secretary of State, 20.9.1920, in *USNA RG-59* 832.00/198.

40. See Table A.16.
41. *RC-JC*, 1920, p. 3.
42. Private sector complaints for an easing of credit conditions had been mounting for some time and even pressures for a moratorium had already begun. See Morgan to Secretary of State, 13.11.1921, in *USNA RG-59* 832.51/217 and *SAJ*, 25.12.1920.
43. SAJ, 16.10.1920.
44. See Law no. 4.182 of 13.11.1920. For the rationale of the proposed amendment see *MFR*, 1920, pp. 135 ff.
45. Ibid. See also *SAJ*, 9.10.1920.
46. J.W.F. Rowe, 'Brazilian Coffee', p. 40.
47. W.G. McCreery and M.L. Bynum, 'The Coffee Industry in Brazil', U.S. Department of Commerce, *Trade Promotion Series no. 92* (USGPO, Washington, 1930) p. 39.
48. See Mensagem Presidencial de 1921, in *DOU*, 4.5.1921 and *Jornal do Commércio*, 13.12.1920.
49. As Augusto Ramos, the President of the Rio Commercial Association sharply observed during the debates on the Bill, 'the creation of the Rediscount Department is a result of the pull of two diverging forces: the first comes from commerce, industry and agriculture, which demand cash to be able to move, to save themselves; the second stems from the casual alliance of two groups: those who, as a matter of principle, attack all and every note issue and those who, even while recognising and accepting the need to help those who complain, saw in the Rediscount Department a strange creature . . . a mock Bank of Issue with all its inconveniences and not a single of its great advantages.' *Jornal do Commércio*, 4.11.1920
50. See mensagem Presidencial de 1921, in *DOU*, 4.5.1921, and Chilton to Curzon, 27.12.1920, in *FO 371/5535*, A 582/263/6.
51. In spite of his reservations in relation to the political character of most of Banco do Brasil's operations and to its strong links with the Treasury, Whitaker was a strong supporter of the creation of a lender of last resort. See J.M. Whitaker, *O Milagre de Minha Vida* (Editora Hucitec, São Paulo, 1978) pp. 33 ff.
52. Ibid. p. 39. See Law no. 4.230, of 31.12.1920 for details.
53. Decree no. 14.635, of 21.1.1921 and C. Pacheco, *História do Banco do Brasil*, p. 174.
54. See the relevant files in *FO 371/5536* and *SAJ*, 29.1.1921.
55. On this see Dillon, Read and Co. to Secretary of State (telegram), 21.10.1920, in *USNA RG-59* 832.51/207 and Morgan to Secretary of State, 24.5.1921, in *USNA RG-59* 832.51/224.
56. See, for instance, *SAJ*, 15.1.1921.
57. See Table A.8.
58. J.W.F. Rowe, 'Brazilian Coffee', p. 22.
59. See Table A.8.
60. Mensagem especial do Sr. Presidente da República ao Congresso Nacional, em 17.10.1921, in Brazil, Câmara dos Deputados, *Documentos Parlamentares: Meio Circulante*, vol. 14 (Typ. do Jornal do Commércio, Rio de Janeiro, 1924) p. 3.

61. At the end of March 1921 domestic prices of Santos 4 type had fallen to 45 milréis per bag as compared with 106 milréis in December 1920. See A.d'E. Taunay, *Pequena história do café*, pp. 373 and 378.
62. *RC-JC*, 1921, p. 19.
63. See Table A.10 and A.11.
64. See Table A.12. The reasons for the severe federal financial disequilibrium from 1919 are discussed below.
65. As presented in the Finance Minister Reports, since the fuller, consolidated, *Balanços Gerais da União* were not published between 1915 and 1923.
66. The outstanding value of federal long-term domestic debt rose by 20.7 per cent in 1921 alone. See Table A.15.
67. See H. Batista to J.M. Whitaker, 11.3.1921, in J.M. Whitaker, *O Milagre de Minha Vida*, pp. 107–8.
68. The discussion which follows concerns only ordinary government debt to the Bank on account of excess budget expenditures. It does not apply to debt arising out of the Bank's acceptance of Treasury *endorsed* coffee bills since these, as 'commercial' paper could be rediscounted by the Department.
69. The President of the Bank was very sensitive to that and on one occasion in 1922 refused to follow the Minister of Finance's instructions to raise the rediscount rate on those grounds. See J.M. Whitaker to H. Batista, undated, in J.M. Whitaker, *O Milagre de Minha Vida*, pp. 106–7.
70. See Table A.17. Voluntary deposits by large national banks at the Banco do Brasil began to be made after the creation of the Rediscount Department and the policy of attracting them was actively pursued by Whitaker, as discussed below.
71. J.M. Whitaker, *O Milagre de Minha Vida*, pp. 36–7.
72. Decree no. 14.898, of 20.6.1921.
73. See Banco do Brasil S/A, Balancetes da Carteira de Redescontos, in *DOU*, several issues.
74. Testimony of Dr. Homero Batista, ex-Minister of Finance, on coffee valorisation operations undertaken during the government of Dr. Epitácio Pessoa, made before the Senate Finance Committee on 24.11.1922, in Brazil. Câmara dos Deputados, *Documentos Parlamentares: Meio Circulante*, vol. 16 (Typ. do Jornal do Commércio, Rio de Janeiro, 1924) p. 1031.
75. As he put it in his memoirs: 'Decidedly against official interventions I was also opposed to this decision at the beginning, all the more so because, knowing the weakness of the Banco do Brasil, I could have no illusions as to the resources upon which I could draw to finance an operation of such a vast scale.' J.M. Whitaker, *O Milagre de Minha Vida*, p. 35.
76. J.M. Whitaker to E. Pessoa, 15.7.1921, in J.M. Whitaker, *O Milagre de Minha Vida*, p. 111.
77. Ibid.
78. *The Commercial and Financial Chronicle*, 6.8.1921.
79. Decree no. 4315, of 28.8.1921.
80. See Table A.8. The authorisation given by the Belgian government for

the purchase of 700 000 bags in July under a bilateral payments agreement may have given an additional fillip to prices. This agreement was part of a larger package signed in 1920, which included granting preferential treatment to certain Belgian exports to Brazil, a privilege until then only granted to the United States. On this see *The Times*, 28.8.1921, and the relevant files in *FO 371*/4432 and 5534.

81. See Table A.10.
82. See *DOU*, 25.8.1921.
83. Pessoa's tour also aimed at obtaining São Paulo's support to go on with the heavy expenditures required by the government's extensive anti-drought works then being carried out in the Brazilian north-east.
84. See Brazil, Câmara dos Deputados, *Documentos Parlamentares: Meio Circulante*, vol. 14, pp. 4. ff.
85. Ibid. pp. 39–44.
86. Ibid. pp. 61 ff.
87. Ibid. *passim*.
88. See Brazilian Warrant Co., Report to Annual Shareholders Meeting, in *SAJ*, 13.5.1922.
89. *The Times*, 6.12.1921 and Tilley to Foreign Office (telegram), 1.12.1921, in *FO 371*/5543, A 8914/8914/6.
90. J.W.F. Rowe, 'Brazilian Coffee', p. 22.
91. See Table A.17.
92. The 1922 crop amounted to 10.2 million bags but it was 'somewhat overestimated until later on when picking was well advanced.' J.W.F. Rowe, 'Brazilian Coffee', p. 23.
93. See Testimony of Dr. Homero Batista, etc., *cit.*, p. 1032.
94. *SAJ*, 6.5.1922. The relevant correspondence relating to the loan negotiations is reproduced in E. Pessoa, *Pela Verdade* (Francisco Alves, Rio de Janeiro, 1925) pp. 197 ff.
95. Testimony of Dr. Homero Batista, etc., *cit.*, p. 1032. As the lessons from the pre-war valorisation recommended, stocks were left in Brazil.
96. See E. Pessoa, *Pela Verdade*, pp. 186–8.
97. Ibid., p. 194. On British Treasury regulations see Norman to Niemeyer, 30.12.1921 and Norman to Blackett, 31.1.1922, in *T 160* F 4319/111/1.
98. J.W.F. Rowe, 'Brazilian Coffee', p. 23.
99. Brazil: Câmara dos Deputados, *Documentos Parlamentares: Meio Circulante*, vol. 14, p. 361.
100. See Decree no. 4.548, of 19.6.1922.
101. J.W.F. Rowe, 'Brazilian Coffee', p. 25. On the behaviour of prices, see Table A.8.
102. See Table A.1.
103. See Table A.2.
104. As measured by the apparent consumption of cement. See Table A.2.
105. Brazil's rapid recovery from the postwar slump, helped by the unforeseen results of economic policy measures has, indeed, a striking similarity with that after the Great Depression, whose causes have been pointed out by Furtado. For a recent restatement of his classic interpretation see A. Fishlow, 'Origins and Consequences'.
106. See Table A.10.

107. For the years 1921 and 1922 taken together Haddad's GDP deflator falls by 7.5 per cent and the Rio cost of living index by 18.7 per cent, while wholesale prices fall by 37.3 per cent in the United States and by 48.3 per cent in the United Kingdom. Data from Table A.3, United States, Department of Commerce, Bureau of the Census, *Historical Statistics of the United States, 1789–1945* (USGPO, Washington, 1959) p. 233, and A.C. Pigou, *Aspects of British Economic History: 1918–1925* (MacMillan, London, 1947) pp. 234–5.

108. See Table A.4.

109. See Table A.11.

110. See Tables A.16 and A.17.

111. Falling from very high levels from the middle of the nineteenth century, the currency ratio reached 2.62 in 1900, 2.32 in 1905, 1.91 in 1910, 1.69 in 1915 and 0.73 in 1920. Data from C.M. Pelaez, and W. Suzigan, *História Monetária do Brasil: análise da política, comportamento e instituições monetárias* (IPEA/INPES, Rio de Janeiro, 1976) Tables A.3 and A.4.

112. Another important innovation introduced into Brazilian banking during 1921 was the installation of a cheque-clearing house at the Banco do Brasil in June. See *BBR*, 1922, pp. 8–9. This was a long-standing demand of banking and business circles, but earlier attempts at implementing it had failed. On this see P. Neuhaus, *Monetary History of Brazil*, p. 60.

113. See Table A.16.

114. C. Pacheco, *História do Banco do Brasil*, p. 169.

115. Total Banco do Brasil deposits rose from 288 000 contos at end-1920 to 1 089 000 by mid-1922, while the value of bills discounted rose from 139 000 to 802 000 in the same period. A very large fraction of this increase was, as shown below, the result of Treasury credit operations. See *BBR*, 1923, p. 7.

116. *BBR*, 1921, p. 8.

117. Foreign banks' reserve ratios remained markedly higher than those of Brazilian-owned banks: at end-1921 reserve ratios were 60.6 for the former and 27.8 for the latter. Data from *MFR*, 1923, pp. 76–7. It should be noted that the increase in the share of deposits held by national banks shown in Table A.2 was, to a large extent, the result of the explosive rise of Banco do Brasil deposits. Cf. Table A.16.

118. Report of the British Financial Mission to Brazil to N.M. Rothschilds & Sons, Messrs Baring Brothers & Co. Ltd., J. Henry Schroeder and Co., Appendix C: Republic of Brazil – Balance Sheet as at 31.12.1923 with relative schedules of Liabilities and Assets, by Sir William McLintock, in *R.A.* 111/220.

119. The total value of bills discounted by the Banco do Brasil amounted to 437 000 contos on 31.12.1921. See *BBR*, 1922, p. 7.

120. This plan originated at the Bank in or before June and was considered by Whitaker as being 'indispensable to have the support from other banks and even to preserve the financial position of the Banco do Brasil.' See J.M. Whitaker to H. Batista, 20.6.1922, in J.M. Whitaker, *O Milagre de Minha Vida*, pp. 108–9.

121. It is patently clear from the records of the Senate debates on the government proposal that very few of its members knew the terms of the Bank-Treasury contract and could gauge the consequences of what they were going to vote for. In the Chamber the Bill had been approved without debate for, so as to avoid having its approval delayed there, the government went as far as to use the tactics of concealing the proposal as an amendment to an otherwise irrelevant finance Bill already in the second round of voting, where it passed unnoticed. See Brazil, Câmara dos Deputados, *Documentos Parlamentares: Meio Circulante*, vol. 16, pp. 65–162.

122. A first draft of 100 000 contos was made in August while the proposal to allow rediscount of these notes was still before Congress. Following Congress approval, 200 000 contos were issued in October and an equal amount in November. See Report of the British Financial Mission, etc., in *R.A.* 111/220.

123. See Table A.16 and A.17.

124. J. Pires do Rio, *A Moeda Brasileira e seu Perenne Caráter Fiduciário* (José Olympio, Rio de Janeiro, n.d.) p. 204. To gauge what these obligations represented, note that total federal government revenue amounted to 972 000 contos in 1922.

5 Attempts at Financial Reconstruction

1. On this see J.M. Bello, *Brazil, 1889–1964*, pp. 248–9.
2. Ibid. pp. 249 ff.
3. See V.A. de Mello Franco, *Outubro 1930* (Nova Fronteira, Rio de Janeiro, 5th edn, 1980) Chapter IV, and E. Carone, *A República Velha (Evolução Política)* Difel, São Paulo, 1971) pp. 345 ff.
4. See Bernardes' platform speech in *Jornal do Commércio*, 19.10.1922.
5. Ibid.
6. Ibid.
7. The emphasis on coal and iron development, although important for balance of payments reasons, was also explained on strategic military grounds as wartime shortages clearly demonstrated. As Bernardes put it 'the solution of the iron problem is closely related to that of coal, both connected with national defence.' Ibid.
8. It was already realised that these public investments 'assist the country to recover and to cut them down often creates a paralysis which does not assist our economic development and civilization.' Ibid.
9. 'If elected, my best efforts will be directed towards the definitive organization of credit. We already owe to President Pessoa's administration the creation of the Rediscount Department, which has rendered and will continue to render great services. It seems, however, that the fundamental and permanent measure should be the creation of a National Bank of Issue and Rediscount. Among civilized nations Brazil is one of the few which does not possess such an institution without which the development of industry and commerce is always precarious.' Ibid.

10. Ibid.
11. See the interview given to the Rio correspondent of the London *Times*. *The Times*, 16.11.1922.
12. See the statement later made by the Minister of Finance in *Jornal do Commércio*, 30.10.1923.
13. On this see E. Pessoa, *Pela Verdade*, pp. 201 ff. and the letter of C. Coelho, former Director of Banco do Brasil's Foreign Exchange Department, in *O Jornal*, 24.2.1923.
14. See 'Exposição apresentada ao Sr. Presidente da República pelo Ministro da Fazenda em 30 de novembro de 1922', in *MFR*, 1923, pp. ix–xi.
15. *SAJ*, 2.12.1922. See also 'Parecer sobre a Mensagem de 30 Novembro e sôbre o Orçamento da Fazenda para 1923', in Brazil, Câmara dos Deputados, *Documentos Parlamentares: Meio Circulante*, vol. 16, *passim*.
16. Although expenditure data presented in Table A.14 for the period after 1923 is not strictly comparable to those for 1915–22, government gross fixed capital formation as a proportion of total expenditure is shown to have fallen from 25.7 per cent in 1922 to 3.7 per cent in 1923 and 5.6 per cent in 1924.
17. See Table A.3 and A.12.
18. See Table A.12.
19. *MFR*, 1923, *passim*.
20. It should be noted that, as Rediscount Department issues had been limited to 400 000 contos and the Treasury short-term liabilities to the Banco do Brasil exceeded twice this amount, this debt froze a large share of the Bank's own resources.
21. See 'Exposição apresentada ao Sr. Presidente da República, etc.', *cit.*, pp. xii–xiii.
22. Ibid.
23. See 'Parecer sobre a Mensagem de 30 de Novembro, etc.', p. 210.
24. *MFR*, 1923, p. xiv.
25. Brazil, Câmara dos Deputados, *Documentos Parlamentares: Meio Circulante*, vol. 16, pp. 222–3.
26. J.M. Whitaker, *O Milagre de Minha Vida*, p. 57.
27. As the report presenting the government central banking reform to Congress argued: 'Moreover the Treasury owes a large sum to the Banco do Brasil. Why not pay a sizeable part of this debt with the Treasury gold, imposing to the Bank, however, the obligation to retain this deposit in Brazil.' See 'Parecer sobre a Mensagem Presidencial de 30 de Novembro, etc.,' *cit.*, p. 222.
28. Besides the sources already quoted, see the long interview given to the Rio *Jornal do Commércio* by Cincinato Braga, the *Paulista* deputy who drafted the government's bill, in *Jornal do Commércio*, 28.4.1923, 29.4.1923, 1.5.1923 and 2.5.1923.
29. Cf., for instance, C.M. Pelaez, 'Consequências econômicas da ortodoxia', pp. 56–7.
30. It is also interesting to note that not even the purely formal aspects of the reform were in tune with contemporary 'gold-exchange standard' principles put forward by the leading creditor nations in the postwar international monetary conferences. The weak current external posi-

tion and the very small relation official reserves bore to the outstanding Treasury currency issue prevented immediate convertibility. Besides, the new central bank's reserves would be kept in Brazil and not in a key-currency centre for, as alleged in the government project, 'the international situation is still too uncertain to allay our fears of seeing this gold suddendly trammeled abroad, in case of war.' See 'Parecer sobre a Mensagem de 30 de Novembro, etc.', *cit.*, p. 222.

31. On this episode, see J.M. Whitaker, *O Milagre de Minha Vida*, pp. 53 ff.
32. *SAJ*, 20.1.1923.
33. See Mensagem Presidencial, in *DOU*, 4.5.1923.
34. See Jewel Tea Co. to Secretary of State, 8.7.1922 and the enclosed Department of State memorandum in *USNA RG-59* 832.61333/189.
35. An American official publication had already openly objected to Brazilian price support as 'an attempt to dominate world markets.' Cf. Trade Information Bulletin, no. 73, October 16, 1922, quoted in J. Brandes, *Herbert Hoover and Economic Diplomacy: Department of Commerce Policy, 1921–1928* (Pittsburgh Univ. Press, 1962) p. 130. In fact, since 1921 the United States government had openly used its veto powers on foreign loans as an instrument of economic policy. On this see J.W. Angell, *Financial Foreign Policy of the United States; a report to the Second International Studies Conference on the State of Economic Life, London* (Council of Foreign Relations, American Committee, New York, 1933) pp. 99–100.
36. 'Exposição do Sr. Presidente da República às Comissões de Finanças do Senado e da Câmara em 20 de outubro de 1923,' in *RC-JC*, 1923, pp. 111 ff.
37. J.W.F. Rowe, 'Brazilian Coffee', p. 25.
38. Numa de Oliveira's telegram, 25.1.1923, in 'Exposição apresentada ao Sr. Presidente da República, etc.,' *cit.*, p. xv.
39. *BBR*, 1924, p. 10.
40. See Table A.8.
41. See, for instance, S.A. Penteado, *A campanha da defesa do café em 1923–24* (Typographia Brasil, São Paulo, 1923) Chaps IV to VI, and I. Costa, *Os Erros da Valorização: subsídios para o estudo da defesa do café* (Seção de Obras d'O Estado de São Paulo, São Paulo, 1925) Chapter IV.
42. J.W.F. Rowe, 'Brazilian Coffee', p. 25.
43. See Table A.6.
44. Confidential Report on the Coffee Situation, by E. Hambloch, Commercial Secretary, H.M. Embassy, Rio de Janeiro, enclosed in Department of Overseas Trade to Foreign Office, 31.7.1923, *FO 371/8432*, A 4636, 4636/6.
45. Ibid. A carefully worded note, taken as having government inspiration, was published by the Rio *Jornal do Commércio* on 28 June to appease the coffee interests but made no reference to the Banco do Brasil's possible indirect involvement in backing the financing of the scheme.
46. See Table A.8.

47. Cf. Tables A.1, A.3 and A.16.
48. *BBR*, 1924, p. 11.
49. C. Braga, 'Brasil Novo' in *Jornal do Commércio*, 28.12.1930.
50. See Table A.16.
51. See Table A.11.
52. *BBR*, 1924, p. 27.
53. See I. de Souza, *Restauração da Moeda no Brasil* (Casa Garraux, São Paulo, 1926) pp. 207–8, who shows that the total value of Banco do Brasil foreign exchange operations fell by almost 50 per cent during 1923. According to official sources, in 1922 the Bank had been responsible for 80 per cent of the total value of foreign exchange operations in Brazil. See 'Parecer sobre a Mensagem de 30 de Novembro, etc.', *cit.*, p. 188.
54. As the President of the Banco do Brasil would later put it, 1923 was 'the most terrible year, regarding foreign exchange, in our history.' See *BBR*, 1924, pp. 10–11.
55. *Memorandum on the Terms of Reference, Financial Mission to Brasil*, in *R.A.*, Box III/220, file no. 6.
56. Ibid.
57. As concisely put in the Mission's terms of reference, as distributed later to its senior members: 'the real aim of the Mission is to furnish the Bankers with information so that with due regard to their own responsibility towards investors here they may be able to assist the Brazilian government.' Ibid.
58. Montagu came from a City family, had a considerable experience in financial matters, was close to Lionel de Rothschild, had recently retired from politics to take business posts in the City and was an experienced negotiator. See S.D. Waley, *Edwin Montagu: A Memoir and an Account of his Visits to India* (Asia Publishing House, London, 1964). A brief psychological portrait of Montagu was drawn by Keynes who, incidentally, was approached by Montagu as a possible member of the mission. See J.M. Keynes, 'Edwin Montagu', in *The Collected Writings of John Maynard Keynes*, volume X: Essays in Biography (published by Macmillan for the Royal Economic Society, Cambridge, 1972) Ch. 6 and King's College, *Keynes Papers*, J.M.K. to Lydia Lopokova, 16.10.1924. I thank Professor D.E. Moggridge for calling my attention to this letter.
59. Lionel de Rothschild to Sperling (Foreign Office), 27.11.1923, in *FO 371*/8430, A 7012/818/6.
60. See the enclosure in N.M. Rothschild & Sons to Sperling (Foreign Office), 12.12.1923, in *FO 371*/8430, A 7294/818/6 and Foreign Office to Tilley (telegram), 27.11.1923, in *FO 371*/8430, A 7012/818/6.
61. See, for instance, the informed article on the British mission appearing in the *Monitor Mercantil*, 14.12.1923.
62. Tilley to Curzon, 17.12.1923, in *FO 371*/9508, A 90/70/6.
63. A fuller account of the negotiations between the Brazilian government and the Montagu Mission than the one presented below is to be found in W. Fritsch, 'The Montagu Financial Mission to Brazil and the Economic Policy Changes of 1924', in *Brazilian Economic Studies, 9* (1985).

64. Montagu's summing up of these discussions is an enlightening account of their early views: 'The extraordinary difficulties of the Constitution' – he wrote to London – 'and the relations between the Federal Government and the States; the conflict of interest between the States and the Federal Government and, therefore, between parts of the Federal Government; the natural divergence of the short-sighted view between the exporter and the importer – all these and many more, add interesting perplexities to the problem the first facet of which is Budget-balancing . . . We all incline a little to find some palatable form of foreign financial control or advice, and, at the same time, we find it extremely difficult to devise one . . . I think our first problem on shore will be to try and understand in detail the nature of the internal floating debt held in Brazil, the funding of which was apparently the main reason for the desire of the Brazilians for that vast loan which led to our appointment.' Montagu to Lionel de Rothschild, 26.12.1923, in *RA* 111/220, file no. 2.

65. Private Diary of the Rt.Hon. Edwin S. Montagu, P.C., (Chairman of the Mission), p. 22, in *RA* 111/220. This source is thereinafter referred to as *Montagu Diary*. Some days later Montagu informed Rothschilds that Vidal has requested 'a written report which shall be frank, but he hopes that if we have anything critical to say we shall not publish it,' and that he replied that 'we are anxious to suit the wishes of the Brazilian government as to the form of our report but that we propose to furnish two reports – one to the Government of Brazil and one to the Bankers . . . It is not for us but for the Bankers to say whether this second report will ever be shown to the Government.' Montagu to Lionel de Rothschild, 19.1.1924, in *RA* 111/220, file no. 2. This settled the issue and from then on Montagu tended to see the drafting of this report to the President as his most important objective during the negotiations. In fact these were conducted with a view to including in this report the maximum number of politically feasible concessions from the government since its final draft would have the President's sanction and thus commit him to putting its proposals into effect. The publication of this report was not decided, however, until much after the mission had left Brazil and then in a slightly revised form, as shown below.

66. *Montagu Diary*, p. 58. When definitive figures were arrived at later, the total of the debt was found to be 884 000 contos of which 451 000 contos represented Treasury Bills and Promissory Notes owing to the Banco do Brasil and 77 000 contos of Treasury Bills owing to the public, mostly arising out of the 1922 transactions described in Chapter 4. The balance of 355 000 contos represented debts to contractors, suppliers, and arrears of several Ministries relating to fiscal years 1922 and 1923. The stated debt to the Bank already excluded 400 000 contos of Treasury Promissory Notes accepted by the old Rediscount Department, which the President envisaged cancelling against the debt formally owed by the Bank to the Treasury on account of the Rediscount Department's issuing of Treasury currency notes. This detail will be further discussed below.

67. Montagu to Lionel de Rothschild, 8.1.1924, in *RA* 111/220, file no. 2.
68. 'Report by the British Financial Mission to Brazil to Messrs. N.M. Rothschild and Sons, Messrs. Baring Brothers and Co. Ltd. and Messrs. J. Henry Schröder and Co.,' in *RA* 111/309. From now on this source will be referred to as *Report to the Bankers*.
69. These additional credits were what in the contemporary Brazilian literature on public finance was referred to as the *cauda do orçamento*, or 'budget tail.'
70. This was how a British government committee on public expenditure presided by Sir Eric Geddes, which proposed wide ranging cuts in February 1922, became known. This proposal was to be put to the Brazilian government in spite of Lynch's misgivings that 'a Geddes Committee is out of the question in this country because there are no impartial Brazilians.' *Montagu Diary*, p. 56. However, Vidal had himself in November 1922 made a speech advocating the creation of a Brazilian version of the Geddes Committee, although this was apparently unknown to the mission. See R. de A.S. Vidal, *Banking Organization and Financial Recovery: Speeches 1922* (Lytho-Typographia Fluminense, Rio de Janeiro, 1923) p. 13.
71. On 5 January, in an interview with the Minister of Justice, Montagu was plainly told that Congress had for many years discussed a Bill submitting state borrowing to federal authorisation but that it was 'a very difficult project to carry into law, because the representatives of each state were inclined to believe that if they were at the moment politically unpopular with the government of the day the loans of their states would not be authorized.' *Montagu Diary*, p. 27.
72. The provisions formally creating the Institute for Permanent Defence of Coffee had been part of the budget law for 1924.
73. *Montagu Diary*, p. 33.
74. Montagu to Lionel de Rothschild, 8.1.1924, in *RA* 111/220, file no. 2.
75. Ibid.
76. 'It does not seem to me good to mix up business with politics. On the other hand what argument is there against suggesting to the Brazilian Government that it might be a good thing to accord to British merchandise most-favoured treatment? Of course Addis would say the City has nothing to do with manufacturers, but is not the time coming when the City would do well to protect itself by showing some identity of interest with the industrial classes?' *Montagu Diary*, p. 36.
77. Also note that the end of the American and Belgian preferential tariff agreements in 1923 greatly diminished the importance of this issue to the British government.
78. *Montagu Diary*, p. 54.
79. These complaints were being loudly voiced by the English financial press. See, for instance, the leader on 'The British Mission to Brazil,' in *SAJ*, 01.12.1923.
80. *Montagu Diary*, p. 80.
81. The Government's iron and steel plan consisted in granting subsidies, mainly in the form of sponsoring the infrastructural investments required, to Brazilian capitalists interested in investing in the industry. It was seen as an alternative to the two existing foreign-sponsored pro-

jects: those of the American Itabira Iron Ore Co., mainly geared to ore exports as the company owned large high-grade deposits in Brazil, and of the Anglo-Brazilian Steel Syndicate, which planned the construction of steel mills near Rio. The former, actually a British-owned concession, but over which an American group had an option of purchase, had been blocked by Bernardes himself at the time he was Governor of Minas Gerais, where the deposits were located, by the imposition of a prohibitive tax on ore exports.

82. As he wrote to London: 'The Government seems to be bent on an increase rather than a diminution of Government trading. They have a project now for the erection of steel factories, from which it will take us all our time to dissuade them, and which will involve them in liabilities the dimensions of which have never been properly calculated, and are perhaps incalculable.' Montagu to Lionel de Rothschild, 8.1.1924, in *RA* 111/220, file no. 2.

83. Montagu to Lionel de Rothschild, 26.12.1923, in *RA* 111/220, file no. 2.

84. *Report to the Bankers*, p. 20.

85. *Montagu Diary*, p. 38. The British were not unaware that this proposal, like many others, would be resisted. Nevertheless on 11 January Addis's moderate suggestion to propose the reduction of the government shareholding at the Bank and an increase in the number of directors elected by private shareholders was turned down by Montagu as 'very timid.' Ibid. p. 49.

86. Mission's Terms of Reference, in *RA* 111/220.

87. As was, in fact, eventually suggested. See *Report to the President*, p. 20.

88. The government shareholding at the Bank, valued at market prices, was then less than the government's liabilities to it.

89. *BBR*, 1922, p. 11, and *BBR*, 1923, p. 44.

90. Montagu to N.M. Rothschild and Sons (telegram), 24.1.1924, in *RA* 111/220, file no. 4.

91. N.M. Rothschild and Sons to Montagu (telegram), 25.1.1924, in *RA* 111/220, file no. 4.

92. Montagu to N.M. Rothschild and Sons (telegram), 26.1.1924, in *RA* 111/220, file no. 4. The Tribunal of Accounts was a body formed by nine members nominated for life by the President *ad referendum* of the Senate, plus six other auditors and representatives of Ministries, also directly appointed by the President, whose duty was to control and authorise public expenditure. Its decisions could, however, still be overruled by the President.

93. N.M. Rothschild and Sons to Montagu (telegram), 1.2.1924 in *RA* 111/220, file no. 4.

94. *Montagu Diary*, pp. 82–3.

95. Ibid. p. 79.

96. Montagu to Lionel de Rothschild, 31.1.1924, in *RA* 111/220, file no. 2. What this visit amounted to was succinctly described by Montagu: 'We had dinner parties, luncheon parties and endless talk: "How do you like Brazil? What will you do for the exchange? Do not put it too high!"'. *Montagu Diary*, p. 198.

97. Ibid. p. 89.

98. Ibid. p. 92.
99. As his personal diary registers, 'I just mentioned it as the third asset which we had discovered which might be disposed of to provide the government with funds.' Ibid. p. 93.
100. Ibid. p. 93.
101. Ibid. p. 93.
102. Ibid. p. 93–4.
103. The abolition of the 'budget tail', for instance, was unconstitutional.
104. As Montagu saw it, the Minister implied that the reforms 'were conditional on his being able to consolidate the [floating] debt.' *Montagu Diary*, p. 99.
105. Ibid. p. 100.
106. Ibid. pp, 101–2.
107. The agreement was already operative but had not yet been fully legalised owing to disagreements over whether the Treasury or the Bank should accept the liability represented by the outstanding 400 000 contos of currency notes issued by the extinct Rediscount Department. Bernardes favoured what Brazilian government officials called a 'cross-entry operation', which would cancel the Bank's liability to the Treasury which these notes legally represented against an equal sum of Treasury short-term debt to the Bank, and consider the notes as part of the total Treasury note liability transferred to the Bank by the 1923 agreement. Vidal and Braga upheld the opposing view that the Treasury should honour its debt to the Bank in full, pointing to the fact that the 1923 agreement did not consider the Rediscount Department notes as part of the Treasury note issue. This issue interested the mission since its outcome would affect the value of the government indebtedness to the Bank. On this, see *Montagu Diary*, p. 104.
108. Ibid. p. 104.
109. Ibid. p. 104.
110. Ibid. p. 104.
111. He left the meeting feeling that he 'must press them to carry out the scheme and press the Banks in London to accept it.' Ibid. p. 105. On the same day he wrote to London informing Rothschild of Vidal and Braga's 'agreement' that it was desirable to sell the Bank. Montagu to Lionel de Rothschild, 18.02.1924, in *RA* 111/220, file no. 2.
112. Ibid. p. 110.
113. *Ibidem*, pp. 110–11. Because inflation and overissue had put the usual 5 per cent *apólices* – *de facto* perpetuities – at a heavy discount, this new kind of higher nominal interest bonds with definite maturity dates had already been recently issued.
114. Ibid. pp. 113–14.
115. Ibid. p. 116.
116. Ibid. p. 116.
117. Ibid. p. 116.
118. *Report to the Bankers*, p. 21.
119. *Montagu Diary*, p. 116.
120. Ibid. p. 117. In their final report to the bankers, although agreeing that 'it should be useful to get such a representative' the mission would,

however, state that it was satisfied that this could not be obtained and that to press the issue 'might have prevented the acceptance of our other proposals.' *Report to the Bankers*, p. 21.

121. *Report to the President*, p. 19.
122. *Montagu Diary*, p. 131.
123. Ibid. p. 132.
124. Ibid. p. 132.
125. 'When Lynch began to interpret, Bernardes turned very red, moved uneasily in his chair, and grinned at me that they were only trying a way for something on which we were in agreement.' Ibid. p. 132.
126. 'I did not move a muscle because I felt that if in this bluff we did not succeed, the situation was really hopeless.' Ibid. p. 132.
127. Ibid. pp. 132–3.
128. Ibid. p. 133.
129. Ibid. p. 133.
130. Ibid. p. 133. Cf. *Report to the President*, p. 20.
131. *Montagu Diary*, p. 133.
132. Ibid. pp. 133–5. The President even agreed with the sale of the Central Railway 'if it could be done.' Curiously enough, after the formal negotiations were wound up, he approached Montagu for financial support for a plan to move the Brazilian capital to the hinterland; the latter politely replied that he 'would look into the matter in London. . . .' Ibid. p. 135.
133. Ibid. pp. 143–4.
134. Ibid. p. 137.
135. Cf. Lionel de Rothschild to Sir W. Tyrell, 15.4.1924, in *FO 371*/9508 A 2427/70/6.
136. *Report to the Bankers*, p. 6.
137. Ibid. pp. 34–5.
138. The *South American Journal*, for instance, reported that 'there are reasons to believe that a big loan for Brazil will be arranged in the near future.' See *SAJ*, 29.3.1924.
139. *BBR*, 1924, pp. 31–2.
140. Mensagem Presidencial de 1924, in *DOU*, 3.5.1924.
141. *SAJ*, 7.6.1924, and Tilley to McDonald, 14.6.1924 in *FO 371*/9508 A 4050/70/6.
142. The first proposals to London were made by Vidal on 16 April. Agreement on a final draft was reached after the second reply with counterproposals from Montagu, undated, but most probably of early June. See *RA* 111/220, file no. 3.
143. Telegram of N.M. Rothschild and Sons to Vidal, undated, but probably of late April, in *RA* 111/220, file no. 3
144. *O Paíz*, 24.6.1924.
145. See, for instance, *Jornal do Commércio*, 28.6.1924.
146. Ibid. For a British view see *The Times*, 30.6.1924.
147. Tilley to McDonald, 5.7.1924, in *FO 371*/9509 A 4650/70/6. For the opposition view, see *O Jornal*, 29.6.1924.
148. W.A. Brown, Jr., *England and the New Gold Standard: 1919–1926* (P.S. King and Son, London, 1929) p. 223.

149. D.E. Moggridge, 'British controls on long-term capital movements, 1924–1931', in D.N. McCloskey (ed.), *Essays on a Mature Economy: Britain after 1840* (Methuen, London, 1971) p. 120.
150. Cf. W.A. Brown Jr., *New Gold Standard*, p. 224. The mistake is repeated in a recent, thorough study on British overseas investment. Cf. J.M. Atkin, *British Overseas Investments, 1918–1931*, Ph.D. Thesis (The London School of Economics and Political Science, London, 1968) p. 49.
151. D.E. Moggridge, 'British controls on capital movements' *op.cit.*, p. 120.
152. D.E. Moggridge, Ibid. p. 120. It should be noted that, according to British usage, Colonial and Dominion governments were not classified as 'foreign' and the restrictive measures did not apply to their loans.
153. W.A. Brown, Jr., *New Gold Standard*, p. 24.
154. See Niemeyer to Chancellor, 5.3.1925, in PRO T 175/4, and Niemeyer Memorandum, 29.11.1924, quoted in D.E. Moggridge, 'British controls on capital movements', p. 121.
155. See R.S. Sayers, *The Bank of England 1891–1944*, Appendices (Cambridge Univ. Press, 1976) p. 289.
156. R.S. Sayers, Ibid. p. 289. Emphasis added.
157. *SAJ*, 5.7.1924.
158. Decrees nos. 16419, of 19 March, and 16524, of 1 July 1924.
159. On this see V. Santa Rosa, *O Sentido do Tenentismo* (Schmidt, Rio de Janeiro, 1933) or B. Fausto, *A Revolução de 1930: historiografia e história* (Brasiliense, São Paulo, 1970) especially Chapter II. For a recent appraisal of the 1924 revolts see A.M. Martinez Correa, *A Rebelião de 1924 em São Paulo* (Hucitec, São Paulo, 1976) especially pp. 45–55.
160. See 'A Palavra da Nação,' in *DOU*, 15.11.1924.
161. *UK-DCR*, 1924, p. 15.
162. Cf. W. Falcão, *O Empirismo Monetário no Brasil* (Cia. Editora Nacional, Rio de Janeiro, 1931) pp. 69–71.
163. See M. Brant, *Economical Fallacies: On the influence of paper-money on foreign exchange, prices, exports, national production, budgets, public finance and national progress* (Casa Leuzinger, Rio de Janeiro, 1931) *passim*.
164. As Vidal qualified his views during the above-mentioned parliamentary debate in 1921: 'Paper-currency issues with productive applications were never prejudicial. When paper is issued to make up for deficits, then, indeed, it is disastrous.' M. Brant, *Economical Fallacies*, p. 17.
165. In an interview given in 1923, defending the government's project for the reorganisation of the Banco do Brasil into a bank of issue he argued: 'Never will the Bank issue a single note without having as assets . . . commercial paper of the most solid houses in Brazil . . . So bridled, the Bank will never be in position to inflate circulation with super-abundant and unnecessary paper-money.' *Jornal do Commércio*, 28.5.1923.
166. See M. Brant, *Economical Fallacies*, p. 18.
167. *Montagu Diary*, pp. 19–20 and 48. The ex-Ministers quoted in the Diary as belonging to what Montagu jokingly referred to as 'the Don

Carlos school of non-emission of currency at any price,' are Leopoldo de Bulhões and the more moderate banker João Ribeiro. Ibid. pp. 48 and 66.

168. This was explicitly admitted even by Antonio Carlos. See the summary of the debates of the Joint Congress Finance Committee in *Jornal do Commércio*, 19.12.1924.

169. *Report to the President*, p. 21.

170. Explaining the decision a few months later, Bernardes would say: 'the perceptible hight cost of living coincided with the emissions of the Banco do Brasil and with the credits which it facilitated, in virtue, perhaps, of its issuing powers . . . Earnestly wishing that this establishment shall withdraw from the path of emissions along which it has advanced too far, the government found it necessary to stop the monetary inflation. . . .' Mensagem Presidencial de 1925, in *DOU*, 4.5.1925.

171. See the summary óf the debates of the Joint Congress Finance Committee in *Jornal do Commércio*, 18.12.1924 and 19.12.1924. Braga and Vidal's exclusion from the process of designing the Bank's reform was explicitly denounced by the former in his resignation letter sent to Bernardes a few days later. See *USNA RG-59*, 832.001143/43, enclosure no. 1.

172. See Table A.16.

173. Decree no. 4.868, of 7.11.1924.

174. For a detailed analysis of the causes of the 1924 coffee price recovery see J.W.F. Rowe, 'Brazilian Coffee', pp. 26–7.

175. Stocks in São Paulo on 1 July 1924 amounted to 4.6 million bags. See Table A.6.

176. 'The resources of the ordinary banks had been hardly adequate, and the planters did not much like the prospect of facing in the future another crop so large as that of 1923. . . .' J.W.F. Rowe, 'Brazilian Coffee', p. 27.

177. Ibid. p. 27.

178. He concludes: 'To a large extent the negotiations were simply a struggle between São Paulo and the federal government as to which party should carry the baby, for it was perfectly clear from the start that São Paulo would never let it drop: on the other hand, if the federal government could be made to act as a nursemaid, so much the better. But a bargainer in such a position is necessarily weaker than his opponent, and President Bernardes, appreciating this, remained adamant.' Ibid. p. 27.

179. Commenting on the resulting state-sponsored coffee defence scheme he would say: 'if the viewpoints of the federal government and of the producing states have substantially differed . . . the disagreements have disappeared with the present organization of coffee defence, which abandoned the recourse to the emission of paper-money. . . .' Mensagem Presidencial de 1926, in *DOU*, 4.5.1926.

180. It was through them that the report reached the American press. See *The New York Times*, 4.7.1924.

181. This last assertion is admittedly conjectural. See, however, the discussion of the United States Department of Commerce actions against the

new coffee defence scheme in 1925 in the following section of this chapter.

182. See the Finance Minister's statement in *RC-JC*, 1925, p. 8.
183. Cf. Tables A.12 and A.15.
184. The contemporary notion, endorsed by Neuhaus, that the 1926 deficit was due to an increase in military expenditure is not correct, since the latter actually fell in nominal terms. Cf. P. Neuhaus, *Monetary History of Brazil*, p. 73 and Brazil, IBGE, *Anuário Estatístico do Brasil*, 1939–40, Table IV, p. 1411.
185. M.A. Phoebus, *Commercial Readjustment in Brazil*, U.S. Department of Commerce, Trade Information Bulletin, no. 560 (USGPO, Washington, 1928) p. 17.
186. Ibid. p. 59.
187. See Table A.1.
188. See Table A.2.
189. See São Paulo State Law no. 2.004 of 19.12.1924 and the regulations appearing in Decree no. 3.082 of 14.2.1925.
190. J.W.F. Rowe, 'Brazilian Coffee', p. 30.
191. Cf. M. Tavares, *Relatório sobre o empréstimo para o Instituto do Café. Apresentado aos membros do Conselho do Instituto do Café . . . em reunião de 23 de janeiro de 1926*, São Paulo, undated, enclosed *in USNA RG-59*, 832.00/551.
192. 'Santos traders knew each day how much coffee had arrived, but no one knew whether the amount would be different on the morrow.' J.W.F Rowe, 'Brazilian Coffee', p. 30.
193. Ibid. p. 30.
194. M. Tavares, *Relatório sobre o empréstimo para o Instituto, etc.*, cit.
195. Interior stocks in São Paulo in July 1925 were just about 1.9 million bags, against a carry over of approximately 4.6 million bags in July 1924. Cf. J.W.F. Rowe, 'Brazilian Coffee', p. 30.
196. See Table A.10.
197. See Table A.3.
198. Balance of trade figures in million pounds for the first three quarters of 1925 were −2.0, −0.3 and 13.1, the last being twice as large as the corresponding figure for the third quarter of 1924. Cf. *BBR*, 1926, p. 8.
199. See Table A.10.
200. S.V.O. Clarke, *Central Bank Cooperation: 1924–31* (Federal Reserve Bank of New York, 1967) p. 22. For a vivid picture of the optimistic mood of the 1924–9 period see J.S. Davis, *The World between the wars 1919–39: an economist's view* (Johns Hopkins, Baltimore, 1975).
201. S.V.O. Clarke, *Central Bank Cooperation*, pp. 22–3.
202. W.L. Schurz's Final Report on the Work of the Coffee Mission, dated 8.7.1925, in Haeberle to Secretary of State, 11.7.1925, *USNA RG-59*, 832.61333/220. See also National Roasters Association to Secretary of State, 31.8.1925, in *USNA RG-59*, 832.51/20.
203. See *USNA RG-59*, 832.51/21, /23, /24, /29 and /30.
204. Attributed to Arthur Young of the Office of the Economic Advisor, in *USNA RG-59*, 832.51/21.

205. State Department Memorandum, 28.10.1925, in *USNA RG-59*, 832.51/34.
206. Kellogg to Hoover, 31.10.1925 in *USNA RG-59*, 832.51/30.
207. Hoover to Kellogg, 4.11.1925, in *USNA RG-59*, 832.51/57.
208. State Department minute, 6.11.1925, in *USNA RG-59*, 832.51/34. See also Hoover's statement in the *New York Journal of Commerce*, 13.11.1925.
209. Tilley to Chamberlain, 30.4.1925, in T160, F 3851/1, A 2560/42/6.
210. The growing outcry from domestic producers in Brazil against the deflation was not, of course, echoed by the City. The latter's extremely favourable opinion of Bernardes's efforts can be illustrated by the *South American Journal's* verdict in an editorial article on 'The Brazilian Outlook,' according to which 'all sound-minded people allow that [Bernardes] has done good work.' *SAJ*, 30.1.1926.
211. Craigie to Leith-Ross, 24.12.1925, in *T 160*/4319/2. The Foreign Office had already made a strong move in this direction in late 1923 but their proposals then found strong opposition from the Department of Overseas Trade and were eventually abandoned owing to the enforcement of the embargo on foreign loans in London. On this see *FO 371*/8430, A 6203/818/6, A 7439/818/6, A 7511/818/6.
212. Brazil Annual Report, 1925, p. 4, in *FO 371*/1118, A 6004/6003/6.
213. Morgan to Secretary of State, 29.9.1925, in *USNA RG-59*, 832.00/533.
214. See *O Jornal*, 25.4.1926.
215. See Sir Cecil Hurst memorandum, in *FO 371*/11893, W 390/223/98.
216. See Sir Victor Wellesley's memorandum on an interview with Rothschilds and Barings representatives, dated 19.4.1926, in *FO 371*/11115, A 2075/9.
217. Ibid.
218. See Sir Austen Chamberlain's memorandum on a meeting with the Brazilian Ambassador in London, dated 16.4.1926, in *FO 371*/11115, A 2075/G.
219. Sir Victor Wellesley's memorandum, in *FO 371*/11115, A 2075/9.
220. Ibid.
221. Chamberlain to Alston, 16.4.1926, in *FO 371*/11115, A 2075/G.
222. Sir Austen Chamberlain's minute, dated 19.4.1926, in *FO 371*/11115, A 2075/G.
223. Sir Victor Wellesley's minute dated 20.4.1926, in *FO 371*/11115, A 2075/G. This 1926 incident has already been analysed by a Brazilian author in an attempt to criticise the widespread view that Britain, unlike other creditor nations, did not try to derive political dividends from her financial dominance. See M. de Paiva Abreu, 'The Niemeyer Mission, an episode of British financial imperialism in Brazil', Univ. of Cambridge, Centre for Latin American Studies, Working Paper no. 10, pp. 20–22. Of course, British government officials contributed to thickening the fog which surrounds the issue for, as Sir Frederick Leith-Ross stated, 'we certainly have no intention of following the Americans in adverting the fact that loans can be discouraged on political grounds.' See Leith-Ross to Craigie, 24.12.1925, in *T 160*/4319/2.

6 The Postwar Gold Standard

1. E. Carone, *A República Velha (Evolução Política)*, p. 391.
2. See Programme of the Economic and Financial Policy etc., in W.L.P. de Souza, *Opinions Regarding Brazilian Economy and Finance of Mr. Washington Luis, President-elect of Brazil for term 1926–1930* (Typographia do Jornal do Commércio, Rio de Janeiro, 1926) pp. 9 ff. This reference will hereafter be referred to as *Opinions*.
3. N.V. Luz, *A Luta pela Industrialização do Brasil* (Alfa-Omega, São Paulo, 2.ª edição, 1975) pp. 159–60, and *RC–JC*, 1926, pp. 48 ff.
4. *Opinions*, p. 11.
5. Cf. C.A. McQueen, *Latin American Monetary and Exchange Conditions*, U.S. Department of Commerce, Trade Information Bulletin no. 430 (USGPO, Washington, 1926) p. 5.
6. 'To the Union finances, to the mass of consumers, to those who live on fixed rents, salaries or wages, to the foreign companies established in Brazil, a high exchange rate is desirable. For the manufacturers, to the states' finances based on *ad valorem* export duties and to debtors a low exchange rate is advantageous.' Mensagem Presidencial de 1926, in *DOU*, 4.5.1926.
7. *Opinions, passim*.
8. Mensagem Presidencial de 1927, in *DOU*, 4.5.1927.
9. Ibid. The current exchange rate was around 7.5d.
10. As Bernardes put it in his May 1926 Presidential Message: 'Resolutely suspending currency issues, the government was aware of the economic phenomena which would ensue from this measure and even predicted, as has happened in other countries which had to curb inflation, a repercussion in trade and industry more considerable than that being verified. Prices fell moderately, significantly ameliorating the people's budget but without increasing the number of ruinous liquidations and without bringing the economic depression which usually marks the two or three years following deflations.' *DOU*, 4.5.1926.
11. Though hardly more than a speculation, one cannot refrain from thinking that there may exist a relation between the banking boom in Minas Gerais in the early twenties – of the twenty-one banks with headquarters in that state in 1925 fourteen had been founded since 1920 – and the very large proportion of *Mineiros* among the leading deflationists. Professor Wirth's statement that 'until the 1930 Revolution, moreover, *Mineiros* preferred to invest in federal bonds,' although put forward without a trace of evidence to support it, also points in the same direction. Cf. J.D. Wirth, *Minas Gerais in the Brazilian Federation, 1889–1937* (Stanford Univ. Press, 1977) pp. 55–6.
12. 'The rise of exchange now', he claimed, 'can only be brought about by voluntary action set deliberately to achieve this fixed object, which it is known will ruin all the production of the country on which the hope, wealth and life of the nation depend . . . Those who have suffered by the fall of exchange have already been sacrificed. For their resurrection we cannot murder the survivors . . . let us weep for the victims; we must not, however, compel the part of the nation which remains to

sacrifice itself in a holocaust for their brothers who have fallen . . . let us bury the dead and take care of the living.' *Opinions*, p. 58.

13. Ibid. pp. 45 ff.
14. Ibid. p. 38.
15. It is interesting to note that, in the twenties, São Paulo's Industrial Associations provided a larger share of the funds to the state's Republican Party than did the traditional *Sociedade Rural*. See N.V. Luz, 'A Década de Vinte e suas Crises', in *Revista do Instituto de Estudos Brasileiros*, no. 6 (1969) p. 69.
16. The expression is Neuhaus's. Cf. P. Neuhaus, *Monetary History of Brazil*, p. 79.
17. As a Brazilian historian put it, his platform speech and the March 1926 elections 'appear as landmarks of the end of an epoch. Never an election aroused such approval and appreciation as that of Washington Luis.' E. Carone, *A República Velha (Evolução Política)*, pp. 391–2.
18. *O Jornal*, 7.10.1926.
19. See Morgan to Secretary of State, 13.10.1926, in *USNA RG-59*, 832.00/597.
20. See Law no. 5.188 of 18.12.1926. The new par in terms of the currency in which the exchange rate was customarily quoted resulted from the definition of the new standard as weighing 0.2 grams of 90 per cent fine gold.
21. For the by-laws regulating the Stabilisation Office operations see Decrees no. 17.617 and 17.618 of 5.1.1927.
22. See Mensagem Presidencial de 1927, in *DOU* 4.5.1927.
23. Washington Luis was reported as having said to Antonio Carlos that 'either Congress gave him the financial reform law or he would go. The Presidency only attracted him as a starting point to implement the monetary reform.' *O Jornal*, 12.12.1926.
24. As Neuhaus, for instance, put it, the reform was 'largely a personal initiative of the President.' Cf. P. Neuhaus, *Monetary History of Brazil*, p. 75.
25. The classic statement on these line is Falcão's. See W. Falcão, *O Empirismo Monetário*, pp. 80 ff. For a recent endorsement of this argument see P. Neuhaus, *Monetary History of Brazil*, pp. 75–7.
26. See, among others, *RC-JC*, 1926; E. Carone, *A República Velha (Instituições e Classes Sociais)* (Difel, São Paulo, 1970) p. 217; H. Silva and M.C. Ribas Carneiro, *História da República Brasileira*, Volume 7: Fim da Primeira República 1927–1930, (Ed. Três, São Paulo, 1975) p. 39; and J.M. Bello, *Brazil, 1889–1964*, pp. 265–6.
27. Cf., for instance, C. Furtado, *Formação Econômica do Brasil* (Cia. Editora Nacional, São Paulo, 11ª edição, 1971) p. 160.
28. P. Neuhaus, *Monetary History of Brazil*, p. 78. For Cassel's views on post-war monetary reform see his *The World's Monetary Problems: two memoranda* (Constable, London, 1921); the best presentation of the purchasing-power-parity theory is perhaps that to be found in his *Money and Foreign Exchange After 1914* (Constable, London, 1922) pp. 137–162.
29. *Opinions*, p. 53.

30. Mensagem Presidencial de 1927, in *DOU*, 4.5.1927. The extraordinary argument that Chile and 'cultivated and experienced Belgium' had also recently stabilised at around 6d was also put forward by the President to justify the new Brazilian par. Ibid.
31. Cf. E. Moreau, *Souvenirs d'un Gouverneur de la Banque de France: Histoire de la stabilisation du Franc (1926–1928)* (M.Th. Genin, Paris, 1954) p. 15.
32. Mensagem Presidencial de 1930, in *DOU*, 4.5.1930.
33. See, for instance, Mensagem Presidencial de 1927, in *DOU* 4.5.1927.
34. For a description of the basic operational features of the so-called Kemmerer (central) banks created in Colombia, Chile, Ecuador, Bolivia and Peru see R. Triffin, 'Central Banking in Latin America', in S.E. Harris (ed.), *Economic Problems of Latin America* (McGraw Hill, New York, 1944) pp. 96–8. It is interesting to notice in this connection that Washington Luis did entertain, in late 1925, but eventually abandoned, the idea of inviting Professor Kemmerer to advise his government on the implementation of monetary reform. On this see the Memorandum from the Office of the Economic Advisor, unsigned, dated 18.2.1925, in *USNA RG-59*, 835.51A.
35. See Tables A.8 and A.10.
36. The governing body of the São Paulo Institute was a five-member Council, presided by the State Secretary of Finance as president of the Institute, and with the State Secretary of Agriculture, two persons nominated by the planters and one representative of the Santos Commercial Association as its other members. The president of the Institute had veto powers over the Council's majority decisions but this was not an effective weapon for, as noted by Rowe, 'the trouble was not what the business men might want to do, but what they would not do.' J.W.F. Rowe, 'Brazilian Coffee', p. 34.
37. W.G. McCreery, and M.L. Bynum, 'Coffee Industry in Brazil', pp. 84–6.
38. Which was only done, however, in August 1926. Ibid. pp. 86–7.
39. See The Defence of Coffee, special memorandum prepared by C.R. Cameron, U.S. Consul in São Paulo, June 1927, in *USNA RG-59* 832.61333/271.
40. M. Tavares, *Relatório sobre o emprestimo para o Instituto, etc.*, *cit.* See also J.W.F. Rowe, 'Brazilian Coffee', p. 33.
41. Morgan to Secretary of State, 16.5.1926, in *USNA RG-59* 832.00/576.
42. J.W.F. Rowe, 'Brazilian Coffee', p. 33.
43. On the partial changes in the organisation of the Institute in the direction of greater state control see State Law no. 2.122 of 29.12.1926, Decree no. 4.031 of 22.3.1926, and Law no. 2.144, of 16.10.1926.
44. As from 25 November 1926, daily coffee releases from the regulating warehouses to Santos were to be one-twenty-fifth of the total exports from Santos during the previous month. Exports, thus, would respond automatically to world absorption with a short lag.
45. J.W.F. Rowe, 'Brazilian Coffee', p. 38.
46. Morgan to Secretary of State, 14.9.1927, in *USNA RG-59*, 832.00/637.
47. Cf. B. Fausto, 'A crise dos anos vinte e a Revolução de 1930', in

B. Fausto, (ed.), *História Geral da Civilização Brasileira*, Tomo III, Volume 2 (Difel, São Paulo, 1977) p. 414.
48. Cf. H. Silva, *1926 – A Grande Marcha*, (Civilização Brasileira, Rio de Janeiro, 1965) p. 218.
49. See Table A.12.
50. Mensagem Presidencial de 1927, in *DOU*, 4.5.1927.
51. See Table A.14.
52. *SAJ*, 15.1.1927. Brazil had by then left the League of Nations and financial relations with London were normalised.
53. *SAJ*, 26.3.1927.
54. M.A. Phoebus, *Commercial Readjustment in Brazil*, U.S. Department of Commerce, Trade Information Bulletin no. 560, (USGPO, Washington, 1928) p. 17.
55. See V.F. Bouças, *Finanças do Brasil*, *passim*.
56. The second half of the twenties also witnessed a significant increase in foreign direct investment. On this see, for instance, D.M. Phelps, *Migration of Industry to South America* (McGraw Hill, New York, 1939). The value of the foreign exchange inflows linked with these direct investments cannot, however, be ascertained.
57. *BBR*, 1928, pp. 5–6.
58. Ibid. p. 6. See also *BBBM*, minutes of meeting held on 7.10.1927.
59. C. Pacheco, *História do Banco do Brasil*, pp. 778–9.
60. *BBR*, 1928, p. 6.
61. Cf. V.F. Bouças, *Finanças do Brasil*, pp. 285–87.
62. For monthly data on Stabilisation Office issues see *RC-JC*, 1930, p. 15.
63. 'In 1927 the situation was marked by tight money and credit stringency during the greater part of the year . . . although some improvement was felt in the latter half of this year, especially in national industries and the year closed with a more optimistic outlook.' M.A. Phoebus, *Commercial Readjustment in Brazil*, p. 59.
64. See Table A.16.
65. Mensagem Presidencial de 1927, in *DOU*, 4.5.1927.
66. J.W.F. Rowe, 'Brazilian Coffee', Table VI, p. 86.
67. Ibid. p. 41.
68. These were resident labourers. Large numbers of day workers were taken on depending on the seasonal demand for labour, especially during the picking of the crop.
69. Rowe's calculations are based on cost of production estimates for São Paulo made by J.C. Muniz for the Coffee Institute during 1928. See J.C. Muniz, 'O Custo de Produção do Café em São Paulo', in *RC-JC*, 1928, pp. 316–22. Other unofficial estimates, which roughly reproduce Muniz's results, can be found in W.G. McCreery and M.L. Bynum, 'Coffee Industry in Brazil', pp. 63–76.
70. J.W.F. Rowe, 'Brazilian Coffee', p. 41.
71. Ibid. p. 43.
72. Ibid.
73. Ibid.
74. Cf., for instance C.M. Pelaez, 'Análise Econômica do Programa Brasileiro de Sustentação do Café, 1906–1945: teoria, política e medição', in

C.M. Pelaez (ed.), *Ensaios sobre Café e Desenvolvimento Econômico* (IBC, Rio de Janeiro, 1973) p. 209.

75. See Table A.7.
76. J.W.F. Rowe, 'Brazilian Coffee', p. 43.
77. See Table A.1.
78. A fact which was underlined by contemporary observers. Cf., for instance, M.A. Phoebus, *Commercial Readjustment in Brazil*, pp. 11–12.
79. See Table A.3.
80. In a normal crop year, under normal world demand conditions, and without a substantial carry-over, this was not likely to exceed one year. The coffee received at the warehouses by October 1926, i.e., the latest arrivals of the 1926 crop, were being released by June 1927. Cf. 'The Defence of Coffee', special memorandum prepared by C.R. Cameron, U.S. Consul in São Paulo, June 1927, p. 6, in *USNA R9-59* 832.61333/271.
81. A worsening of international economic conditions and, especially a tightening of credit conditions in the central countries, would affect the demand for coffee not only through the effect of falling incomes upon final demand. An important short-run effect was the fall of roasters' demand following an increase in interest rates in the consuming centres. This point is elaborated below, in the context of the 1929–30 world depression.
82. This interpretation of the timing of the downswing of the Brazilian economy in the late twenties is not original and was shared by most contemporary observers. Cf., for instance, *SAJ*, 5.1.1929, 4.5.1929, 6.7.1929, 27.1.1929, and *UK-DCR*, 1928, pp. 2 ff. However, it is strangely absent from recent writings which usually place it after the collapse of coffee price support in October 1929.
83. For a discussion of this issue see C.P. Kindleberger, *The World in Depression 1929–1939* (Allen Lane and The Penguin Press, London, 1973) pp. 74 ff, and the references quoted therein.
84. Cf. C.P. Kindleberger, ibid. pp. 113–14, and S.V.O. Clarke, *Central Bank Cooperation*, pp. 147–8.
85. See Table A.11.
86. Cf. V. Bouças, *Finanças do Brasil, passim*.
87. Dawson to Secretary of State, 16.3.1929, in *USNA RG-59*, 832.61333/296.
88. Brazil, Ministério do Trabalho, Indústria e Comércio, *Movimento Bancário, 1929–1930* (Oficinas do DNE, Rio de Janeiro, 1932) p. 50. Although contemporary conservative critics blamed the Banco do Brasil for overextending its commercial operations, it was the private banking sector which led the boom, their deposits growing by 17.4 per cent in 1927 against only 5.1 per cent for the Banco do Brasil. For the critics, see *RC-JC*, 1928, *passim*.
89. Cf., for instance, *BOLSA Monthly Review*, July 1929, pp. 297–8.
90. The Banco do Brasil was to be a creditor in no less than 60 per cent of the compositions and 30 per cent of the backruptcies occurring in Rio in 1928, mostly during the last quarter of the year. Its share in their liabilities was certainly much higher. Cf. *BBR*, 1929, p. 11.

91. Data sources as from Table A.16.
92. *BBR*, 1929, pp. 13–14.
93. *RC-JC*, 1928, p. 11 and C. Pacheco, *História do Banco do Brasil*, p. 239.
94. *BBBM*, minutes of meeting of 13.9.1929 and *BBR*, 1929, p. 13–14.
95. See Tables A.16 and A.17.
96. *RC-JC*, 1928, p. 12.
97. There can be no doubt that the government was fully aware of the position and of the role played by the Bank's policy in it. Washington Luis himself, confidentially briefing a leading politician on the economic situation in early 1929, would clearly state that an 'evident crisis' had hit the country mainly through balance of payments difficulties and that as a 'preventive measure, the Banco do Brasil had to hold its transactions, limiting them to the indispensible and very secure. As a consequence, the other banks acted in the same way. Then, the anguishing situation of debtors, the bankruptcies, in a word, the crisis. It happens, though, that with several factors persisting, the Banco do Brasil cannot change its orientation. It is, moreover, clearing its commercial porfolio to adapt itself, without danger, to its role as a Central Bank of Issue;' but, concluding in an optimistic tone, he assured 'he would not leave office without achieving full convertibility as soon as Stabilisation Office reserves reach 50 per cent [of the outstanding note issue] or a little over.' Letter of João Neves da Fontoura to Getúlio Vargas, 23.5.1929, in H. Silva, *A Grande Marcha*, pp. 224–5.
98. See Table A.1.
99. See Table A.11.
100. J.C. Muniz, 'O Custo da Produção do café em São Paulo', in *RC-JC*, 1928, pp. 321–2.
101. The stretch between the cities of Daurú and Araçatuba along the Noroeste, has been cited 'as Eldorado for the new planters.' W.G. McCreery and M.L. Bynum, 'Coffee Industry in Brazil', p. 57.
102. 'Weather conditions certainly played a far more important part in the creation and maintenance of the very high price level from 1924 to 1926 than the São Paulo Institute.' J.W.F. Rowe, 'Brazilian Coffee', p. 147.
103. Cf., for instance, A.V. Villela and W. Suzigan, *Política do Governo e Crescimento*, p. 147.
104. J.W.F. Rowe, 'Brazilian Coffee', p. 48.
105. Dawson to Secretary of State, 16.3.1929, in *USNA RG-59* 832.61333/296.
106. J.W.F. Rowe, 'Brazilian Coffee', p. 44.
107. Ibid. p. 50.
108. As the president of the Coffee Institute himself recollected, in 1929, the planters, when they started to feel the effects of the longer retention, 'cried that it was necessary to reduce prices to sell everything.' M.R. Telles, *A Defesa do Café e a Crise Econômica de 1929* (n.r.e., São Paulo, 1931) p. 19.
109. M.R. Telles, ibid. pp. 23 and 31–2.
110. Ibid. p. 32.

111. For the behaviour of future prices see *BOLSA Monthly Review*, several issues.
112. *BOLSA Monthly Review*, May 1929, p. 223.
113. *BBBM*, minutes of meeting of 22.4.1929 and M.R. Telles, *A Defesa do Café*, p. 35.
114. *BOLSA Monthly Review*, May 1929, p. 223.
115. For a detailed description of the so-called 'series system' then introduced, see J.W.F. Rowe, 'Brazilian Coffee', p. 50.
116. *BOLSA Monthly Review*, August 1929, p. 338.
117. J.W.F. Rowe, 'Brazilian Coffee', p. 47.
118. *BOLSA Monthly Review*, July 1929, p. 303.
119. See Table A.6.
120. See Mensagem Presidencial de 1929, in *DOU*, 4.5.1929.
121. Quoted in J.W.F. Rowe, 'Brazilian Coffee', p. 47.
122. Schoenfeld to Secretary of State, 24.7.1929, in *USNA RG-59*, 832.00 Political Reports/22.
123. Coffee for 90-day delivery fell 6 per cent during May and was falling again in July. See *BOLSA Monthly Review*, several issues.
124. Letter of Silva Gordo to Rolim Telles, 2.1.1931, reproduced in M.R. Telles, *A Defesa do Café*, pp. 31–2.
125. Ibid.
126. On June 1929, the Chancellor 'Cautioned the City to watch its steps in lending overseas.' R.S. Sayers, *Bank of England 1891–1944*, p. 227. On the British balance of payments strains from mid-1929 see R.S. Sayers, ibid., pp. 226 ff. and S.V.O. Clarke, *Central Bank Cooperation*, pp. 159 ff. On the constraints on foreign lending in London see D.E. Moggridge, *British Monetary Policy 1929–1931: The Norman conquest of $4.86* (Cambridge Univ. Press, 1972) pp. 212–13.
127. Castle's memorandum to the Secretary of State, 23.5.1929, in *USNA RG-59*, 832.51 Sa./144.
128. M.R. Telles, *A Defesa do Café*, p. 34.
129. Ibid. pp. 30–31.
130. This figure was calculated taking into account that, given the usual behaviour of importers under the defence system, Brazil supplied the margin between total world absorption and other producers' deliveries. Note that the financing of the Institute's July 1929 stock had been guaranteed by the postponement, for one more year, of Lazards' customary £5 million advances.
131. This argument was publicly put forward by the president of the Institute at that time. Cf. A. d'E. Taunay, *Pequena história do Café*, p. 425.
132. Letter of Rolim Telles to Julio Prestes, 2.10.1929, reproduced in M.R. Telles, *A Defesa do Café*, p. 221.
133. Ibid.
134. J. Neves da Fontoura, *Memórias*, Volume 2 (Ed. Globo, Porto Alegre, 1963) p. 25.
135. L.P. Raja Gabaglia, *Epitácio Pessoa*, Volume 2 (José Olympio, Rio de Janeiro, 1951) p. 785.
136. H. Silva, *A Grande Marcha*, p. 218.
137. Actually the agreement allowed the choice of the Rio Grande do Sul

candidate between Vargas and Borges de Medeiros, the old local political boss who had governed the state for twenty-three consecutive years before Vargas. See H. Silva, *A Grande Marcha*,pp. 240–2.
138. Ibid. *Passim.*
139. As the courier of Vargas' letter recollected: 'Mr. Washington Luis quickly read the letter. By his startled face, I felt I was before a man who had fallen from the clouds of his dreams to the hard ground of reality. He murmured, prostrated by the shock produced by reading the letter: "It can't be . . . it can't be . . . ". A. Carrazoni, *Depoimentos* (Typ. do Jornal do Commércio, Rio de Janiero, 1932) pp. 140–41, quoted in H. Silva, *A Grande Marcha*, p. 278.
140. H. Silva, *A Grande Marcha*, p. 288 ff.
141. See Schoenfeld to Secretary of State, 18.12.1929, in *USNA RG-59*, 832.00 Political Reports/10, and *SAJ*, 5.7.1930.
142. *RC-JC*, 1929, p. 21. See also A. d'E. Taunay, *Pequena história do Café*, p. 425.
143. *Diário de São Paulo*, 20.9.1929, and Cameron to Secretary of State, 20.8.1929, in *USNA RG-59*, 832.61333/300.
144. As stated by Washington Luis even after the crash, 'the 20 million bags of coffee stored in the country, even if acquired just to build up stocks and at the very low price of £1.5 per bag, would add 30 to 40 million pounds sterling to our reserves.' Mensagem Presidencial de 1930, in *DOU*, 4.5.1930.
145. M.R. Telles, *A Defesa do Café*, p. 33.
146. Ibid. p. 34.
147. Ibid. p. 36. A vivid testimony of the uncompromising stance taken by the government can also be found in a letter written by Roberto Simonsen – the influential manager of the Institute's coffee brokerage firm and an important liaison between the Institute and London financiers – to Washington Luis, recalling these crucial days: 'I can never forget', Simonsen wrote, 'the meeting I had with you on the day following my arrival from Europe, the 14th of October 1929, and the long conference I subsequently had, on your advice, with the President of the Banco do Brasil. To the arguments I presented pointing to the terrible crisis which, in the opinion of the London experts I had just heard, was near and inevitable, Dr. Guilherme da Silveira answered by showing me a copy of Juglar's "Theory of Crisis", adding that, as a good doctor, he was not fearful of what was going to happen for he was holding his scalpel awaiting the developments.' Roberto Simonsen to Washington Luis, 28.12.1936, Washington Luis Papers.
148. Ibid. pp. 36–7.
149. J.W.F. Rowe, 'Brazilian Coffee', p. 53.
150. See Table A.8.
151. While the American wholesale price index fell by 16 per cent in 1930 and 25 per cent in 1931, world coffee prices fell by 40 and almost 60 per cent, respectively. Cf. A. Delfim Netto, *O Problema do Café op. cit..* p. 131.
152. J.W.F. Rowe, 'Brazilian Coffee', p. 56.
153. However, there would be few failures among banks and *comissários*

during the early stages of the crisis for, as noted by Rowe, 'when all are frozen in together no one dares to act precipitately.' See J.W.F. Rowe, 'Brazilian Coffee', p. 57 and *BBR*, 1930, p. 10.

154. J.M. Whitaker, *O Milagre de Minha Vida*, p. 137.
155. *RC-JC*, 1929, p. 23.
156. See, for instance, *SAJ*, 17.12.1927, 31.3.1928, 28.7.1928, 6.10.1928 or 5.10.1929.
157. As Deputy Lindolfo Collor wrote after the crash: 'The Bank, in fact, is not in a position, without the gravest risk, to support the defence of coffee . . . the time has come for the divorce between exchange stabilization and coffee defence. Either the government supports coffee and becomes unable to maintain the exchange rate, or maintains the exchange rate and the defence of coffee crumbles.' *Jornal do Commércio*, 14.10.1929.
158. *RC-JC*, 1929, p. 23.
159. M.R. Telles, *A Defesa do Café*, p. 33.
160. *BBBM*, minute of meeting held on 26.11.1929.
161. *RC-JC*, 1929, p. 23.
162. *BBR*, 1930, p. 8.
163. As the bankers' statement announcing the issue of the short-term loan read, they had 'satisfied themselves that the government has already taken steps to permit increase in daily entries into Santos available for export from 30 000 to 40 000 bags of coffee and that the government is now engaged in working out a comprehensive scheme to deal with the present situation, with a view to facilitating the gradual liquidation of the large accumulations of coffee stocks in the interior.' Quoted in *BOLSA Monthly Review*, December 1929, p. 26.
164. Speyer and Co. to Secretary of State, 19.11.1929, in *USNA RG-59*, 832.51Sa/150.
165. See Table A.11.
166. See Morgan to Secretary of State, 17.12.1929, in *USNA RG-59*, 832.61333/311.
167. See Thompson to Secretary of State, 17.12.1929, in *USNA RG–59*, 832.5151/32 and M. de A. Ramos, *A Situação Econômica e Financeira do Brasil e a Execução da Lei no. 5.108* (Typ. do Jornal do Commércio, Rio de Janeiro, 1930) pp. 27 ff.
168. For a description of the regulations see *SAJ*, 25.1. 1930.
169. On 5 April 1930, the Bank's net short-term foreign liabilities reached the incredible figure of £18.2 million. Cf. C. Pacheco, *História do Banco do Brasil*, p. 281.
170. That is, by using the gold backing its own holdings of Stabilisation Office notes to settle drafts issued against it. The Bank's holding of offices notes were estimated at 50 per cent of the issue, while a large fraction of the rest was held by the state governments' banks. Cf. *BOLSA Monthly Review*, 1929, p. 27.
171. See Tables A.16 and A.17.
172. *BOLSA Monthly Review*, March 1930, p. 160.
173. A. d'E. Taunay, *Pequena História do Café*, p. 428.
174. The official figures gave Prestes 59 per cent of the votes cast for the two candidates.

175. *SAJ*, 26.4.1930.
176. As the London bankers argued against their critics in the London Stock Exchange, 'it must be remembered, firstly, that a large proportion of the funds now being raised . . . is destined to repay advances made by British lenders against coffee, and secondly, that it is a matter of great importance both to British exporters and to British investors that the coffee situation should be cleared up, in order that Brazil should be able to continue to make remittances to this country, and to place orders for British goods, for British exports to Brazil enormously exceed our imports from that country.' Schroeders and Co., *Quarterly Review*, June 1930, quoted in J.W.F. Rowe, 'Brazilian Coffee', p. 59.
177. Cf. *SAJ* 12.7.1930.
178. Compare the following statement made in April 1930, by the president of the Banco do Brasil: 'One can say that Brazilian stabilization was put to a rude test from which it emerged absolutely victorious. The first phase of the reform is done and, certainly, one can affirm that the conversion of our currency can be done on safe conditions, within a short period, after the creation of the Central Bank". *BBR*, 1930, p. 18.
179. See the British Embassy's Commercial Secretary Memorandum, dated 20.3.1930, in *FO 371*/14205, A 3040/727/6.
180. See *FO 371*/14199, A 3964/106/6, and Seeds to Henderson, 16.9.1930, in *FO 371*/14206, A 6070/2833/6. The British Ambassador assured his government that he was confidentially informed that during Prestes' visit 'discussions actually took place with the Bank of England, which agreed to send an expert to look into the affairs of the Banco do Brasil if invited to do so by the President.'
181. Ibid.
182. *SAJ*, 12.7.1930. The instructions were allegedly made by Prestes from London.
183. For the monthly issues of Stabilisation Office notes see *RC-JC*, 1930, p. 15.
184. See Tables A.1 and A.2.
185. Collected federal revenue in 1930 totalled only three-quarters of budget estimates. The aggregate revenue of the states fell by almost one-fifth as compared with 1929. See Table A.12 and Brazil, IBGE, *Anuário Estatístico do Brasil*, 1939/40, (Servico Gráfico do IBGE, Rio de Janeiro), p. 1409.
186. Sir W. Seeds to Henderson, 7.8.1930, in *FO 371*/14206, A 5343/2833/6.
187. Ibid.
188. Sir W. Seeds to Henderson, 16.9.1930, in *FO 371*/14206, A 6070/2833/6.
189. Sir W. Seeds to Henderson, 24.9.1930, in *T 160*/639/F 8351/1.
190. On this see, for instance, H. Silva, *1930 — A Revolução Traída* (Civilização Brasileira, Rio de Janeiro, 1966) p. 185 ff.

7 Conclusions

1. A. Gramsci, *The Modern Prince and Other Writings* (International Publishers, New York, 1970) pp. 154–5.

2. Cf., for instance, R. Prebisch, *The Economic Development of Latin America and its Principal Problems* (United Nations, Lake Sucess, 1950) p. 57.
3. Referring to the various primary product price support schemes organised during the twenties, Keynes sustained that 'in certain cases valorization schemes to provide by concerted action for the carrying of stocks are inevitable and defensive . . . Where production is inelastic, or where a particular product is so large a proportion of the national business that alternative occupations cannot be found, a miscalculation leading to heavy redundant stocks may prove ruinous if matters are allowed to take their course on principles of *laissez-faire* . . . The coffee valorization of the Brazilian government . . . brought into existence by the post-war troubles and the slump of 1920–21 were fully justified on the same grounds.' J.M. Keynes 'A Treatise on Money, Volume 2: The Applied Theory of Money', in Royal Economic Society, *The Collected Writings of John Maynard Keynes*, Volume VI (MacMillan, Cambridge, 1971) pp. 126–7.
4. B. Eichengreen, Editor's introduction, in B. Eichengreen, *The Gold Standard in Theory and History* (Methuen, London, 1985) p. 3.
5. A.G. Ford, *The Gold Standard: 1880–1914*, Chapter VII. The emphasis on the role of income-induced changes in imports as part of the trade balance adjustment mechanism derives from the fact that, given the wide differences between the structures of domestic supply and demand and, thus, the relatively small number of import-competing products, the role of relative price changes in the adjustment process should be small.

Bibliography

This list includes only references to public archives, private papers, newspapers, periodical official publications, books and articles quoted in the footnotes of this book. It is not a list of all sources consulted nor a comprehensive bibliography on the subject.

I. Public Archives and Private Papers

The archives to which references were made are listed below. In the footnotes to the text, references to Public Record Office material preceded by the class-mark FO 371 refer to *Foreign Office (Brazil, General Correspondence) Political* files, those preceded by FO 368 refer to Foreign Office (*Brazil, General Correspondence) Commercial* files, while those preceded by T 160 refer to *Treasury (Finance)* files; all references to papers in the National Archives of the United States refer to *Record Group 59: Records of the Department of State Relating to Internal Affairs of Brazil.*

Archives of N.M. Rothschild and Sons. London.
Arquivo do Banco do Brasil. Brasília.
Public Record Office. London.
The National Archives of the United States. Washington.
Washington Luis Papers, held by Mr. W.L.P. de Souza Neto. Rio de Janeiro.

II. Newspapers, Yearbooks and Periodical Official Publications

Banco do Brasil. *Relatório do Banco do Brasil.* Typ. do Jornal do Commércio, Rio de Janeiro, yearly.
Bolsa Monthly Review. London, monthly.
Brazil. Câmara dos Deputados. *Documentos Parlamentares: Meio Circulante.* Typ. do Jornal do Commércio, Rio de Janeiro, issued irregularly.
Brazil. Câmara Syndical dos Corretores de Fundos Públicos da Capital Federal. *Relatório.* Imprensa Nacional, Rio de Janeiro, yearly.
Brazil. Departamento Nacional do Café. *Anuário Estatístico do Café.* DNC, Rio de Janeiro, yearly.
Brazil. Imprensa Nacional. *Diário Oficial da União.* Rio de Janeiro, daily.
Brazil. Instituto Brasileiro de Geografia e Estatística. *Anuário Estatístico do Brasil.* Serviço Gráfico do IBGE, Rio de Janeiro, yearly.
Brazil. Ministério da Agricultura, Indústria e Commércio (Diretoria Geral de Estatística). *Resumo de Várias Estatísticas Econômico-Financeiras.* Typ. da Estatística, Rio de Janeiro (1924).
Brazil. Ministério da Fazenda. *Balanço Geral da União.* Imprensa Nacional, Rio de Janeiro, yearly.
Brazil. Ministério da Fazenda (Directoria de Estatística Commercial).

Commércio Exterior do Brasil. Oficinas de Estatística Commercial, Rio de Janeiro, issued irregularly, issuing agency changes.

Brazil. Ministério da Fazenda (Secretaria Técnica do Conselho de Economia e Finanças). *Finanças do Brasil.* Imprensa Nacional, Rio de Janeiro (1932) volume 3.

Brazil. Ministério da Fazenda. *Relatório Apresentado ao Presidente da República dos Estados Unidos do Brasil pelo Ministro de Estado dos Negócios da Fazenda.* Imprensa Nacional, Rio de Janeiro, yearly.

Brazil. Ministério da Fazenda. *Relatório da Caixa de Amortização.* Imprensa Nacional, Rio de Janeiro, issued irregularly.

Brazil. Ministério do Trabalho, Indústria e Commércio (Departamento Nacional de Estatística). *Movimento Bancário.* Oficinas do DNE, Rio de Janeiro, yearly.

Brazilian Review (title changes to *Wileman's Brazilian Review*). Rio de Janeiro, weekly.

Diário de São Paulo. São Paulo, daily.

Federal Reserve Bulletin. New York, monthly.

India Rubber Journal. London, weekly.

Jornal do Commércio. Rio de Janeiro, daily.

Jornal do Commércio. Retrospecto Commercial. Typ. do Jornal do Commércio, Rio de Janeiro, yearly.

Monitor Mercantil. Rio de Janeiro, daily.

Monthly Investor's Manual. London, monthly.

New York Journal of Commerce. New York, daily.

O Jornal. Rio de Janeiro, daily.

O Paiz. Rio de Janeiro, daily.

The Commercial and Financial Chronicle. New York, daily.

The New York Times. New York, daily.

The South American Journal and Brazil and River Plate Mail. London, weekly.

The Times. London, daily.

United Kingdom. Foreign Office and the Board of Trade. *Diplomatic and Consular Reports (Annual Series); Brazil.* HMSO, London, yearly, title changes.

United States. Department of Commerce. Bureau of the Census. *Historical Statistics of the United States, 1789–1945.* USGPO, Washington (1959).

United States. Department of State. *Foreign Relations of the United States.* USGPO, Washington, yearly.

Who's Who. London, yearly.

III. Books and Articles

ABREU, M. de PAIVA. (1973) *The Niemeyer Mission: an episode of British financial imperialism in Brazil* (University of Cambridge, Centre of Latin American Studies, Working Paper no. 10, Cambridge).

ALDCROFT, D. (1977) *From Versailles to Wall Street, 1919–1929* (Allen Lane, London).

ALMEIDA, C.J.C. de, (1906) *Banco da República do Brasil: Relatório apresentado ao Exmo. Sr. Ministro da Fazenda pelo Director da Carteira de Câmbio, 1902–1906* (Typ. do Jornal do Commércio, Rio de Janeiro).

ANGELL, J.F. (1933) *Financial Foreign Policy of the United States: a report to the Second International Studies Conference on the State of Economic Life, London, 1933* (Council of Foreign Relations, American Committee, New York).

ATKIN, J.M. (1968) 'British Overseas Investment, 1918–1931', The London School of Economics and Political Science, London. Unpublished Ph.D. Dissertation.

ATKIN, J. (1970) 'Official Regulation of British Overseas Investment, 1914–1931', in *Economic History Review*, July.

BARBOSA, F. de Assis (1968) 'A presidência Campos Salles', in *Luzo-Brazilian Review*, volume V, June.

BASTER, A.S.J. (1935) *The International Banks* (P.S. King and Son, London).

BELLO, J.M. (1966) *A History of Modern Brazil, 1889–1964* (Stanford Univ. Press).

BLOOMFIELD, A.F. (1959) *Monetary policy under the international gold standard, 1880–1914* (Federal Reserve Bank of New York).

BOUÇAS, V.F. (1955) *Finanças do Brasil: Dívida Externa, 1824–1945* (Ministério da Fazenda, Secretaria do Conselho Técnico de Economia e Finanças, Rio de Janeiro).

BRANDES, J. (1962) *Herbert Hoover and Economic Diplomacy: Department of Commerce Policy, 1921–1928* (Univ. of Pittsburgh Press).

BRANT, M. (1931) *Economical Fallacies: on the influence of paper-money on foreign exchange, prices, exports, national production, budgets, public finance and national progress* (Casa Leuzinger, Rio de Janeiro).

BROWN Jr., W.A. (1929) *England and the New Gold Standard: 1919–1926* (P.S. King and Son, London).

BUARQUE de HOLANDA, S. (1972) 'Do Império à República' in *Buarque de Holanda, S.* (ed.) *História Géral da Civilização Brasileira*. Tomo II, volume 5 (Difel, São Paulo).

CALÓGERAS, J.P. (1960) *Política Monetária do Brasil* (Cia. Editora Nacional, São Paulo).

CARONE, E. (1971) *A República Velha (Evolução Política)* (Difel, São Paulo).

CARONE, E. (1970) *A República Velha (Instituições e Classes Sociais)* (Difel, São Paulo).

CARRAZONE, A. (1932) *Depoimentos* (Typ. do Jornal do Commércio, Rio de Janeiro).

CASSEL, G. (1922) *Money and Foreign Exchange after 1914* (Constable, London).

CASSEL, G. (1921) *The World's Monetary Problems: two memoranda* (Constable, London).

CAVALCANTI, A. (1891) *A Reforma Monetária* (Imprensa Nacional, Rio de Janeiro).

CLAPHAM, J.H. (1944) *The Bank of England: a History* (Cambridge Univ. Press).

CLARKE, S.V.O. (1967) *Central Bank Cooperation: 1924–31* (Federal Reserve Bank of New York).

CORRÊA do LAGO, L.A.C., ALMEIDA, F.L. de and LIMA, B.M.F.

(1979) *A Indústria Brasileira de Bens de Capital: origens, situação recente, perspectivas* (FGV, Rio de Janeiro).

COSTA, I. (1925) *Os Erros da Valorização: subsídios para o estudo da defesa do café* (Seção de Obras d'O Estado de São Paulo, São Paulo).

DEAN, W. (1971) *A Industrialização de São Paulo (1880–1945)* (Difel, São Paulo).

DELFIM NETTO, A. (1979) *O Problema do Café no Brasil* (FGV/ SUPLAN, Rio de Janeiro).

DOWIE, J.A. (1975) '1919–1920 is in Need of Attention', in *Economic History Review*, August.

EICHENGREEN, B. (1985) *The Gold Standard in Theory and History* (Methuen, London).

FALCÃO, W. (1931) *O Empirismo Monetário no Brasil* (Cia. Editora Nacional, Rio de Janeiro).

FAUSTO, B. (1977) 'A crise dos anos vinte e a Revolução de 1930', in Fausto, B. (ed.), *História Geral da Civilização Brasileira*, Tomo III, volume 2 (Difel, São Paulo).

FAUSTO, B. (1970) *A Revolução de 1930: historiografia e história* (Brasiliense, São Paulo).

FAUSTO, B. (n.d.) 'Pequenos Ensaios de História da República (1889–1945)', *Cadernos CEBRAP* no. 10, 2ª edição (Brasiliense, São Paulo).

FAUSTO, B. (1977) *Trabalho Urbano e Conflito Social (1890–1920)* (Difel, São Paulo).

FERREIRA, E.F. (1974) *A Administração da Dívida Pública e a Política Monetária no Brasil* (IBMEC, Rio de Janeiro).

FERREIRA RAMOS, F.F. (1907) *La question de la valorisation du café au Brésil*, Conférence faite au Cercle d'Etudes Coloniales d'Anvers le 29 Janvier 1907 (Imprimerie J.E. Buschmann, Anvers).

FISHLOW, A. (1972) 'Origins and Consequences of Import Substitution in Brazil' in Di Marco (ed.), *International Economics and Development: Essays in honour of Raul Prebisch* (Academic Press, New York).

FONTOURA, J. NEVES da (1963) *Memórias*, volume 2: A Aliança Liberal e a Revolução de 30 (Globo, Porto Alegre).

FORD, A.G. (1962) *The Gold Standard: 1880–1914. Britain and Argentina* (Clarendon Press, Oxford).

FRANCO, G.H.B. (1982) '*Reforma Monetária e Instabilidade Durante a Transição Republicana*', Rio de Janeiro, PUC. Unpublished M.Sc. Dissertation.

FRIEDMAN, M. and A.J. SCHWARTZ (1963) *A Monetary History of the United States, 1860–1960*, N.B.E.R. Studies in Business Cycles no. 12 (Princeton Univ. Press).

FRITSCH, W. (1983) 'Brazil and the Great War: 1914–1918', in *Rivista di Storia Economica*, Second Series, vol. 2 (International Issue).

FRITSCH, W. (1985) 'The Montagu Financial Mission to Brazil and the Economic Policy Changes of 1924', in *Brazilian Economic Studies*, 9.

FURTADO, C. (1971) *Formação Econômica do Brasil* (Cia. Editora Nacional, São Paulo, 11ª edição).

GRAMSCI, A. (1970) *The Modern Prince and Other Essays* (International Publishers, New York).

HADDAD, C.L.S. (1980) 'Crescimento Econômico do Brasil, 1900–76', in Neuhaus, P., *Economia Brasileira: Uma Visão Histórica* (Campus, Rio de Janeiro).

HADDAD, C.L.S. (1974) '*Growth of Brazilian Real Output, 1900–47*', University of Chicago. *Unpublished Ph.D. Dissertation*.

HARDACH, G. (1977) *The First World War, 1914–1918* (Allen Lane, London).

HOLLOWAY, T.H. (1975) *The Brazilian Coffee Valorization of 1906* (Logmark Edition, Madison).

HOWSON, S. (1975) *Domestic Monetary Management in Britain, 1919–1938* (University of Cambridge, Department of Applied Economics Occasional Paper no. 48, Cambridge).

HOWSON, S. (1974) 'The Origins of Dear Money, 1919–1920', in *Economic History Review*, February.

JOSLIN, D. (1963) *A Century of Banking in Latin America* (Oxford Univ. Press).

KEYNES, J.M. (1972) 'Edwin Montagu', in *The Collected Writtngs of John Maynard Keynes*, volume X: Essays in Biography (Macmillan for the Royal Economic Society, Cambridge).

KEYNES, J.M. (1971) 'A Treatise on Money', in *The Collected Writings of John Maynard Keynes*, volume II: The Applied Theory of Money (Macmillan for the Royal Economic Society, Cambridge).

KINDLEBERGER, C.P. (1973) *The World in Depression 1929–1939* (Allen Lane and The Penguin Press, London).

LALIÈRE, A. (1909) *Le café dans l'état de Saint Paul, Brésil* (Augustin Challamel, Paris).

LEAGUE OF NATIONS (1942) *Economic Fluctuations in the United States and the United Kingdom, 1918–1922*, (Geneva).

LEWIS, W.A. (1949) *Economic Survey, 1919–1939* (Allen and Unwin, London).

LOUGH, W.H. (1915) *Financial developments in South American countries*, U.S. Department of Commerce, Special Agents Series no. 103 (U.S.G.P.O., Washington).

LUZ, N.V. (1969) 'A Década de Vinte e suas Crises', in *Revista do Instituto de Estudos Brasileiros*, no. 6.

LUZ, N.V. (1975) *A Luta pela Industrialização no Brasil*, (Alfa-Omega, São Paulo, 2.ª edição).

MACEDO SOARES, J.C. de (1927) *A Borracha: Estudo Econômico e Estatístico* (L. Chauny et L. Quinsac, Paris).

MARTINEZ CORREA, A.M. (1976) *A Rebelião de 1924 em São Paulo* (Hucitec, São Paulo).

McCREERY, W.G. and BYNUM, M.L. (1930) *The Coffee Industry in Brazil*, U.S. Department of Commerce, Trade Promotion Series no. 92 (U.S.G.P.O., Washington).

McQUEEN, C.A. (1926) *Latin American Monetary and Exchange Conditions* U.S. Department of Commerce, Trade Information Bulletin no. 430 (U.S.G.P.O., Washington).

MELLO FRANCO, V.A. de (1980) *Outubro 1930* (Nova Fronteira, Rio de Janeiro, 5ª edição).

MOGGRIDGE, D.E. (1971) 'British controls on long-term capital movements, 1924–1931', in McCloskey, D.N. (ed.), *Essays on a Mature Economy: Britain after 1840* (Methuen, London).

MOGGRIDGE, D.E. (1972) *British Monetary Policy, 1924–1931: The Norman Conquest of $4.86* (Cambridge Univ. Press).

MOREAU, E. (1954) *Souvenirs d'un Gouverneur de la Banque de France: Histoire de la stabilisation du Franc (1926–1928)* (M.Th, Genin, Paris).

NEUHAUS, P. (1974) 'A Monetary History of Brazil, 1900–1945', Chicago. Unpublished Ph.D. Dissertation.

NORMANO, J.F. (1935) *Brazil, a study of economic types* (Univ. of North Carolina Press, Chapel Hill).

NUNES, F.C.B. and J.R. SILVA (1929–32) *Tarifa das Alfândegas* (A. Coelho Branco, Rio de Janeiro).

ORTIGÃO, R. (1914) *A Moeda Circulante no Brasil* (Typ. do Jornal do Commércio, Rio de Janeiro).

PACHECO, C. (1979) *História do Banco do Brasil (História Financeira do Brasil desde 1808 até 1951)*, volume IV (AGGS, Rio de Janeiro).

PARRINI, C.P. (1965) *Heir to Empire: United States Economic Diplomacy, 1916–1923* (Univ. of Pittsburgh Press).

PELAEZ, C.M. (1971) 'As consequências econômicas da ortodoxia monetária, cambial e fiscal no Brasil entre 1889–1945', in *Revista Brasileira de Economia*, Jul/Sep.

PELAEZ, C.M. (1973) 'Análise Econômica do Programa Brasileiro de Sustentação do Café, 1906–1945: teoria, política e medição' in Pelaez, C.M. (ed.), *Ensaios sobre Café e Desenvolvimento Econômico* (I.B.C., Rio de Janeiro).

PELAEZ, C.M. and SUZIGAN, W. (1976) *História Monetária do Brasil: análise da política, comportamento e instituições monetárias* (IPEA/ INPES, Rio de Janeiro).

PENTEADO, S.A. (1923) *A Campanha da Defesa do Café em 1923–24*, (Typographia Brazil, São Paulo).

PESSOA, E. (1925) *Pela Verdade* (Francisco Alves, Rio de Janeiro).

PHELPS, C.W. (1927) *The Foreign Expansion of American Banks: American Branch Banking Abroad* (The Ronald Press, New York).

PHELPS, D.M. (1939) *Migration of Industry to South America* (McGraw Hill, New York).

PHOEBUS, M.A. (1928) *Commercial Readjustment in Brazil*, U.S. Department of Commerce, Trade Information Bulletin, no. 560 (U.S.G.P.O., Washington).

PIGOU, A.C. (1947) *Aspects of British Economic History: 1918–1925* (Macmillan, London).

PIRES DO RIO, J. (n.d.) *A Moeda Brasileira e seu Perenne Caráter Fiduciário* (José Olympio, Rio de Janeiro).

PREBISCH, R. (1950) *The Economic Development of Latin America and its Principal Problems* (United Nations, Lake Sucess.)

RAJA-GABAGLIA, L.P. (1951) *Epitácio Pessoa* (José Olympio, Rio de Janeiro).

RAMOS, M. de A. (1930) *A Situação Econômica e Financeira do Brasil e a Execução da Lei no. 5.108* (Typ. do Jornal do Commércio, Rio de Janeiro).

RIBEIRO de ANDRADE, A.C. (1923) *Bancos de Emissão no Brasil* (Liv. Leite Ribeiro, Rio de Janeiro).

ROWE, J.W.F. (1932) 'Brazilian Coffee', London and Cambridge Economic Service, Special Memorandum no. 35, Studies in the Artificial Control of Raw Materials no. 3, London.

SALTER, J.A., (1921) *Allied Shipping Control: an experiment in international administration* (Oxford Univ. Press).

SANTA ROSA, V. (1933) *O Sentido do Tenentismo* (Schmidt, Rio de Janeiro).

SAYERS, R.S. (1976) *The Bank of England, 1891–1944* (Cambridge Univ. Press).

SCHURZ, W.L. (1922) *Valorization of Brazilian Coffee*, United States Bureau of Foreign and Domestic Commerce, Supplement to Commerce Reports, Trade Information Bulletin no. 73, October 16, 1922, (U.S.G.P.O., Washington).

SILVA, H. (1966) *1930 – A Revolucão Traída*, Civilização Brasileira, Rio de Janeiro.

SILVA, H. (1965) *1926 – A Grande Marcha*, Civilização Brasileira, Rio de Janeiro.

SILVA, H. e RIBAS CARNEIRO, M.C. (1975) *História da República Brasileira*, Editora Três, São Paulo.

SIMON, M. (1967) The pattern of new British portfolio foreign investment 1865–1914, in Adler, J.R. (ed.), *Capital Movements and Economic Development* (St. Martin's Press, New York).

SIMONSEN, R. (1939) *A evolução industrial do Brasil* (Empresa Gráfica Revista dos Tribunais, São Paulo).

SOUZA, I. de (1926) *Restauração da Moeda no Brasil* (Casa Garraux, São Paulo).

SOUZA, W.L.P. de (1926) *Opinions Regarding Brazilian Economy and Finance of Mr. Washington Luis, President-Elect of Brazil for Term 1926–1930* (Typ. do Jornal do Commercio, Rio de Janeiro).

SUBERCASEAUX, G. (1920) *Le Papier-monnaie* (Giard, Paris).

TAUNAY, A. d'E. (1945) *Pequena história do café no Brasil (1727–1937)* (INC, Rio de Janeiro).

TAUSSIG, F.W. (1927) *International Trade* (Macmillan, New York).

TELLES, M.R. (1931) *A defesa do café e a crise econômica de 1929* (n.r.e., São Paulo).

TRIFFIN, R. (1944) 'Central Banking in Latin America', in Harris, S.E. (ed.), *Economic Problems of Latin America* (McGraw Hill, New York).

TRIFFIN, R. (1964) *The Evolution of the International Monetary System: Historical Reappraisal and Future Perspectives*, Princeton Studies in International Finance no. 12 (Princeton Univ. Press).

VIANA, V. (1926) *O Banco do Brasil: sua formação, seu engrandecimento, sua missão nacional* (Typ. do Jornal do Commércio, Rio de Janeiro).

VIDAL, R. de A.S. (1923) *Banking Organization and Financial Recovery: Speeches 1922* (Lytho-Typographia Fluminense, Rio de Janeiro).

VIEIRA SOUTO, L.R. (1925) *O Papel-Moeda e o Câmbio* (Imprimerie de Vaugirard, Paris).

VILLELA, A.V. (1972) 'Surto industrial durante a Guerra de 1914–1918', in

Ensaios Econômicos: homenagem a Octávio Gouvêa de Bulhões (APEC, Rio de Janeiro).

VILLELA, A.V. e SUZIGAN, W. (1973) *Política do governo e crescimento da economia brasileira* (IPEA/INPES, Rio de Janeiro).

WALEY, S.D. (1964) *Edwin Montagu: A Memoir and an Account of his Visits to India* (Asia Publishing House, London).

WHITAKER, J.M. (1978) *O Milagre de Minha Vida* (Editora Hucitec, São Paulo).

WILEMAN, J.P. (1896) *Brazilian-Exchange: the study of an inconvertible currency* (Galli Brothers, Buenos Aires).

WILLIAMS, J.H. (1919) 'Latin American Foreign Exchange and International Balances During the War', in *The Quarterly Journal of Economics*, volume XXXIII, May.

WIRTH, J.D. (1977) *Minas Gerais in the Brazilian Federation, 1889–1937* (Stanford Univ. Press).

Index